INTERPERSONAL COMMUNICATION

INTERPERSONAL COMMUNICATION

Stewart L. Tubbs
General Motors Institute

Sylvia Moss

Random House   New York

First Edition
98765432
Copyright © 1974, 1977, 1978 by Random House, Inc.

All rights reserved under International and Pan-American Copyright Conventions. No part of this book may be reproduced in any form or by any means, electronic or mechanical, including photocopying, without permission in writing from the publisher. All inquiries should be addressed to Random House, Inc., 201 East 50th Street, New York, N.Y. 10022. Published in the United States by Random House, Inc., and simultaneously in Canada by Random House of Canada Limited, Toronto.

Library of Congress Cataloging in Publication Data

Tubbs, Stewart L., 1943-
  Interpersonal communication.

  Based on the 2d ed. of the authors' Human communication.
  Bibliography: p.
  Includes index.
  1. Interpersonal communication. I. Moss, Sylvia, 1937-   joint author. II. Title.
BF637.C45T82   301.14   77-27280
ISBN 0-394-32201-0

Manufactured in the United States of America

Since this page cannot legibly accommodate all the copyright notices, the following pages constitute an extension of the copyright page.

Acknowledgments

Grateful acknowledgment is made to the following illustrators and agencies for permission to reprint illustrations from copyright material:

Drawing by Charles M. Schultz © 1970 United Feature Syndicate, Inc.

Drawing by Art Sansom. Reprinted by permission of NEA.

"Short Ribs" Reprinted by permission of NEA.

"Frank & Ernest" Reprinted by permission of NEA.

Drawing by Charles M. Schulz © 1972 United Feature Syndicate, Inc.

Drawing by Charles M. Schulz © 1974 United Feature Syndicate, Inc.

"Frank & Ernest" Reprinted by permission of NEA.

GRIN AND BEAR IT by George Lichty and Fred Wagner, Courtesy of Field Newspaper Syndicate.

Drawing by Whitney Darrow, Jr.; © 1976 *The New Yorker Magazine,* Inc.

Reproduced by special permission of PLAYBOY Magazine; copyright © 1975 by Playboy.

Drawing by Handelsman; © 1972 *The New Yorker Magazine,* Inc.

Grateful acknowledgment is made to the following authors and publishers for permission to reprint selections from copyright material:

From Dean C. Barnlund, "Toward a Meaning-Centered Philosophy of Communication," *Journal of Communication,* 12 (1962), p. 199. Copyright © 1962 by the International Communication Association, and reproduced by permission.

From A RAP ON RACE by Margaret Mead and James Baldwin. Copyright © 1971 by J. B. Lippincott Company. Reprinted by permission of J. B. Lippincott Company.

From David Jenkins, "Prediction in Interpersonal Communication," *Journal of Communication,* 11 (1961), p. 134. Copyright © 1961 by the International Communication Association. Reprinted by permission of the publisher.

From T. George Harris, "To Know Why Men Do What They Do: A Conversation with David McClelland," *Psychology Today* Magazine (January 1971). Copyright © 1970 Ziff-Davis Publishing Company. Reprinted by permission of *Psychology Today* Magazine.

Adapted from Robert Leeper, "A Study of a Neglected Portion of the Field of Learning—The Development of Sensory Organization," *Journal of Genetic Psychology,* 46 (1935), pp. 41–75. Reprinted by permission of The Journal Press.

PERMISSIONS ACKNOWLEDGMENTS

From Abraham S. Luchins, "Primary-Recency in Impression Formation," in *The Order of Presentation in Persuasion*, Vol. 1, edited by Carl I. Hovland *et al.*, pp. 35–36. Copyright © 1957 by Yale University Press. Reprinted by permission of the publisher.

Portion of Tables 1 and 4 (pp. 54 and 58) under the title "The Twelve Most Frequent Communicative Traits," from INTERRACIAL COMMUNICATION by Andrea L. Rich. Copyright © 1974 by Andrea L. Rich. Reprinted by permission of Harper & Row, Publishers, Inc.

Reprinted from OF HUMAN INTERACTION, by Joseph Luft, by permission of Mayfield Publishing Company (formerly National Press Books). Copyright © 1969 by The National Press.

From Anatol Rapoport and Albert Chammah, *Prisoner's Dilemma: A Study in Conflict and Cooperation*, p. 24–25. Copyright © 1965 by The University of Michigan Press. Reprinted by permission.

From Malcolm P. McNair, "What Price Human Relations," *Harvard Business Review*, March-April 1957. Copyright © 1957 by the President and Fellows of Harvard College; all rights reserved.

From Claude Brown, *Manchild in the Promised Land*, p. 171. Copyright © Claude Brown 1965. Reprinted by permission of Macmillan Publishing Co., Inc.

From David Smith and Clark Sturges, "The Semantics of the San Francisco Drug Scene," *ETC.: A Review of General Semantics*, 26, no. 2 (1969), pp. 168–173. Copyright © 1969 by the International Society for General Semantics. Reprinted by permission of the International Society for General Semantics.

From Sam Glucksberg, Robert M. Krauss, and Robert Weisberg, "Referential Communication in Nursery School Children: Method and Some Preliminary Findings," *Journal of Experimental Child Psychology*, 3 (1966), p. 335. Copyright © 1966 by Academic Press, Inc. Reprinted by permission of the publisher and the authors.

From John Haller, "The Semantics of Color," *ETC.: A Review of General Semantics*, 26, no. 2 (1969), p. 203. Copyright © 1969 by the International Society for General Semantics. Reprinted by permission of the International Society for General Semantics.

From Dominick Barbara, "Nonverbal Communication," *Journal of Communication*, 13 (1953), p. 167. Copyright © 1953 by the International Communicaiton Association. Reprinted by permission of the author and the publisher.

From Albert E. Scheflen, "Quasi-Courtship Behavior in Psychotherapy," *Psychiatry* (1965) 28: 245–257. Copyright © 1965 by The William Alanson White Psychiatric Foundation, Inc. and reprinted by permission.

From Gerald M. Goldhaber, "Gay Talk: Communication Behavior of Male Homosexuals." Paper presented at the annual convention of the Speech Communication Association, Chicago, December 27, 1974. Reprinted by permission of the author.

From *My Fair Lady* by Alan Jay Lerner and Frederick Loewe. Copyright © 1956 by Alan Jay Lerner and Frederick Loewe.

From Florence Xerxa, "Encounter: A Greek Mission Impossible," *The New York Times*, January 18, 1976. Copyright © 1976 by The New York Times Company. Reprinted by permission.

From Donald Hebb, *A Textbook of Psychology*, 3rd ed., p. 235. Copyright © 1972 by W. B. Saunders Company. Reprinted by permission of the author and the publisher.

PERMISSIONS ACKNOWLEDGMENTS

From David W. Johnson, *Reaching Out: Interpersonal Effectiveness and Self-Actualization*, p. 35. Copyright © 1972 by Prentice-Hall, Inc. Reprinted by permission of the publisher.

From Muriel James and Dorothy Jungeward, *Born to Win*, p. 18. Copyright © 1971 by Addison Wesley Publishing. Reprinted by permission of the publisher.

Adapted from Cal Downs and Wil Linkugel, "A Content Analysis of Twenty Selection Interviews." Paper presented to the annual conference of the International Communication Association, April 1971, in Phoenix, Arizona, and later published in *Personnnel Administration/Public Personnel Review*, September-October 1972. Reprinted by permission of the authors.

From Edgar H. Schein, "The Chinese Indoctrination Program for Prisoners of War," *Psychiatry* (1956), 19: 149–172. Copyright © 1956 by The William Alanson White Psychiatric Foundation, Inc., and reprinted by permission.

From PERSONALITY AND INTERPERSONAL BEHAVIOR by Robert Freed Bales. Copyright © 1970 by Holt, Rinehart and Winston Inc. Reprinted by permission of Holt, Rinehart and Winston.

From Herbert Thelen and Watson Dickerman, "Stereotypes and the Growth of Groups," *Educational Leadership*, 6 (1949), pp. 309–316. Reprinted by permission.

From UP THE ORGANIZATION, by Robert Townsend. Copyright © 1970 by Robert Townsend. Reprinted by permission of Random House, Inc.

From Carl Larson, "Forms of Analysis and Small Group Problem Solving," *Speech Monographs*, 36 (1969), pp. 452–453. Reprinted by permission.

The Conflict Grid figure from "The Fifth Achievement," Robert R. Blake and Jane Srygley Mouton, *The Journal of Applied Behavioral Science*, pp. 413–426, 1970. Reprinted by permission of the authors and the publisher.

From Dennis Gouran, "Group Communication: Perspectives and Priorities for Future Research," *Quarterly Journal of Speech*, 59 (1973), p. 25. Reprinted by permission.

Photos
6 © J. Tobias; 12 Charles Gatewood; 20 The American Museum of Natural History; 26 Virginia Hamilton; 28 Charles Gatewood; 29 Paolo Koch/Rapho/Photo Researchers; 51 Charles Gatewood; 61 Charles Gatewood; 81 Charles Gatewood; 85 Charles Gatewood; 100 George W. Gardner; 125 Charles Gatewood; 134 UPI; 156 Charles Gatewood; 176 Charles Gatewood; 186 Charles Gatewood; 187 © J. Tobias; 188 Charles Gatewood; 189 UPI; 202 Charles Gatewood; 225 Charles Gatewood; 242 Charles Gatewood; 253 UPI; 263 UPI; 276 George W. Gardner.

To
    Gail, Brian, and Kelly
Harry, Michael, and Sara

Preface

Our first book, *Human Communication: An Interpersonal Perspective* (Random House, 1974), was designed to meet a growing need for quality textbooks in interpersonal communication. The second edition of that book had two objectives. The first objective was to revise, improve, and update the material in the original edition; the second was to broaden its scope by including more material on public communication as well as entirely new chapters on organizational and mass communication. The reception to the second edition has been extremely encouraging. Moreover, a substantial number of our colleagues from across the country feel there is also a need for a compact, more narrowly focused text—one that combines the style and strengths of the second edition with an exclusively interpersonal framework. The present book is designed to serve that need. We have taken Chapters 1 through 10 from our second edition and rewritten Chapters 1, 2, 9, and 10 to suit the course in interpersonal communication. In preparing this text we have retained the many photographs and additional illustrative material of the second edition as well as our new material on intercultural communication and on the receiving functions of communication.

The book's organization is straightforward. Chapters 1 through 8 lay out the principles of communication; Chapters 9 and 10 deal with their application. Chapter 1 covers important conceptual issues and provides working definitions of key terms that appear throughout the book. Chapter 2 presents a process model of interpersonal communication and goes on to explore the way in which the individual communicator as both sender and receiver learns communication behaviors. Chapters on person perception and the bases of human attraction are followed by a chapter on the relationship aspects of interpersonal communication. The latter subject, originally discussed in Chapter 12 of our first edition, is given a much more central place in our present text, and we have added to it a discussion of empathic listening. The chapters on verbal and nonverbal messages include a substantial amount of material on interpersonal communication between people with different cultural backgrounds. Chapter 9 is concerned with the two-person communication context and its unique aspects. The final chapter focuses on the small-group context with three or more participants.

As in our other books, our aim has been to interpret the current state of knowledge about communication and to synthesize and clarify material from several sources including anthropology, linguistics, psychology, sociology, and organizational theory. Moreover, we have tried to impart to the student some sense of the dynamic nature of modern communication study. Where research appears inconclusive or contradictory, we still prefer to note this rather than force a point or make easy generalizations. It has been our aim in this way to better present the current state-of-the-art to today's introductory students, who are becoming intensely concerned about communication and whom we hope to interest in our field.

Stewart L. Tubbs
Sylvia Moss

Contents

Chapter 1   **THE PROCESS OF INTERPERSONAL COMMUNICATION**   **1**

    WHAT IS INTERPERSONAL COMMUNICATION?   3

    WHAT IS EFFECTIVE INTERPERSONAL COMMUNICATION?   8

    Understanding/Pleasure/Attitude Influence/Improved Relationships/Action

Chapter 2   **A MODEL OF INTERPERSONAL COMMUNICATION**   **17**

    SENDER/RECEIVER   21

    Input/Filters

    COMMUNICATIVE STIMULI   29

    Verbal Stimuli/Nonverbal Stimuli

    CHANNELS   32

    INTERFERENCE   34

    Signal-to-Noise Ratio/Technical and Semantic Interference

    RECEIVER/SENDER   37

    TIME   39

CONTENTS

xiv

Chapter 3 SOCIAL BEHAVIOR AND MOTIVATION — 45

LEARNING TO COMMUNICATE — 47
Classical Conditioning/Instrumental Learning/Social Learning/Social Facilitation

FEEDBACK AS A REINFORCER — 57
Influencing Through Feedback/The Information Value of Feedback

REWARDS AND MOTIVATIONS — 61
The Need for Affiliation/The Need for Achievement/Dogmatism/Machiavellianism

Chapter 4 PERSON PERCEPTION — 71

PERCEIVING PEOPLE AND OBJECTS: A COMPARISON — 73

FORMING IMPRESSIONS OF OTHERS — 77
A Private Theory of Personality/The First Impression/Trait Associations/Personal Generalizations and Stereotypes

CHARACTERISTICS OF ACCURATE PERCEIVERS — 89

IMPROVING PERCEPTION AND COMMUNICATION — 91

Chapter 5 BASES OF HUMAN ATTRACTION — 97

PROXIMITY — 99
Theories About the Effects of Proximity/Proximity and Intercultural Communication

SIMILARITY	104

Balance Theory/Qualifications of Similarity Predictions

SITUATION	111

Anxiety/Changes in Self-Esteem/ Isolation

POPULAR AND UNPOPULAR PEOPLE	114

The Sociogram/Overchosen People and Isolates

Chapter 6 SELF AND OTHERS: RELATIONSHIP ASPECTS OF COMMUNICATION 121

CONFIRMATION AND DISCONFIRMATION	123
AWARENESS OF SELF AND OTHERS	127

The Johari Window/Metacommunication/ Self-Disclosure

TRUST	134

Game Behavior/Some Effects of Distrust/ Reducing Defensiveness/Empathic Listening

Chapter 7 THE VERBAL MESSAGE 147

WORDS AND MEANINGS	150

Symbols and Referents/Denotation and Connotation/Private and Shared Meanings

MESSAGE ENCODING	160
LANGUAGE AND THOUGHT	165

Inferences/Dichotomies/Word Power/ Single Meanings

CONTENTS

xvi

Chapter 8 THE NONVERBAL MESSAGE — 181

SPATIAL AND TEMPORAL CUES — 185
Space/Time

VISUAL CUES — 193
Facial Expression/Eye Contact/Body Movements/Hand Gestures/Physical Appearance and the Use of Objects

VOCAL CUES — 204
The Information in Vocal Cues/Volume Rate and Fluency/Pitch/Quality

INTERPRETING NONVERBAL MESSAGES — 211

Chapter 9 TWO-PERSON COMMUNICATION — 219

THE SOCIAL SETTING — 221
Norms/Roles

UNSTRUCTURED TWO-PERSON COMMUNICATION — 226
Involvement and Arousal/Some Dimensions of Interpersonal Relations/Transactional Analysis

STRUCTURED TWO-PERSON COMMUNICATION: THE INTERVIEW — 237
Standardized and Unstandardized Interviews/Questions and Answers/Interview Structure

Chapter 10 SMALL GROUP COMMUNICATION — 249

GROUP DYNAMICS — 253
Conformity/Social Influence/The Quality of Group Problem Solving/The

Role of Group Member/Cohesiveness/
The Phases of Group Development

GROUP STRUCTURE　　　　　　　267

Group Size/Communication Networks/
Leadership

CORRELATES OF EFFECTIVE
GROUPS　　　　　　　　　　　　273

Idea Developments and Problem
Solving/Resolution of Conflict/Patterns
of Decision Making/Testing the Group's
Effectiveness

REFERENCES　　　　　　　　283

APPENDIX　　　　　　　　　305

ROLE PLAY EXERCISES　　　　　307

Two-Person Role-Play Exercises

GROUP ROLE-PLAY EXERCISES　　308

The Sinking Ship/Ability Grouping
Meeting

CASE PROBLEMS　　　　　　　309

DISCLOSURE GAMES　　　　　　312

A DISCLOSURE GAME FOR TWO
PLAYERS　　　　　　　　　　　312

Procedure

A SHORTER DISCLOSURE GAME　318

Interpersonal Yoga

INDEX　　　　　　　　　　　321

INTERPERSONAL COMMUNICATION

Chapter 1: The Process of Interpersonal Communication

OBJECTIVES

After reading this chapter the student should be able to:
1. Define the term "communication."
2. Define the term "interpersonal communication."
3. Identify and describe three characteristics of interpersonal communication.
4. Define the term "intercultural communication."
5. Define effective communication in terms of five possible outcomes of interpersonal communication.

1

He: Mind if I sit here too?
She: (*Smiling*) Why not?
He: (*Encouraged*) You know we're in the same English class. E 201.
She: I know. I remember you asked the instructor a question yesterday.
He: That's funny. I didn't think you'd noticed me too.
She: What do you mean, "*too*"?
He: Well I've been trying to "accidentally" run into you for over a week.
She: (*Skeptical*) Oh *sure* you have.
He: It's true. I have.
She: Prove it.
He: What about dinner tonight over a bottle of cheap but potent wine?
She: It's a date.

This exchange between two college students in a local coffee shop is not very different from thousands of other first encounters between two people that occur daily. At this point the students think that they may like each other. And perhaps in the future they will spend many, many pleasurable hours in each other's company. Or perhaps after longer exposure to one another, they will find that there is not so much to like after all. The vehicle through which human relationships are developed or destroyed is interpersonal communication. In this book we shall explore many aspects of this subject—all the way from the first impressions we have of one another to how human relationships are maintained and sometimes terminated.

WHAT IS INTERPERSONAL COMMUNICATION?

What do you think of when the word "communication" is used? Students answering this question may mention anything from the use of electric circuits to prayer (that is, communication with God). Communication is a subject so frequently discussed that the term itself has become *too* meaningful—that is, it has too many different meanings for people. Agreeing on a working definition is the first step toward improving our understanding of this complex phenomenon.

Communication has been broadly defined as "the sharing of experience," and to some extent all living organisms can be said to share experience. What makes human communication unique is the superior ability to create and to use symbols, for it is this ability that enables humans to "share experiences indirectly and vicariously" (Goyer, 1970, pp. 4–5). Let us keep this reference to human beings, the symbol-making animals,* in mind as we consider an alternate definition:

> Communication, as I conceive it, is a word that describes the process of creating a meaning. Two words in this sentence are critical. They are "create" and "meaning." Messages may be generated from the outside—by a speaker, a television screen, a scolding parent—but meanings are generated from within. This position parallels that of Berlo when he writes, "Communication does not consist of the transmission of meaning. Meanings are not transmitted, or transferable. Only messages are transmittable and meanings are not in the message, they are in the message-users." Communication is man's attempt to cope with his experience, his current mood, his emerging needs. For every person is a unique act of creation, involving dissimilar materials. But it is, within broad limits, assumed to be predictable or there could be no theory of communication. (Barnlund, 1962, p. 199)

For the time being, then, let us say that **communication** is *the process of creating a meaning between two or more people*. This is at least a partial definition, one we shall want to expand in discussing communication outcomes.

The term "interpersonal communication" may still be confusing to you. Does interpersonal communication occur anytime two or more people interact? Does it occur when people exchange letters or talk on the phone? Does it include communication between author and reader, playwright and actor, and telecaster and viewer? As we use the term in this book, it does not include those kinds of contracts. **Interpersonal communication** refers to *face-to-face, two-way communication* only. This distinction limits our discussion by omitting written communication and public (or speaker-audience) communication as well as a formal discussion of organizational and mass communication. Keep in

---

* Although we have emphasized the human ability to create and use symbols as distinctive, the issue of whether animals other than humankind are capable of communicating by symbolic means is controversial. One researcher (Premack, 1970) has taught a chimpanzee named Sarah to read and make up sentences on a magnetic board. The words are represented by plastic pieces of different shapes and colors. Washoe, another chimpanzee (Gardner and Gardner, 1969), has learned to use sign language. Yet, when the New York Academy of Sciences sponsored a conference on language and speech in 1975, experts on animal communication were unable to reach agreement on the question of whether animals could be taught to use language.

mind, however, that interpersonal communication often takes place within organizations and that it is an important part of the social influence process in mass communication (see Tubbs and Moss, 1977).

How much of our time is involved in interpersonal communication? One study examined how 173 people from various occupations spent their time (Samovar et al., 1969). Every person kept a log of his or her communication activities for each fifteen-minute period throughout the day. These activities included conversing, listening, reading, and viewing television. (In this study, writing was not considered a communication behavior.) The respondents estimated that almost three-quarters (72.8 percent) of their waking hours involved communication activities. Members of certain occupations—salesmen, teachers, and administrators—averaged even more. Excluding the time the subjects spent reading and viewing television, the study still showed an average of 52.4 percent of the subjects' waking hours was devoted to listening and conversing. These are the activities we classify as interpersonal communication.

Interpersonal communication events are informal, everyday exchanges. Thus they include most of the communication activities we engage in from the time we get up until we go to bed. Such activities can be thought of as **transactions**. Harris offers a simple but very useful definition of a transaction as a situation in which "I do something to you and you do something back" (Harris, 1967, p. 12). We enter into and move out of such encounters several times each day, with little or no prior arrangement, and many of the rules regulating behavior in these encounters are not even known to us, at least on a conscious level. There are exceptions. In an interview, for example, the roles of interviewer and respondent are fairly well defined. And as members of groups we may have to follow an agenda. Although the contexts, or situations, in which interpersonal communication occurs are extremely diverse, we can say that an activity is interpersonal communication if it meets three criteria: (1) *all parties are in close proximity,* (2) *all parties send and receive messages,* and (3) *these messages include both verbal and nonverbal stimuli.*

That all parties must be in close proximity follows from our definition of interpersonal communication. We have to be within a somewhat limited physical distance of one another to communicate face-to-face. This point seems obvious. Less obvious, but no less important, is the fact that there seems to be an informal distance classification to which we adhere, usually without being aware of it. Chapter 8, on the nonverbal message, describes how physical distance between people affects their communication. Different distances seem appropriate for different messages. If you doubt the validity of this statement, try discussing an intimate subject with someone who is standing five feet away from you.

INTERPERSONAL COMMUNICATION

Many of the informal exchanges of daily life are interpersonal communication events.

We expand our definition still further when we observe that both parties send and receive messages. You are sitting in a booth having coffee with someone you hardly know but think you might like to go out with. Each of you is both a sender and a receiver of messages; the interaction depends on the two of you. As you start to talk, one of you usually asks about the other's hometown, interests, activities, friends, and so on. As you hit on mutually interesting topics, you tend to steer your conversation in those directions and to drop other subjects that seem to lead nowhere. If you can't find topics that are mutually satisfying or if you find you are really at opposite poles on a number of issues, you may want to terminate the exchange altogether, as these people did:

Larry: So you're an art major, huh?
Gail: Yes, I really feel this is the only major that gives me the freedom to *create*.
Larry: I really don't know too much about artists or art.
Gail: Well, I'm also interested in music. In fact, I play the guitar.
Larry: Do you like John Denver? I think he's far out.

Gail: Oh, I can't stand John Denver.
Larry: Oh. Sorry.
(*Silence.*)

We can see now how the outcome of interaction constantly changes as a result of the responses of both parties. What each says—indeed whether he or she continues to say anything—depends to a great extent on what the other person says and does. That is, each relies on feedback from the other communicator, or, as one author has defined it, "the return to you of behavior you have generated" (Luft, 1969, p. 116).

Compare any recent face-to-face encounter you have had with your present activity—sitting and reading a book. Are there times when you would like us to back up and explain something over again? Or do you wish you could change the subject? Can a member of the audience change the script of a play by interacting with the playwright? Obviously not. But how an actor interprets the script may be influenced by feedback from the audience. It is true that television viewers may write letters to a network concerning a given program and that enough letters or responses to a rating survey will affect the future of the program. But this interaction is not so immediate as the interaction that results from a conversation, and the viewers are not face to face with the television personality. Thus, although playwright and telecaster both originate messages, their communication would not be considered interpersonal.

We have shown that all parties involved in interpersonal communication send and receive messages at close proximity. Our third point is that these messages include both verbal and nonverbal stimuli. We tend to think of such communication solely as speech communication. Yet we respond to a person's facial expressions, eye movements, hand gestures, dress, and posture as well as to other nonverbal stimuli he or she transmits. Sometimes nonverbal stimuli supplement verbal stimuli; sometimes they contradict them; sometimes they replace them entirely.

If you want to see how dependent we are on nonverbal cues, strike up a conversation with someone you know well. Then give that person absolutely no response, verbal or nonverbal. Just look at the person and listen. After a while he or she starts saying things like "You know what I mean?" "What do you think?" and "Do you follow me?" If you don't look at the person, his or her reaction is likely to be even more rapid and intense. If you try this technique on someone you don't know (a stranger seated next to you on a plane, for example), the response is likely to be silence after a relatively short time. When we are face to face, our behaviors really do have an immediate effect on others.

In the chapters that follow, we shall examine each of the three criteria of interpersonal communication in much greater detail. Our discussion will also relate interpersonal communication to an area of rapidly increasing interest: **intercultural communication**—that is, *communication between members of different cultures (whether defined in terms of racial, ethnic, or socio-economic differences, or a combination of these differences)*. A similar definition is proposed by Samovar and Porter: "Whenever the parties to a communication act bring with them different experiential backgrounds that reflect a longstanding deposit of group experience, knowledge, and values, we have intercultural communication" (1972, p. 1). Since intercultural communication can occur in any interpersonal context, we shall be making frequent references to this dimension of experience throughout our text.

WHAT IS EFFECTIVE INTERPERSONAL COMMUNICATION?

Students sometimes say that interpersonal communication is effective when a person gets his or her point across. This is but one measure of effectiveness. More generally, **interpersonal communication is effective** *when the stimulus as it was initiated and intended by the sender corresponds closely with the stimulus as it is perceived and responded to by the receiver*. We can also represent effectiveness by an equation. If we let G stand for the person who generates the response and P for the perceiver of the response, then communication is whole and complete when the response G intends and the response P provides are identical (Goyer, 1970, p. 10):

$$\frac{P \text{ meaning}}{G \text{ meaning}} = 1$$

We rarely reach 1—that is, perfect sharing of meaning. As a matter of fact, we never reach 1. We approximate it. And the greater the correspondence between our intention and the response we receive, the more effective we have been in communicating. At times, of course, we hit the zero mark: there is absolutely no correspondence between the response we want to produce and the one we receive. The drowning man who signals wildly for help to one of his friends on a sailboat only to have his friend wave back is ineffective, to say the least.

We can't judge our effectiveness if our intentions are not clear; we must know what we are trying to do. What makes that first definition of effectiveness inadequate ("when a person gets his or her point across") is that in communicating we may try to bring about one or more of several possible outcomes. We shall consider five of them here: understanding, pleasure, attitude influence, improved relationships, and action.

Understanding

Understanding refers primarily to *accurate reception of the content of the intended stimulus.* In this sense, a communicator is said to be effective if his or her receiver has an accurate understanding of the message the communicator has tried to convey. (Of course, the communicator sometimes conveys messages unintentionally that are also understood quite clearly.)

The primary failures in communication are failures to achieve content accuracy. For example, the service manager of an oil company had a call one winter morning from a woman who complained that her oil burner was not working. "How high is your thermostat set?" he asked. "Just a moment," the woman replied. After several minutes she returned to the phone. "At 4 feet $3\frac{1}{2}$ inches," she said, "same as it's always been." This confusion is typical of a failure to achieve understanding. Like most misunderstandings of this kind, it should be relatively easy to remedy through clarifying feedback and restatement.

As we add more people to a communication context, it becomes more difficult to determine how accurately messages are being received. This is one of the reasons that group discussions sometimes turn into free-for-alls. Comments begin to have little relation to each other, and even a group with an agenda to follow may not advance toward the resolution of any of its problems. Situations such as these call for more clarifying, summarizing, and directing of group comments (see Chapter 10).

Pleasure

Not all communication has as its goal the transmission of a specific message. In fact, the goal of the newly emergent transactional analysis school of thought is simply to communicate with others in a way that ensures a sense of mutual well-being (Harris, 1967, p. 50). This is sometimes referred to as phatic communication, or maintaining human contact. Many of our brief exchanges with others—"Hi"; "How are you today?"; "How's it going?"—have this purpose. Casual dates, cocktail parties, and rap sessions are more structured occasions on which we come together to enjoy the company and conversation of others. (Some think that the word "rap" comes from the word "rapport," which refers to a sympathetic relationship between people.) The degree to which we find communication pleasurable is closely related to our feelings about those with whom we are interacting. If

INTERPERSONAL COMMUNICATION

10 you repeatedly find that your communication with a particular person is not enjoyable, you may discover some of the reasons why in Chapters 5 and 6.

Attitude Influence

Suppose that five politicians meet to determine the best way to reduce cost overruns on military contracts and that they reach a stalemate because of their extreme differences of opinion. Such situations are often erroneously referred to as "communication breakdowns." If the disputing parties understood each other better, it is assumed, their differences would be eliminated and an agreement would be reached. But understanding and agreement are by no means synonymous outcomes. When you understand someone's message, you may find that you disagree with him or her even more strongly than you did before.

Drawing by Charles M. Schulz. © 1970 United Feature Syndicate, Inc.

In many situations we are interested in influencing a person's attitude as well as in having him or her understand what we are saying. As we shall see in Chapters 3 and 4, the process of changing and reformulating attitudes, or **attitude influence,** goes on throughout our lives. In two-person situations, attitude influence is often referred to as "social influence," the dynamics of which are discussed in Chapter 5. Attitude influence is no less important in the small-group or the organizational setting. For example, consensus among group members is an objective of many problem-solving discussions (see Chapter 10).

In determining how successful your attempts to communicate have been, remember that you may fail to change a person's attitude but still get that person to understand your point of view. In other words, a failure to change someone's point of view should not necessarily be written off as a failure to increase understanding.

Improved Relationships

It is commonly believed that if a person can select the right words, prepare his or her message ahead of time, and state it precisely, perfect communication will be ensured. But total effectiveness requires a positive and trusting psychological climate. When a human relationship is clouded by mistrust, numerous opportunities arise for distorting or discrediting even the most skillfully constructed messages. A young man will probably discount his date's assurances that she is very interested in him after she cancels an appointment for the third or fourth time. A professor may begin to doubt the excuses of a student whom she sees holding court at the student union an hour after the student was too sick to take the midterm.

We mentioned that the primary failures in communication occur when the content of the message is not understood accurately. By contrast, secondary failures are disturbances in human relationships that result from misunderstandings. They stem from the frustration, anger, or confusion (sometimes all three) caused by the initial failure to understand. Because such failures tend to polarize the communicators involved, they are difficult to resolve. By acknowledging that the initial misunderstandings are a common occurrence in daily communication, we may be able to tolerate them better and avoid or at least minimize their damaging effects on interpersonal relationships.

There is another kind of understanding, of course, that can have a profound effect on human relationships: understanding another person's motivations. At times each of us communicates not to convey information or to change someone's attitude but simply to be "understood" in this second sense. Throughout this text we shall discuss various facets of human relationships: motivation (Chapters 3 and 9); social choice (Chapter 5); confirmation, self-disclosure, and trust (Chapter 6); and group cohesiveness (Chapter 10). We hope to show that all these concepts are bound together by a common theme: the better the relationship between people, the more likely it is that other outcomes of effective communication in the fullest sense will also occur.

Action

Some would argue that all communication is useless unless it brings about a desired action. Yet all the outcomes discussed thus far—understanding, pleasure, attitude influence, improved relationships—are important at different times and in different places. There are instances, however, when action is an essential determinant of the success of a communicative act. An automobile salesman who wants you to think more favorably of his car than his competitor's also wants you to act by buying the car; his primary objective is not attitude change. A math tutor is far from satisfied if the student she is coaching says he understands how to do a set of problems but fails to demonstrate that understanding on his next exam. And we might question the effectiveness of a finance committee that reaches consensus on how to balance a budget yet fails to act on its decision.

Eliciting action on the part of another person is probably the

INTERPERSONAL COMMUNICATION

communication outcome most difficult to produce. In the first place it seems easier to get someone to understand your message than it is to get the person to agree with it. Furthermore, it seems easier to get that person to agree—that he or she should exercise regularly, for example —than to get the person to act on it. (We realize that some behaviors are induced through coercion, social pressure, or role prescriptions, and do not necessarily require prior attitude change. Voluntary actions, however, usually follow rather than precede attitude changes.) If you are trying to prompt action on the part of the receiver, you increase your chances of getting the desired response if you can (1) facilitate his or her understanding of your request, (2) secure his or her agreement that the request is legitimate, and (3) maintain a comfortable relationship with him or her. This is not to say that the desired action will automatically follow, but it is more likely to follow if these three intermediate objectives have first been accomplished.

In short, the five possible outcomes of effective human communication are understanding, pleasure, attitude influence, improved relationships, and action. At different points in this book, we shall give special attention to each of them. For example, the concepts of dogma-

Although this salesman may be trying to influence attitudes, his primary objective is action.

tism (Chapter 3), attitude similarity (Chapter 5), status (Chapter 9), and social influence and consensus (Chapter 10) all have some bearing on attitude influence. Similarly, the concepts of trust (Chapter 6) and cohesiveness (Chapter 10) are relevant to improved human relationships.

The five outcomes we have discussed are neither exhaustive nor mutually exclusive. Thus a look at the relationship aspects of communication in Chapter 6 will illustrate that defensive behaviors distort understanding, that the so-called disconfirming responses are not pleasurable, and that negative feedback makes for resistance to attitude influence. In the chapters that follow we hope to show some of the many ways in which communication outcomes are interdependent and to demonstrate that this is true for many different communication settings.

Summary

Human communication is unique because the superior ability of human beings to create and make use of symbols enables them to share their experiences indirectly. In studying interpersonal communication we limit ourselves to a portion of that experience: face-to-face, two-way communication. All interpersonal communication events fulfill three conditions. First, all parties are in close proximity. Second, all parties send and receive messages, and the outcome of interaction constantly changes as a result of their responses. And third, these messages include both verbal and nonverbal stimuli.

In the second half of this chapter we turned to an examination of what constitutes effective communication. We established that interpersonal communication is effective to the degree that the stimulus as it is intended by the sender corresponds with the stimulus as it is perceived and responded to by the receiver. We learned that effectiveness is closely linked to intention and that in communicating we usually want to bring about one or more of several possible outcomes. Five of the major communication outcomes—understanding, pleasure, attitude influence, improved relationships, and action—were considered.

Review Questions

1. Provide your own personal definition of communication. How is it similar to or different from the definitions given in the text?
2. State three characteristics of interpersonal communication. How does interpersonal communication differ from other types of communication?

3. What is intercultural communication?
4. List five outcomes of interpersonal communication. Give an example of each.
5. What is effective communication? Think of arguments for and against the types of communication effectiveness that have been described in this chapter. Are there some that the text has not included? Are there some it has discussed that you think should not be included? What do you think is the most important outcome of interpersonal communication?

Exercises

1. Start a personal log in which you record your daily reaction to perhaps ten members of your class. Only some will impress you (favorably or unfavorably) at first. Note details of their behavior. Describe your own responses as candidly as possible.
2. Observe several communication events and keep a record of their outcomes. Which outcomes occurred most frequently? Under what conditions did these outcomes appear to occur? How can you explain these results?
3. Write a one-page case study of a communication failure that you have experienced or observed. Then write an analysis of its causes and suggest a way to resolve it.

Suggested Readings

Barnlund, Dean C. *Interpersonal Communication: Survey and Studies*. Boston: Houghton Mifflin, 1968. This book is perhaps the single most comprehensive one available on the subject of interpersonal communication. A valuable in-depth sourcebook, it contains summaries of many points of view, along with thirty-seven articles covering a wide range of topics.

Berne, Eric. *Games People Play*. New York: Grove Press, 1964. This delightful best seller offers a framework for analyzing human interaction. Part I presents the Parent, Adult, Child mode of psychiatry, a neo-Freudian formula that is easy to follow and use. In Part II, Berne explains certain recognizable behaviors in terms of games, including such notable ones as, "Now I've Got You, You Son of a Bitch," "Ain't It Awful," and "Rapo."

Tubbs, Stewart and Carter, Robert (Eds.). *Shared Experiences in Human Communication*. Rochelle Park, N.J.: Hayden, 1977. This book is a collection of thirty-five articles on communication. The selections include a number of popularly written articles and chapters from books along with a few research articles. Among the topics discussed are transactional analysis, profane language, bralessness and eye contact, women's liberated role in communication, Parkinson's laws in groups, and listening.

Watzlawick, Paul, Beavin, Janet, and Jackson, Don. *Pragmatics of Human Communication.* New York: Norton, 1967. The authors offer an excellent explanation of several basic principles of communication, relating them to such areas as psychiatry and existentialism. In chapter five, the principles are applied in an analysis of the interaction in Edward Albee's play "Who's Afraid of Virginia Woolf?"

Chapter 2: A Model of Interpersonal Communication

OBJECTIVES

After reading this chapter the student should be able to:
1. List at least two characteristics of models.
2. State two criteria that may be used to evaluate models.
3. Describe what is referred to by the term "input" as it is used in the communication model.
4. Define the term "selective attention" and give an example of its relevance to communication.
5. Distinguish between physiological filters and psychological filters.
6. List four types of communicative stimuli and give an example of each type.
7. Identify three primary channels of interpersonal (that is, face-to-face) communication.
8. Explain the term "signal-to-noise ratio."
9. Distinguish between technical and semantic interference and give an example of each.
10. Identify the four processes involved in the act of listening.
11. List the three systems of human memory and indicate their functions.
12. Describe two concepts about the nature of interpersonal communication that are emphasized by spiral (or helical) models.
13. Describe three effects of time on interpersonal communication.
14. Draw and label a model of interpersonal communication using the following terms: sender/receiver, receiver/sender, input, filters, communicative stimuli, channels, interference, and time.

2

In both the physical and the social sciences, it is now popular to talk about "models." We are all familiar with the term "model" as it refers to a line-for-line replica of a thing—a building, an airplane, or even a living cell. But when scientists speak of models, they refer to something broader and more abstract. Some equate "model" with "theory"—a kind of theory in miniature. Simon and Newell (1963) have argued that there are three main kinds of theories: verbal, mathematical, and analogical theories. They illustrate with an example from economics. A verbal theory might include the statement: "Consumption increases linearly with income, but less than proportionately." In a mathematical theory, a corresponding statement would be given in the form of an equation: "$C = a + bY; a > 0; 0 < b < 1$." An analogical theory might relate the way goods and money move within an economy to the way liquid flows through a pump (Simon and Newell, 1963, p. 81).

Other writers feel that it is more precise to consider a model not as a theory but as a scientific metaphor—that is, an extended comparison between the subject we want to study and some object or process. For example, we might use a computer system as a model of the human memory and the way it processes information; in this case, the comparison would be drawn from computer technology. Kaplan has tried to refine the concept of the scientific metaphor even further by suggesting that it is more accurate to view "as models only those theories which explicitly direct attention to certain resemblances between the theoretical entities and the real subject-matter" (1964, p. 265).

Lately, the communication process itself has served as a model for explaining other phenomena. Thus the transmission of nerve impulses has been described in terms of a communication model. And in discussing human behavior, one writer refers to communication as "the only scientific model which enables us to explain physical, intrapersonal, interpersonal, and cultural aspects of events within one system" (Ruesch, in Ruesch and Bateson, 1968, p. 5).

Unlike the metaphors of literature, those of science need not consist of words. They may be equations. Or they may be made out of paper, wire, wax, steel, or any other material. The important thing to remember is that models are *made* by human beings. They do not exist in nature, though their terms may be drawn from nature. They

Helical models can apply to both chemistry—as in this DNA helix—and communication.

are abstractions. Thus many models can describe the same object or process or series of events. Each offers us another way to organize and classify data, another way to see relationships between parts. Each identifies and makes explicit the elements—or, to use a scientific term, the "variables"—to be studied. Kaplan explains this advantage of a model succinctly: "As inquiry proceeds, theories must be brought into the open sooner or later; the model simply makes it sooner" (1964, p. 269).

"If so many models exist, then how do I know which one is correct?" you might ask. This is an important question, for many models have been proposed to describe the communication process. Theorists agree that there is no single true model, just as there is no single correct metaphor. They propose instead that we evaluate models in terms of two criteria. First, how effectively does the model permit us to organize data and then make successful predictions about such data? And second, how much research does the model generate? Keep in mind that the model can prove valuable even if the research simply uncovers that it is a misleading one. In both criteria the primary concern is with utility. The question, then, is not "Is this the right model?" but "Is this the most useful model?"

One advantage of using a model is that it makes explicit the assumptions and interests of the model builder. It tells you what elements he or she intends to examine; indirectly, it also tells you what he or she is not examining. For example, the model of interpersonal communication in Figure 2.1, which we shall explore in some detail, is primarily concerned with directly observable and measurable experience—what happens *between* communicators and how their interaction evolves and changes over time. Instead of presenting a cross-section of one moment in a communication event, the present model tries to give you a sense of the movement of communication in time. This is called a **process model** of communication.

Some of the terms in which our model is explained—the metaphors, if you will—are taken from the study of the computer (for example, "input" or "information"), and others are from telecommunication (for example, "channel" and "interference"). This does not mean that interpersonal communication is synonymous with the operation of either a computer or a telephone. A model cannot be taken literally or applied rigidly to all phenomena. It is a framework from which we are able to generalize; it simplifies reality. Therefore, to explain a given communication event, we may have to put back the particulars of that event. We may even have to revise our model to accommodate new experiences. With these warnings in mind, let us turn to Figure 2.1.

This is a model of the most basic interpersonal communication event; it involves only two people. Initially, we shall call them the sender/receiver and the receiver/sender. In actuality, both are sources of communication, and at different times each originates and receives communicative stimuli. The sender/receiver may originate the first message and the receiver/sender may be the first to perceive the transmitted stimuli, but in most of our daily communication activities (which are spontaneous and relatively unstructured), this order is dictated by chance. Thus, as represented in the present model, a great many transactions can be initiated from either the right or left side. For example, when you got up this morning, did you speak to someone first or were you spoken to first? You probably don't even remember, because who spoke first was a matter of chance. In an important sense, it is arbitrary to call yourself either a sender or a receiver: you are both. Even while you are speaking, you are simultaneously observing the other person's behavior and reacting to it. This is also true of the other person as he or she interacts with you.

SENDER/RECEIVER

Let us take a closer look at the sender/receiver as he or she tries to transmit a message. What kinds of human characteristics does the

INTERPERSONAL COMMUNICATION

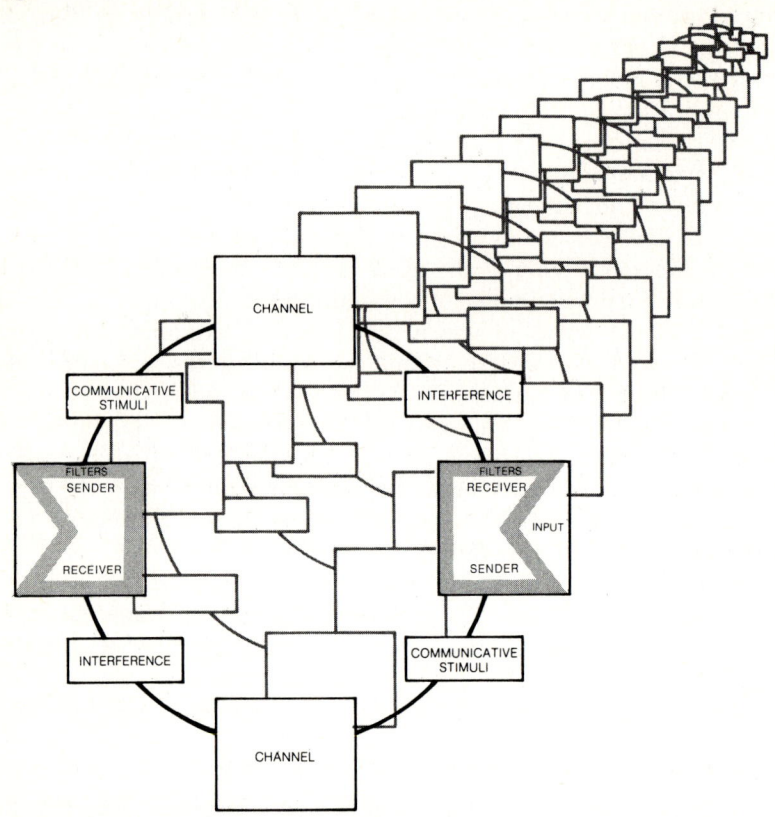

Figure 2.1

THE TUBBS COMMUNICATION MODEL

sender/receiver have that would be important in the communication process? Obviously, mental capacities are of central importance. Inside this person's brain are millions of nerve cells that function together to store and utilize knowledge, attitudes, and emotions. We want to know what makes this communicator distinct from any other communicator—in effect, what makes the sender/receiver the person he or she is.

Input

Like those of any other human being, the sender's senses are continually bombarded by a wealth of stimuli from both inside and outside the body. All that he or she knows and experiences—whether of the physical or the social world—comes initially through the senses.

Borrowing from computer terminology, we call these raw data **input,** *all the stimuli—both past and present—that give us our information about the world.*

From the accounts of explorers, castaways, and prisoners of war, we can learn what it is like to experience a long period of isolation, but even such people ordinarily have some sensory stimulation. The effect of radically decreased input—in solitary confinement, for example—is more difficult to imagine. You can get some notion of how dependent you are on a steady flow of stimuli by supposing that your senses were shut off one by one. Imagine what it would be like to be without them for a day or just an hour or even fifteen minutes.

To make the situation concrete, suppose a psychologist hires you to participate in a controlled experiment in which you must spend several days (probably three or four) lying on a bed in a cubicle that measures eight by four by six feet. To limit your tactile sensations, you wear cotton gloves and cylinders of cardboard on your arms from below your elbows to beyond the tips of your fingers. Translucent goggles allow you to see diffused light but no patterned stimuli. Your perception of sound is also cut to a minimum. You can speak with the experimenter by using an intercom, but such exchanges are not frequent. The only breaks in this routine are eating or going to the toilet. How long do you think you would last, and how would you feel during and after the experiment?

We know the answers to these questions because in 1953 a group of researchers at McGill University, in Montreal, performed this experiment. They wanted to study the effects of **sensory deprivation,** or *extremely limited sensory intake,* on normal human beings. From the description in the preceding paragraph, you can see that the test conditions were monotonous but not frightening. There were simply very few stimuli. Yet most of the subjects felt their experience had been unpleasant, and few lasted longer than two or three days. Some felt disoriented and were easily upset. Some daydreamed much of the time. Others had blank periods. One remarkable finding was that many people experienced hallucinations; these ranged from geometric patterns to actual scenes. Not all the hallucinations were visual. Some participants heard speech or music. One reported that his head felt detached from his body. It seems as though when input is limited, people start creating it for themselves.

Several sensory deprivation studies were done at McGill during the 1950s, and research is still going on in Canada and the United States. Although much remains to be learned about the effects of limited sensory input, it has been shown that we depend on stimuli not only for our initial knowledge about the world but also for our daily functioning. One psychologist sums up the findings of sensory deprivation research this way: "human beings are individually, socially, and physiologically dependent not only upon stimulation, but upon a continually varied and changing sensory stimulation in order to maintain normal, intelligent, coordinated, adaptive behavior and mental functioning" (Brownfield, 1965, pp. 74–75).

The reason you find it so difficult to imagine yourself in a situation that provides little or no input is that most of the time you do receive "varied and changing sensory stimulation." In fact, you receive more input than you can possibly handle, and there are specific cells in the nervous system, inhibitory neurons, that filter out some of these incoming stimuli to keep them from your conscious awareness. Were it not for inhibitory neurons, says Kern (1971), we would experience something comparable to an epileptic seizure every time we opened our eyes.

Despite these neurological checks on our perception, there are still times when there seem to be too many stimuli. In addition to the normal input of human life, city dwellers are besieged by the noises and distractions of an urban environment. And wherever we live, mass communication provides us with a deluge of information. Under ordinary circumstances, then, so many stimuli assail us at a conscious level that we can experience only a small portion of the total. You can illustrate this for yourself. Right now you are primarily aware of reading this page in this book. Try moving your toes. Are you now aware of your shoes, socks, or bare feet? You have just brought this sensory input to the conscious level. The sensations are always there, but you probably were not consciously experiencing them.

Because your capacity to register sensory stimuli is limited, you cannot take in everything. Nor do you always want to. You choose certain aspects of your environment over others. What you are aware of at any time is determined in part by what you as a receiver *select* out of the total input. "You hear what you want to hear," mutters the irritated father to his teen-age son. "This is the third time this afternoon I've asked you when you're going to get around to washing the car." Later that day the same man may sit at the dinner table reading the Sunday paper, oblivious to a family quarrel that is taking place across the room. The American philosopher and psychologist William James has explained the process of selection that is at work here in terms of interest or attention: "Millions of items of the outward order are present to my senses which never properly enter into my experience. Why? Because they have no *interest* for me. *My experience is what I agree to attend to*. Only those items which I *notice* shape my mind—without selective interest, experience is an utter chaos" (James, 1950, p. 402).

It was more than eighty years ago that James referred to "selective interest." Today the name given to the receiver's ability to process certain of the stimuli available to him or her while filtering out others is **selective attention**. As receivers we attend selectively to all sensory stimuli. One area of special interest for the student of interpersonal communication is selective listening, which during the past twenty-five years has been the subject of considerable research.

In the 1950s researchers began studying the so-called cocktail party problem—how a person manages to listen to a single voice when several other people are speaking simultaneously. They found that a person will try to focus on one voice at a time rather than shift his or her attention from one person's voice to another (Broadbent, 1958). This is probably due in part to greater interest in a continuous message than in several interrupted messages. Another finding was that the receiver is able to sort out one voice much more easily when it enters only one ear, with a competing message coming in the other ear, than if both messages are heard by the same ear (Moray, 1969, p. 17).

One of the most popular techniques of listening research is speech shadowing, which requires that a listener wearing headphones repeat a message presented to one ear and ignore a second message presented simultaneously to the other ear. Since this task requires a great deal of concentration, for some time most researchers believed that information in the rejected message was completely ignored. It was found, however, that a person completely involved in listening to the speech presented to one ear will be responsive to the sound of his or her own name in the other ear, even if that person is unresponsive to all the other words in this second message. It was also true that "speech entering the rejected ear can break through to the subject's attention if it consists of words that would probably follow the words that have just been heard by the ear that is receiving attention" (Broadbent, in Smith, 1966, p. 282). In other words, as receivers we are more likely to attend to messages that have emotional value for us or to messages that are highly probable (that is, those we expect to hear). From his survey of listening research, Moray concludes that "a listener *is* able to exercise considerable voluntary control over what he will hear" (1969, p. 88). Bear in mind, however, that selective attention is not always a totally conscious process.

Filters

No two people—not even identical twins—have the same input, even when their environment seems constant. In addition, no two people perceive in exactly the same way. That is why they often disagree even when they are given what seems to be the same information. In our model, selective attention is represented by the filters through which all input or sensation must pass. Simply put, a **filter** is *a limit on our capacity to sense or perceive stimuli*. Filters are of two kinds: physiological and psychological. We shall call them "perceptual filters" and "sets," respectively.

A MODEL OF INTERPERSONAL COMMUNICATION

26

Our sets about how people should speak, look, and act sometimes interfere with the ability to perceive them accurately.

Perceptual Filters. How far do you trust your senses? Most of us trust our senses so much that we are offended at the suggestion that we might have observed something inaccurately. "But I saw it with my own eyes," we counter. Yet we are often unaware of the many stimuli that are filtered out of our experience. To begin with, all living creatures have upper and lower limits (thresholds) of stimulus intensity above and below which they are unable to perceive. Human beings cannot see infrared and ultraviolet light rays. Nor can they hear the sound of a dog whistle: it has too high a frequency for human ears. These **perceptual filters** are *biological limitations that are built into human beings* and cannot be reversed. Moreover, they vary somewhat from one person to another so that we differ in the degree to which our various senses are accurate.

To the human communicator one extremely troublesome perceptual filter is the limit on one's ability to hear. Sometimes we think we hear a person say one thing when actually he or she said another. We then act on the basis of what we think that person said. Or we may act without hearing what a person said at all. Many communication

A MODEL OF INTERPERSONAL COMMUNICATION

difficulties are rooted in this kind of misunderstanding. For example, one woman found out through a third party that she had antagonized her next-door neighbor by "cutting her dead." It turned out that the neighbor had walked by and said hello while the woman was standing at her front door anxiously awaiting her young son. This was the first day she had allowed him to walk home himself from his first-grade class, and the boy was late. Apparently, she was staring in the direction of the school and never even heard the neighbor's greeting. The neighbor, who was rather new to the community, interpreted the woman's unresponsiveness as a snub.

Sets. Other forms of selection can be just as strong as perceptual filters. For example, ask someone to complete the following sentence:

> *P-o-l-k* is pronounced *poke,* and *f-o-l-k* is pronounced *foke,* and the white of an egg is pronounced . . . ?

Although the white of an egg is called "albumen," you will find that most people answer "yolk." Miller (1965, p. 22) explains this reaction as a verbal habit. Because of what precedes the last part of the sentence, we expect a word that will rhyme with "polk" and "folk." **Set** is the word used to describe this *expectancy* or *predisposition to respond.* Here is how set functions when we look at a piece of sculpture:

> When we step in front of a bust we understand what we are expected to look for. We do not, as a rule, take it to be a representation of a cut-off head; we take in the situation and know that this belongs to the institution or convention called "busts" with which we have been familiar even before we grew up. For the same reason, we do not miss the absence of color in the marble any more than we miss its absence in black-and-white photographs (Gombrich, 1961, p. 60).

One of the most powerful determinants of set is culture. Consider the two parallel straight lines in Figure 2.2. Which would you say is longer? Chances are that if you live in a Western culture, you will perceive the top line as being the longer of the two. If you measure them, though, you will see that they are actually the same length. This is a well-known phenomenon known as the Müller-Lyer illusion. It is an illusion in visual perception that Western peoples are particularly likely to experience, and one to which certain non-Western peoples are much less susceptible.

Figure 2.2

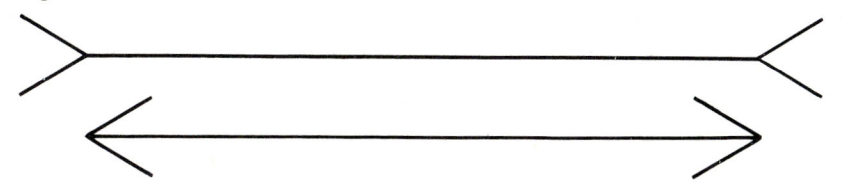

One explanation for the Müller-Lyer illusion is that people who live in a visual environment in which straight lines and right angles prevail—a "carpentered world" constructed with tools such as the saw, the plane, and the plumb bob—learn to make certain visual inferences. For example, they tend to interpret acute and obtuse angles as right angles that are extended in space. This is what happens when Westerners look at Figure 2.2. From the two-dimensional drawing they make inferences about perspective, thus seeing the two lines as unequal in length. People who live in a culture that has very few structures made up of straight lines and corners—people from Ghana, for example—are not likely to experience the Müller-Lyer illusion because they do not tend to make such inferences about perspective (Segall, Campbell, and Herskovits, in Price-Williams, 1969). This is just one way in which culture influences our perception. We shall examine others in Chapter 4.

We have sets not only about objects and words but about other human beings—what they should look like, how they should act, and what they will say. In our culture a businessperson expects people who have appointments at his or her office to be on time, and in turn those people do not expect to be kept waiting for long periods of time. When these expectancies are shared by all involved, they are often useful in facilitating communication. Other sets interfere with our ability to perceive accurately and respond appropriately. For example, some people—especially in telephone conversations—are so accustomed to being asked how they are that after saying "Hi" or "Hello" they answer "Fine" to whatever the other party has just said.

A great deal of interpersonal conflict stems from people's unaware-

The carpentered world; straight lines and corners predominate in most Western cultures.

The uncarpentered world: Zulu villagers see few structures with straight lines or corners.

ness of the limits on their perceptual capacities. If they do realize the fallibility of their senses, they may be too defensive to acknowledge their mistakes. There is now convincing evidence that in some situations, if such a person is pressed, his or her opposition to our point is likely to be reinforced instead of changed, even though the person appears to be agreeing with us.

As two people communicate, each formulates ideas that become the content of the communication event. How accurately a message is received depends on the other person's perceptual filters and sets. Remember that psychological and physiological characteristics will influence which stimuli are selected and how they are perceived.

COMMUNICATIVE STIMULI

Looking again at the model in Figure 2.1, we can think of the message that the sender/receiver transmits as being conveyed in the form of communicative stimuli. These stimuli may be verbal or nonverbal, and they may be intentional or unintentional. Thus four types of stimuli are possible: (1) intentional verbal, (2) unintentional verbal, (3) intentional nonverbal, and (4) unintentional nonverbal. As we examine these categories individually, keep in mind that most messages contain two or more types of stimuli and that they often overlap.

Verbal Stimuli

A verbal stimulus is *any type of spoken communication that uses one or more words*. Most of the communicative stimuli we are conscious of fall within the category of **intentional verbal**; these are *the conscious attempts we make to communicate with others through speech*.

Intentional verbal stimuli may be classified according to the elements in the message that influence how it is received. Suppose that Sharon, a college sophomore, wants to persuade her younger brother to stop taking drugs. She has several options. She can warn him that he is going to be arrested. She can threaten to tell their parents. She can cite the opinion of a psychiatrist. She can present him with some medical statistics and let him draw his own conclusions. She can sum up both sides of the issue by stating its pros and cons or just state her own point of view. In short, she must choose among **message variables,** or *alternate ways of presenting a single message*.

Much of the research on human communication concerns verbal message variables. Among the questions that have been studied are whether scare tactics or emotional appeals are persuasive, whether you should state both sides of an issue or give a simple statement of your own viewpoint, and whether you should allow the other person to draw his own conclusions from your argument or draw them yourself. The relative effectiveness of the variables is usually measured by which persuades people most readily to change their attitudes.

Unintentional verbal stimuli are *the things we say without meaning to*. Freud argued that all the apparently unintentional stimuli we transmit—both verbal and nonverbal—are unconsciously motivated. We cannot discuss the merits of this argument here, but we can cite an amusing example of a slip of the tongue described by one of Freud's colleagues: "While writing a prescription for a woman who was especially weighed down by the financial burden of the treatment, I was interested to hear her say suddenly: 'Please do not give me *big bills,* because I cannot swallow them.' Of course, she meant to say *pills*" (Brill, quoted in Freud, 1938, p. 82).

Everyone makes slips occasionally. For example, one of the authors heard a young man say that on a scale from one to five, he rated the college football team seven. He probably intended to say "on a scale from one to ten." A speech professor once explained to his students that "With a singular subject you must use a plural verb." He did not realize what he had said until his students started to laugh. Sometimes it is only when we get feedback from others (in this instance, laughter) that we become aware we have even transmitted such stimuli. In general, unintentional stimuli, both verbal and nonverbal, tend to increase in number if the person is a poor communicator.

Nonverbal Stimuli

Nonverbal stimuli cannot be described as easily as verbal stimuli, probably because the category is so broad. They include all the nonverbal aspects of our behavior: facial expression, posture, tone of voice, hand movements, manner of dress, and so on. In short, *they are all the stimuli we transmit without words or over and above the words we use.*

Let us first consider **intentional nonverbal stimuli,** *the nonverbal stimuli we want to transmit.* Sometimes we rely exclusively on nonverbal stimuli; sometimes we use them to reinforce verbal stimuli. For example, you can greet someone by smiling and nodding your head, or you can say "Hello" and also smile or wave. At times we deliberately use nonverbal stimuli to cancel out a polite verbal response and indicate our true feelings: the verbal message may be positive, but the tone of voice and facial expression indicate that we mean something negative. Maintaining eye contact with a person who is speaking to you is another nonverbal stimulus. It conveys interest and attention. It also offers feedback to the speaker, and in some cases it tells the speaker whether you understand or agree with what he or she is saying.

Interpreting nonverbal stimuli can be difficult, and it may require some insight to determine whether or not they are intentional. Many expressions that seem unintentional are in fact deliberate. Think of a weary clerk in the complaint department of a large store. She has been told that the customers must be treated politely—even when they are offensive. There must be many times when she would like to express her annoyance. She can do this by speaking politely but purposely conveying her mood through her tone of voice. Similarly, a friend who assures you that "Nothing is wrong" lets you know that something is very wrong by casually dropping his lip and lowering his voice. Most of us use such tactics from time to time, which makes them easier to spot in others.

Thayer (1963) has stressed the notion that much of what we are as a person "communicates" itself every time we behave. A great deal of this behavior is unintentional. Some writers on the subject go so far as to assert that what we communicate is what we are. **Unintentional nonverbal stimuli** are *all those nonverbal aspects of our behavior transmitted without our control.* For example, one of the authors once told a student speaker to relax. "I am relaxed," the student replied in a tight voice, speaking over the rattling of a paper he was holding. A problem frequently raised in management classes is that store managers unintentionally communicate anger or impatience to their customers. This is a situation different from that of the angry clerk in the complaint department: she does not depend on the good will of the customer, but the store manager does, and she wants to control her nonverbal cues.

Controlling nonverbal stimuli is a very difficult task. Facial expressions, posture, tone of voice, hand gestures—what some writers have called "body language"—often give us away. Ralph Waldo Emerson phrased it well when he remarked to a speaker, "What you are speaks so loudly that I cannot hear what you say." And of course the better a person knows you, the more likely he or she is to pick up your nonverbal expressions—even if you don't want that to happen. Lest we paint too dark a picture, however, we should add that as your communication skills improve, you may find that the number of unintentional stimuli you transmit will decrease significantly.

CHANNELS

If you are talking on the telephone, the channels that transmit the communicative stimuli are the telephone wires. The **channels** of face-to-face communication are the sensory organs. Although all five senses may receive the stimuli, you rely almost exclusively on three: hearing, sight, and touch. For example, you listen to someone state an argument, or you exchange knowing glances with a friend, or you put your hand on someone's shoulder.

In the less formal contexts of communication we rarely think about communication channels. Usually, a person becomes aware of them only when one or more are cut off or when some sort of interference is present. For example, if there is a large vase of flowers between two people trying to talk across a dinner table, both lose a lot because they are unable to see each other's faces. They may even find it too unsettling to carry on a conversation without the presence of facial cues. In other words, face-to-face communication is a multichannel experience. Simultaneously, we receive and make use of information from a number of different channels. In general, the more channels being used, the greater the number of communicative stimuli transmitted.

It follows that the more channels being used, the greater the possibility of transmitting unintentional stimuli. At times, the receiver finds himself or herself confronted with contradictory messages, and he or she has to decide which channel is likely to carry the most accurate information. Weitz found, for example, that within a group of white "liberals," tone of voice and behavior were much more accurate channels in reflecting friendliness toward blacks than was verbalized attitude. In fact, there was a significant negative correlation between verbal attitude and actual behavior: "the more friendly the attitude, the less friendly the behavior" (Weitz, 1972, p. 20).

Both individual and cultural preferences exist in our choice of channels. Dittmann (1972) observes, for example, that in conveying emotion the members of some cultures favor the voice over the face. In *A Rap on Race,* Margaret Mead and James Baldwin speak about cultural differences with respect to the sense of touch:

Mead: . . . Now one thing I'd like to ask you about is the whole role of touch. It seems to me that the average middle-class American is exceedingly inhibited about touching other people.
Baldwin: He's frozen, really.
Mead: He's frozen. He maybe shakes hands.
Baldwin: Even that is done nervously.
Mead: He doesn't really enjoy it. Now my general experience in working with black people is that I always have to touch them, or they touch me if we are going to get anywhere.
Baldwin: Oh, yeah.
Mead: I feel, if I don't touch them, I haven't communicated with them at all. I could sit across the room and make beautiful speeches forever, but one touch makes the difference, just one touch.
Baldwin: I don't know why that is. I remember once in Africa I watched the way Africans carried their babies; they wrapped them in this thing on their backs. Somebody said it's almost the key to the African psychology, because when the baby needs something all the baby's got to do is knock. (Mead and Baldwin, 1971, pp. 45–46)

Note here that even for Mead, who is not black, touch is a preferred channel of communication in her exchanges with black people. Both as senders and receivers many of us have strong preferences for a particular channel of communication.

INTERFERENCE

Once the sender has initiated a message, he or she almost always assumes that it has been received. The sender is puzzled or annoyed if he or she is misinterpreted or gets no response. The sender may even have taken special pains to make the message very clear. "Isn't that enough?" the sender asks. In effect, he or she wants to know what went wrong between the transmission and reception of the message.

The communication scholar would answer, **interference,** or **noise**—that is, *anything that distorts the information transmitted to the receiver or distracts him or her from receiving it.* In communication theory the terms "interference" and "noise" are synonymous. "Interference" is probably a more appropriate word, but because "noise" was the term first used in studies of telecommunication, you should be familiar with it too. Claude Shannon and Warren Weaver, the authors of one of the earliest communication models, spoke of the noise that could interfere with the transmission of a signal. And in discussing the problem of noise in relation to television, Cherry indicates its broader meaning by saying that " 'noise' refers to any disturbance or interference, apart from the wanted signals or messages selected and being sent" (1966, p. 42).

If you think of noise as "any disturbance or interference," you will soon realize that noise need not be sound. It can be visual, for example. Winston Churchill was once quite successful in creating a lot of noise without uttering a word. The members of Parliament were being addressed by a speaker of an opposing party. Looking very intent, Churchill bent down and groped along the floor, pretending to search for a missing collar button. He succeeded in distracting almost all the members of Parliament from listening to the speech. Whether Churchill accomplished what he intended is another question. Festinger and Maccoby (1964) have found that under some circumstances people who are distracted when listening to a communication tend to change their attitudes more in the direction of the communication.

Signal-to-Noise Ratio

We can think of noise, or interference, in terms of how it affects information. Cherry writes, "Noise is the destroyer of information and sets the ultimate upper limit to the information capacity of a channel." (1966, p. 176) **Signal-to-noise ratio** is the term often used to denote *the relationship between the essential information in a message and the extraneous or distracting factors.* You may know people whose communication is characterized by a little signal and much noise. Occasionally, they are charming. More often they are boring and annoying. In effect, they tell you more than you want to know.

Shakespeare was a master at portraying the exasperating quality of "noisy" replies. This is the way that Polonius, the lord chamberlain, tells the king and queen that Hamlet is mad:

> My liege, and madam, to expostulate
> What majesty should be, what duty is,
> Why day is day, night night, and time is time,
> Were nothing but to waste night, day and time.
> Therefore, since brevity is the soul of wit,
> And tediousness the limbs and outward flourishes,
> I will be brief: your noble son is mad:
> Mad call I it; for, to define true madness,
> What is't but to be nothing else but mad?
> But let that go.

To which the queen briskly answers: "More matter, with less art" (*Hamlet,* Act 2, Scene 2).

Let's consider a more familiar kind of dialogue:

Fred: How do you get to Detroit from Flint?
Sam: Well, gosh, I've taken several ways. Back in the 1950s I used to go along Dixie Highway, but that isn't as good any more. I remember that road because that's where I learned to drive. I still enjoy driving on a Sunday afternoon. Do you?
Fred: Yes, but how do I get to Detroit?
Sam: Detroit—oh, yes, Detroit. Now there's a real city. Some people wouldn't agree with me, but I've always liked Detroit. Say the best way to get to Detroit might be to take Interstate 75.

To Fred, Sam's last sentence is signal; all the rest is noise. Fred asks a simple question and gets far more than he wants. For his purposes, much of the information Sam provides is useless. At first glance, we might say that Sam is a bore or that he can't concentrate because his mind wanders. Yet the reasons Sam supplies all the detail about himself may be complex. He may feel that this is the way to be friendly. He may be trying to communicate something more about himself so that Fred will take greater interest in him. He may be stalling for time as he tries to remember the name "Interstate 75" so that he won't lose face. Certainly, he is unaware of the poor impression he is making on Fred.

Technical and Semantic Interference

We can also distinguish between two kinds of interference: technical interference and semantic interference. **Technical interference** refers to *the factors that cause the receiver to perceive distortion in the intended information or stimuli.* And the sender too may create the distortion: if he or she has a speech impediment or even simply mumbles, he or she may have difficulty making words clear to another person. Someone at a party may not be able to hear the response of the other person because the stereo is blaring or because other people standing nearby are speaking so loudly. In this case, the interference is simply the transmission of the sounds of other people in conversation.

The second type of interference is **semantic interference,** which occurs when *the receiver does not attribute the same meaning to the signal that the sender does.* For example, a city official and a social worker got into a heated argument over the causes of crime. The city official argued that the causes were primarily "economic," and the social worker maintained, quite predictably, that they were largely "social." Only after considerable discussion did the two begin to realize that although they had been using different terms, essentially they were referring to the same phenomena.

Disagreements about meaning are so common that one writer makes the distinction between meaning to the speaker and meaning to the listener (Cherry, 1966, pp. 116–117). The closer the fit between the two meanings, of course, the more complete the communication. Bear in mind, however, that no two people will attribute exactly the same meaning to any word and that it is also possible for people to attribute meanings to nonverbal messages. We said in Chapter 1 that we can never reach 1—the perfect sharing of meaning. We can only approximate it. For meanings, as Berlo has emphasized, "are not in the message, they are in the message-users" (in Barnlund, 1962, p. 199).

We shall have a great deal more to say about meaning and sources of interference in Chapters 7 and 8, when we discuss verbal and nonverbal messages.

As we have seen, interference can exist in the context of the communication, in the channel, in the communicator who sends the message, or in the one who receives it. Some interference will always be present in human communication.

RECEIVER/SENDER

Traditionally, emphasis has been given to the communicator as message sender, but equally important to any viable model of interpersonal communication is an analysis of the communicator as receiver. For most communication, visual perception will be an essential aspect of message reception, one that will be discussed further in Chapters 4 and 8. Another critical aspect of message reception is **listening**.

Listening and hearing are far from synonymous. To quote Barker, listening is "the selective process of attending to, hearing, understanding, and remembering aural symbols" (1971, p. 17). In other words, when the receiver/sender listens, four different yet interrelated processes will be involved: attention, hearing, understanding, and remembering.

We have already discussed *attention* on pp. 24–25. The second element in the act of listening is **hearing**, "the physiological process of receiving aural stimuli" (Barker, 1971, p. 17). We hear when sound waves are received by the ear and stimulate neurological impulses to the brain. (Listening may also involve visual communication, so that the eyes may also serve as message receptors.) The assumption is that in most human communication a receiver's physical hearing apparatus is functioning adequately and that therefore listening problems cannot be identified with hearing problems.

Understanding, sometimes referred to as "auding," is the process by which the communicator assigns a meaning to the aural stimuli he or she receives. That meaning may or may not correspond closely to the meaning intended by the person who sends the message, as we have already emphasized.

Remembering, the final element in the listening process, involves the storage of information for later retrieval. If someone gives you directions to her house and you understand them but forget the directions halfway to your destination, then your listening was still not as useful as it might have been. To some extent most listening tests are tests of how much we remember of what we have heard and understood.

Human memory involves at least three different memory systems. The first is **sensory information storage,** a system in which an accurate image of the events the receiver has experienced at the sensory level is maintained for a very short time period (approximately .1 to .5 seconds). The information the receiver maintains in *short-term memory,* the second memory system, would be "the immediate **interpretation** of these events" (Lindsay and Norman, 1972, p. 288). Short-term memory can handle about six or seven items of information at a time. For example, it is short-term memory that allows you to remember the digits of a new telephone number long enough to dial it after you get it from information. A constant rehearsal of the items is required to keep them in short-term memory. In contrast with the very limited capacity of this system, the capacity of *long-term memory* seems to be virtually unlimited. "Everything that is retained for more than a few minutes at a time obviously must reside in the long-term memory system. All learned experiences, including the rules of language" (Lindsay and Norman, 1972, p. 288). Of course, the various memory systems play a part in all forms of message reception—not just in listening. Often it is important to recall not only what was said but how the person looked when he or she said it, whether the person reached out and touched you to emphasize some point, and so on. Moreover, Barker astutely reminds us that "the information you remember may not be the same message you heard initially" (1971, p. 34).

Thus far we have discussed the transmission and reception of a single message. At this point, however, our model departs from several current models which create the illusion that all communication has a definite starting point with a sender and a termination point with a receiver. When the second communicator in Figure 2.1 has received a message, we have come only halfway through the continuous and ongoing process that is communication. For each receiver of a message is also a sender of messages—hence, the term "receiver/sender." Moreover, that person's uniqueness as a human being ensures that his or her attempts to communicate will be very different from those of the other person in the model. For example, that person's cultural input may be quite unlike that of the first communicator. His or her filters, both physiological and psychological, will be different. The stimuli he or she transmits will be different. Even the selection of channels and sources of difficulty, or interference, may differ.

The present model includes these differences as inherent parts of the communication process. Although the lower half of the circle lists the same elements as the upper half—input, filters, communicative stimuli, channels, interference—and these elements are defined in the same way, they are always different in content from those in the upper half. The transmission and reception of a single message is only one part of our model. Face-to-face communication in particular is characterized by its interdependent participants and the explicit and immediate feedback between them.

TIME

Once the receiver/sender responds to the first communicator, their interaction can be represented by a circle. But as their exchange progresses in time, the relationship between them is more accurately described by several circles. In fact, all but the briefest exchanges entail several communication cycles. Thus time itself becomes the final element in our model.

We have tried to convey the presence of time in Figure 2.1 by representing communication in the form of a spiral, like an uncoiled spring. Some writers prefer to symbolize time as a helix; the only difference between these forms is that the spiral is usually regarded as two-dimensional whereas the helix is thought of as three-dimensional. We shall treat them as identical.

Spiral (or helical) models emphasize the effect of the past on present or future behavior. Dance sums up this emphasis in the following way:

> At any and all times, the helix gives geometrical testimony to the concept that communication while moving forward is at the same moment coming back upon itself and being affected by its past behavior. . . . The communication process, like the helix, is constantly moving forward and yet is always to some degree dependent upon the past, which informs the present and the future (Dance, 1967, p. 295).

The spiral also illustrates that participants in the communication process can never return to the point at which they started. Their relationship must undergo change as a result of each interaction. Let us look briefly at some of the ways in which time changes communication.

First, time affects the *intensity* of human relationships. Marathon encounter groups tacitly acknowledge this principle. The participants are brought together for an extended period—usually six to twenty-four hours. As they learn to express themselves more openly, the interaction reaches a high level of intensity. If the group were to meet only one hour a week for six to twenty-four weeks, such intensity would be difficult to achieve. In terms of the model, it is as though we were pulling the ends of the spring farther and farther apart. In other words, a human relationship is not constant; its intensity is affected by the amount of time that passes between encounters.

The effect of time is often dramatized in relationships between people who are far apart in age. Consider communication between mother and child. The *mode,* or form, of their communication changes over time. At first the communication is essentially nonverbal. The infant signals need for food and comfort by wailing, but cannot use language. A mother responds by satisfying these needs; she may speak to the infant as she does this, but she does not expect a response. Slowly the child learns to communicate in other ways. It begins to smile when it is happy or amused. Even the pattern of crying changes. Later the child learns to point toward desired objects. At about age one he or she learns to walk and can lead the mother toward things that are out of reach. By this time the child often can say two or three words and shows clear evidence that many more are understood. The mother has already begun to use some discipline and whether the child listens or not—probably not—the word "no" is understood. By the end of the second year, the child's vocabulary has expanded to such a degree that he or she can sometimes make up simple two- or three-word sentences such as "Give cake" or "Me cup." Once language is mastered, mother and child can communicate in new ways. Nonverbal communication still takes place, but the shift in emphasis from non-verbal to verbal makes possible a change in the kind of relationship that evolves between mother and child.

In addition to changing intensity and mode, time can also change the *style* of communication. When two people first meet, they usually try to be as explicit as possible in their communication. Even if the two share several interests, one does not assume that the other knows what he or she is thinking or trying to say. This kind of insight develops only after long acquaintance. Sometimes two people get to know each other so well that each can anticipate much of what the other is trying to communicate. We frequently see this relationship in married couples or very close friends; to use the term of the Russian psychologist Vygotsky, their speech becomes "abbreviated" (1962, p. 141).

Communication of this kind can have its limitations. For example, at home Nick and Marie had often discussed the unit they intended to buy that would accommodate their stereo and speakers. The only obstacle was money. Then an unexpected dividend check appeared in the mail one morning, and that afternoon the couple visited a large showroom of stereophonic equipment:

Salesman: May I help you?
Nick: Yes. We'd like to see a console for keeping stereo equipment and records.
Marie: A console? I don't want a console. They're big and ugly. I don't like them.
Nick: Well, I *thought* that was what you wanted.
Marie: I never said that. We said when we got the money we would buy a unit.

Whereupon husband and wife, completely ignoring the salesman, launched into a private argument about what each thought the other had had in mind. In such instances, speech has become too abbreviated: one person takes for granted that he or she knows what the other is thinking, and that person turns out to be wrong. Even when the two parties who use abbreviated speech are in agreement, they can unwittingly alienate a third party by making that person feel left out; he or she may be at a loss to understand much of what the other two are talking about.

Thus the effect of time on communication is not always constructive. It would be ideal if time always moved interpersonal transactions toward greater and greater effectiveness. But we know, for example, that communication between parent and child becomes more difficult as the child reaches adolescence. Time does not always erase differences. Indeed, it can have a negative effect on communication. If two friends quarrel bitterly, the passage of time may help transform their anger into total alienation because it incorporates repeated misunderstandings that reinforce the original disagreement.

Throughout this text we shall try to point out the effects of time on communication. Implicit in this emphasis is our belief that time is one of the most relevant variables in the study of interpersonal communication. If it does nothing else, the spiral model should remind us that communication is not static and that it thus requires different methods of analysis from a fixed entity. Dance sums up the problem so well that we simply quote his statement here:

> The means of examining something in a quiescent and immobile state are quite different from the means of examining something that is in constant flux, motion, and process. If communication is viewed as a process, we are forced to adapt our examination and our examining instruments to the challenge of something in motion, something that is changing while we are in the very act of examining it. (Dance, 1967, pp. 293–294)

The model identifies some of the major elements that exist in all interpersonal communication. We have discussed such communication only in its simplest form. As we add more communicators, change the kind or amount of interference, or vary the stimuli transmitted, our subject increases in complexity.

As you read on you may want to look at other models, some of which are mentioned in the books at the end of this chapter. You may even want to try your hand at developing a model of your own. In either case remember that each communication event you will study has something unique about it, and no model can be used as a blueprint of the communication process.

Summary

In this chapter we defined models as scientific metaphors and discussed some of their advantages and limitations. We presented a model to help us conceptualize the relationships between the elements of interpersonal communication. Like all human beings, both communicators in our model originate and perceive communicative stimuli. Both depend on the steady flow of physical, social, and cultural input, and both select from the total input through their perceptual filters and sets.

We then discussed the components of a message in terms of the types of stimuli transmitted: verbal and nonverbal, intentional and unintentional. We learned that though all five senses are potential channels for receiving stimuli, face-to-face communication relies primarily on hearing, sight, and touch and is usually a multichannel experience. Anything that distorts the information transmitted through the various channels or that distracts the receiver from getting it would be considered interference. Moreover, a distinction can be made between technical and semantic interference.

We saw that all the elements in the sender/receiver's half of our communication cycle—input, filters, communicative stimuli, channels, and interference—are different for the receiver/sender because of his or her uniqueness as a human being. Emphasis was given to the receiver as listener, and four processes involved in the act of listening were discussed. Finally, we examined the effect of time, represented in the model by a spiral, as a crucial variable in all studies of communication.

Review Questions

1. What are two characteristics of models? What criteria may be used to evaluate the worth of models?

2. What is input and how does it influence a person's communication?
3. What is selective attention? Give an example of its relevance to communication.
4. How do physiological and psychological filters differ?
5. Name the four types of communicative stimuli. Give a specific example of each from your own experience.
6. What are the three primary channels of interpersonal communication?
7. What is the signal-to-noise ratio?
8. Explain the difference between technical and semantic interference and give an example of each.
9. Name the four processes involved in the act of listening.
10. Identify the three systems of human memory and explain their functions.
11. What do spiral (or helical) models suggest about the nature of interpersonal communication?
12. Discuss intensity, mode, and style of face-to-face communication as functions of time.

Exercises

1. a. Draw and label a model of interpersonal communication. If possible, include components that can be appropriately labeled as sender/receiver, receiver/sender, input, filters, communicative stimuli, channels, interference, and time.
b. Examine the model carefully and formulate five statements that describe how two or more components of the model may influence communication effectiveness as defined in Chapter 1 (see objective 5, p. 2).
c. To what extent would your model meet the criteria for evaluating models?
2. Select a group of about ten students and ask them to discuss one of the case problems listed in the Appendix. Observe the group and, if possible, tape-record the discussion. Analyze the group's communication in terms of intentional, unintentional, verbal, and nonverbal stimuli.
3. Write a short paper in which you analyze the strengths and weaknesses of the communication model in this chapter. Compare and contrast it with some other models that may be found in the books in the Suggested Readings.

Suggested Readings

Budd, Richard, and Ruben, Brent (Eds.). *Approaches to Human Communication.* Rochelle Park, N.J.: Hayden, 1973. The editors of this excellent sourcebook have brought together a vast array of articles on communication theory. Communication theory is applied to such diverse subject areas as art, economics and marketing, general systems theory, history, international behavior, nonverbal behavior, organizational behavior, and therapeutic transaction.

Dance, Frank E. X. (Ed.). *Human Communication Theory: Original Essays.* New York: Holt, Rinehart, and Winston, 1967. This important collection of essays contains interesting articles that cover communication theory from the various perspectives of anthropology, neurophysiology, psychiatry, psychology, sociology, and other fields of study.

Ronald L. Smith. "Theories and Models of Communication Processes," in Larry L. Barker and Robert T. Kibler (Eds.). *Speech Communication Behavior: Perspectives and Principles.* Englewood Cliffs, N.J.: Prentice-Hall, 1971. An article that surveys a wide variety of communication models. Different models representing the various communication contexts (including organizational and mass) are illustrated and explained.

Chapter 3 Social Behavior and Motivation

OBJECTIVES

After reading this chapter the student should be able to:
1. Distinguish between classical conditioning, instrumental learning, and social learning.
2. Distinguish between the concepts of generalization and discrimination as they apply to learning.
3. Describe how modeling and vicarious reinforcement might influence communication style.
4. Discuss two methods by which people have been trained to be more assertive.
5. Describe the phenomenon of social facilitation and give at least two examples of how it affects behavior.
6. Explain how the concepts of reinforcement (both positive and negative) and feedback operate in communication.
7. Define the terms "comparison level" and "comparison level for alternatives" and give an example of each.
8. Describe how need for affiliation, need for achievement, dogmatism, and Machiavellianism influence communication style.

3

A human being can be a human being only because other people have taught him, directly and indirectly, explicitly and implicitly, how to be human and what the important characteristics of the world, human and nonhuman, are that he is going to have to live with. (Church, 1961, p. 137)

Writers in many disciplines have repeatedly emphasized the importance of social interaction as an influence on the developing individual. Studies of infants raised in orphanages and monkeys raised in isolation show us that interaction is a necessity of life. In fact, some theorists have argued that mind and self actually emerge as a result of social experience and that communication is responsible for that emergence.

Essentially, this chapter is concerned with the first element of our model: the communicator as both sender and receiver and the learning processes by which his or her communication behaviors develop out of interactions with other human beings. Our interest in learning is twofold: we want to know how communication behaviors, like other social behaviors, are learned, and we want to suggest how some of these behaviors can be modified through new experiences.

LEARNING TO COMMUNICATE

"The exam questions I do poorly on are the ones based on class lectures."

"In a group I sometimes make comments that other people have already made but that I haven't heard."

"When other people are talking, I find myself worrying about my personal problems."

"When I'm called on in class, I often have to ask the instructor to repeat the question."

"While my boss explains how I should do a certain job I can follow his instructions, but once I go back to my desk I just can't seem to keep them in my mind."

"Listening to someone else talk makes me drowsy."

For many of us such difficulties in learning to listen are "other people's problems," for we tend to overestimate our own listening effectiveness. We assume that listening is essentially a matter of intelligence and that we are skilled listeners because all our lives we've been getting plenty of practice. Both assumptions are easily disproved by empirical findings. For example, one group of studies (Nichols and Stevens, 1957) has shown that in the first eight-hour period after hearing someone give a brief talk, you will forget from 33 to 50 percent of what has been said. And after two months you will remember only 25 percent of the total message. Numerous other studies indicate that dramatic improvements in listening behavior are possible with even a minimum of training (Keller, 1960).

So listening is not a skill to be taken for granted; it is a learned pattern of response that can be improved just like writing or speaking. And like all our other communication behaviors, it is learned in one of three ways: by classical conditioning, by instrumental learning, or by social learning.

Classical Conditioning

The basic principles of **classical conditioning** are all present in Pavlov's famous experiments with the hungry dog. In these experiments, the dog was shown a light just before it received food. The food, an unconditioned stimulus, always produced a salivating response in the dog, but the light was a neutral stimulus. After the two stimuli, food and light, had been paired a number of times, the dog salivated whenever it saw the light—even if it received no food. Such a response is said to be "conditioned."

Many human responses are conditioned in a similar way. For example, you learn to respond emotionally to the name of a loved one; the name, which was once a neutral stimulus, elicits a positive response because of the pleasurable experience with which it has come to be associated. We find many examples of conditioned responses in an organizational setting. In one industrial plant the supervisors learned that before the plant manager was going to give someone a real dressing down, he would put his arm around the man and then speak into his ear in a very low voice. Whenever the plant manager put his arm around a supervisor, the supervisor would brace himself for some harsh words (Tubbs, in Patterson, Hain, and Zima, in manuscript).

These responses are of limited usefulness because they are not adaptive—that is, they do not produce changes in the environment. The dog will not always receive food if it salivates when it sees a light. The supervisor will not avoid criticism just because he braces himself for a lecture by the plant manager. Although many communication behaviors are conditioned, our primary concern is with those that can produce change and to find out about these we must look to a second type of learning.

Instrumental Learning

A good part of the learning that does produce environmental change is **instrumental learning.** We can best explain its principles by describing another animal experiment, this one derived from the work of B. F. Skinner.

In front of you is a box that contains a hungry pigeon. Aimlessly, the bird pecks around the box, scouting for food. In time it pecks at a window in the box that happens to be illuminated, and it is immediately given a pellet of food. The food is its **reinforcement,** or *reward for giving the desired response.* After a number of such reinforcements, the pigeon learns that it is possible to get food simply by pecking at the window when it is lighted. This behavior is *instrumental* in getting the reward. Incidentally, the reward, or reinforcer, need not be a positive stimulus. It can be the removal of some unpleasant stimulus: for example, a pigeon may learn to peck at the window in order to avoid an electric shock.

Although the pigeon in the Skinner box sounds somewhat remote from human concerns, the same learning principles can be used to explain much about human behavior. For instance, one team of researchers (Rheingold, Gewirtz, and Ross, 1959) found that infants would make sounds if they were reinforced by the adults who took care of them. In this case the reinforcement was not food; it was human contact (smiling, stroking, and speaking on the part of the adult). During the last two days of the experiment, the researchers "extinguished" this vocalizing response by remaining silent and expressionless whenever the infant made sounds. **Extinction,** *the elimination of a response by withholding reinforcement,* can modify communication behaviors of many kinds. For example, in certain social situations people are reinforced for being polite to others—even at the expense of truth. Ann, a well-mannered and somewhat meek young woman in her mid-twenties, would never venture a comment that was in the least critical of another. When she started group therapy, however, she soon found that it was candor, not politeness, that was regarded as appropriate social behavior. Whenever she made one of her characteristically "sweet" remarks, other group members responded with comments like "Oh, come off it" and "Are you kidding? You're just saying that." Because she was no longer being reinforced for masking her true feelings, this now-ineffective pattern of behavior was extinguished and new, more desirable behavior within the group was reinforced.

Applications of instrumental learning to the complexities of interpersonal communication are clearer if we consider the nature of reinforcers. Food is a reinforcer for the pigeon in the Skinner box. Smiles, caresses, and human sounds are the reinforcers for the infants in the vocalizing experiment. Reinforcers for an adult might be smiles, eye contact, praise, agreement, higher grades, money, social acceptance, or job promotions. Even being listened to by a person important to you is a powerful reinforcer. It is for this reason that the teacher who listens selectively is able to modify nonverbal as well as verbal behavior within the classroom. Barker observes that there are teachers who, "either consciously or inadvertently, use failure to listen as punishment by ignoring certain pupils who attempt to communicate with them" (1971, p. 39).

The basic principle is always the same. Each of us emits hundreds of responses. Some are reinforced, others discouraged. The reinforcement of a given behavior increases the probability that the behavior will occur again. In a busy, competitive law firm, one young lawyer found that the way to get what she wanted—whether it was a larger office, a raise, or more secretarial help—was to make demands very insistently. "Well," she was fond of saying, "it's true. The squeaky wheel gets the most grease." As she moved on to other jobs, this became her style. She was quite vocal in expressing her dissatisfactions, and professionally she always seemed to get what she wanted.

Indirectly, the concept of reinforcement suggests one possible reason that so many of us are poor listeners. Several studies show that, generally, listening is not as reinforcing as speaking. In one study (Crane, Dieker, and Brown, 1970), listening was rated second only to reading as the least arousing of four activities—speaking, writing, listening, and reading. Another study (Bostrom, 1970) has shown that in a small-group discussion those who talk most frequently have the highest satisfaction with the group discussion; those who participate least are the least satisfied. In other words, for most of us talking is more enjoyable than listening to someone else talk.

But let us return to the example of the lawyer who became so insistent and assertive in her job demands. Once she acquired this new response, she began to **generalize** it—to *apply it to situations that were similar but not identical* to those in which she learned it. Since no two stimuli are identical, generalization has an important function. It has been proposed, for example, that without the ability to generalize, it would be impossible to learn language. On the other hand, it is through generalization that we come to stereotype groups of people, and not all these stereotypes are accurate.

How then do we learn which behaviors are appropriate for which situations? A successful debater who has been reinforced for his rigorous use of logic, his verbal aggression, and his criticism of his opponent's weaknesses, may have a hard time adapting to the cooperative spirit of a problem-solving discussion if he applies his debating behavior in this setting. Debating and problem solving both require communication skills, but the differences in situation require differences in behavior. Similarly, the insistent lawyer may find that her sharp, assertive style at the office doesn't work at home when she has to cope with her teen-age daughters. The principle involved here is **discrimination,** *learning that a behavior has different consequences in different situations.* To some degree all social learning depends on our ability to discriminate and react selectively.

Social Learning

Skinner and his followers believe that virtually all human behavior can be accounted for by the principles of instrumental learning. **Social learning,** *a much broader-based theory of how behavior is acquired* (Bandura and Walters, 1963), emphasizes that we also learn many new responses through **modeling,** or *imitation.* In other words, it is not always necessary for us to perform behaviors and be reinforced for them; we can learn many new responses simply by observing them in others.

According to this theory, from the time we are very young much of our communication style is shaped by modeling. Our parents are usually our first and most significant models. Perhaps you have met a

Even children have many models in addition to their parents.

child of five or six who might be described as a "forty-year-old kid." By imitating many adult facial expressions and mannerisms and picking up a great deal of adult vocabulary, the child models himself or herself so closely on an adult pattern that he or she seems to be a walking parody of one of the parents. Yet a child rarely grows up to be a carbon copy of any single human being. As he or she develops, numerous models become available: brothers and sisters, other relatives, friends, neighbors, and teachers. The child also reads stories and sees movies or television programs that dramatize the behavior of symbolic models. Out of all the behavior the child observes, only selected responses are imitated. For example, in certain respects a child may pattern himself or herself after a favorite uncle. If he or she notices that a kid brother gets his own way by throwing temper tantrums, the child may also give temper tantrums a try. If the tantrums get the child what he or she wants, they will probably persist. Incidentally, the way we communicate anger is often learned from our parents. In one parents' discussion group about how to give constructive criticism to teen-age children, the following comments were not atypical:

Mrs. A: When I get angry, certain phrases come to my mind full-blown. I don't have to compose them. I even use the same tone my mother did thirty years ago.

Mrs. B: My father used to call me "stupid" and I hated it. Now I find myself using the same epithet with my son. I don't like it at all. I don't like myself when I do it.

Mrs. C: . . . I use exactly the same words my mother used against me, when I was a child. I never did anything right and she always made me do things over. I do the same to my children. (Ginott, 1969, pp. 79–80)

Modeling goes on throughout our lives. For example, the way students dress and speak on campus is regulated to a great degree by the way they observe their peers dress and speak. And on the job employees often take their cues from the boss. The director of a prestigious brokerage firm was a man who always wore colored shirts and loud ties. Each time a new man came to work at the firm the employees would observe the same slow shift in his style of dressing. The new man would start the job dressing in a conservative business suit and white button-down shirt. Over the months his clothes would become more bold and informal until at last he had what the elevator operator used to refer to as "the uniform." In general, it is the person we perceive as most powerful who becomes a model for our behavior. This may not be the person who receives the greatest rewards; instead, we imitate the person who has the power to grant these rewards (Bandura, Ross, and Ross, 1963).

We have already suggested that a model need not be directly observed (Bandura, 1965). The mass media provide us with an overwhelming number of sources for modeling—beauty queens, athletes, television personalities, and so on. There are also many other situations that provide us with sources for modeling. For example, most introductory speech and communication courses make use of both live and symbolic models to teach communication skills. Students in such courses watch fellow students give speeches that are then critiqued; they see videotapes of actual speeches that are later evaluated in class; and they read and analyze the merits of various printed speeches.

Another social learning concept is **vicarious reinforcement,** the principle that *when we observe others being reinforced for a given behavior we are more likely to perform that behavior ourselves.* Vicarious reinforcement has been used as a technique for reducing speech anxiety in college students (Giffin and Bradley, 1969). Students who observe others communicating successfully are more likely to try these communication behaviors themselves. Apparently, we expect to receive the same reinforcement as others do. Miller reports that the delivery of a speaker who has observed an audience reaction to a preceding speaker will become disrupted and nonfluent if he or she receives an audience response different from that of the first speaker. In fact, "the sequence of responses to the two speakers had greater impact upon delivery than did approval or disapproval of the speaker himself" (Miller, 1964, p. 114).

Thus social learning theorists explain social behavior in the language of learning theory, but in doing so they broaden the definition of learning considerably. For them socially accepted and/or adaptive behavior is acquired not only through reinforcement, generalization, and discrimination, but through modeling and vicarious reinforcement.

We have been talking not only about the learning of specific communication skills such as listening and speaking, but about communication style itself. In the past few years, a question that has become increasingly relevant is whether certain broad differences in communication style between the sexes are learned. While they do not dismiss the biological differences between males and females, social learning theorists have argued quite persuasively that many of the psychological differences between the sexes are learned during early childhood both by direct reinforcement and by modeling. Thus they speak of certain **sex-typed behaviors**—that is, *behaviors that typically elicit different rewards for each sex.*

Consider aggressive behavior. At age three, boys show more aggressive and hostile behavior than girls. This difference seems to exist among children from many cultures, and it is often said that males are "instinctively" more aggressive than females. Social learning theorists remind us, however, that aggression is likely to bring different consequences for a boy than for a girl, even at the tender age of three. Children are quick to learn that the girl who never hits other children is a "little lady" but that the boy who never answers back and can't handle his own fights is a "sissy." Differential reinforcement of aggressive behavior becomes even more pronounced as children grow older. Seven-year-old Billy may be encouraged to "hit back" by his father, but Billy's sister is likely to be told that girls "don't fight." "I love fresh little boys," says the doting grandmother, but she doesn't expect her granddaughter to be that way. Apparently, little girls are still expected to be made of "sugar and spice and everything nice."

This is not to say that girls do not know how to express aggression or that they are incapable of acting aggressively. We have to distinguish between *acquisition* of a new response and its *performance*. Girls observe a great many aggressive models, just as boys do. They perform less aggressively because they receive more negative consequences (criticism, rejection, and so on) for such behavior. On the other hand, dependency behaviors seem to work in reverse: girls perform more dependent behaviors than boys do because the former receive more positive consequences for such behavior. Achievement is another behavior that seems to be sex-typed, as we shall see when we discuss motivation.

A direct outgrowth of such differential reinforcement may be the traditionally unassertive communication style of many women. Increasing numbers of people—including counselors and psychologists—argue that most women have been brought up to be compliant, unassertive, and dependent on others. They have been brought up to feel, for example, that assertiveness in any sphere is unfeminine. According to this view, it is not only aggressive but assertive behavior that is sex-typed. One specialist in assertiveness training for women distinguishes between aggressive behavior, in which you stand up for your rights in a way that violates the rights of the other party, and assertive behavior, in which you stand up for your legitimate rights in a way that does not violate the rights of the other party. In these terms, **assertiveness** is *"a direct, honest, and appropriate expression of one's feelings, opinions, and beliefs"* (Jakubowski-Spector, 1973, p. 2).

Right now we are experiencing a vogue for **assertiveness-training** workshops and classes of every description. Some are daylong workshops; some are groups that meet for one hour each week for a ten- or twenty-session course. Although many of the programs are designed with women in mind, there are some classes for men, too. Counselors use a wide range of techniques, some self-styled, some very closely following the techniques of behavior modification or behavior therapy. The aims are to extinguish unassertive behaviors and patterns of response and to develop and reinforce more assertive ones, often by teaching new communication skills that involve persuasion and confrontation. Assertiveness training is also concerned with correcting nonverbal behaviors that undercut what we think of as assertive statements. For example, a person who is being interviewed for a job might be speaking about her qualifications but avoiding eye contact with the interviewer or speaking in a voice that is almost inaudible.

Some counselors advise the client to tape-record conversations with people with whom she is likely to have assertiveness problems and then analyze her own responses. Often, the client is asked to participate in exercises with others that involve confrontation. Some confrontation exercises take place within the class or workshop. Others are to be enacted at home or in other settings outside the group meeting. It took Joanne, a graduate student in history, several weeks to work up to this declaration to her husband: "When you asked me to type your master's essay, you said you'd try to help with the house so I wouldn't fall behind in my classes. But you've seen me stay up late night after night and haven't offered to do any of the chores. Finals are coming up soon. Now that your paper is typed, I really need some help from you."

Among the most popular techniques for teaching assertiveness skills is **behavioral rehearsal,** *"a special kind of roleplaying experience in which the individual practices or rehearses those specific assertive responses which are to become part of her behavioral repertoire"* (Jakubowski-Spector, 1973, p. 12; italics added). Together counselor and participant choose some situation in which the latter has had difficulties in being assertive. For example, a young woman in her early twenties who felt that her mother was treating her like a child chose to role-play a recent argument. In that conversation the mother had reminded her daughter of a dentist appointment the following day, and then went on to also remind her to tell the dentist about a chipped tooth, and—adding insult to injury—mentioned that there was free parking in the back of the dentist's office. During the first role play the counselor plays the mother and the young woman plays herself. A discussion of her responses follows with some suggestions for more effective behaviors on her part. Participant and counselor then reverse roles with the counselor showing the participant other, more assertive ways to respond to the situation. For example, instead of the participant's, "Ma, I know that. Listen, I can take care of myself," the counselor's comment is

> Ma, I think it's time that I told you how I feel. I know that you're just trying to be helpful but, to tell you the truth, when you tell me what to do—like you just did—I feel as though I'm two years old and I find myself resenting it. I would like you to stop treating me that way. (Jakubowski-Spector, 1973, p. 14)

In the next discussion the participant reacts to how she has seen the counselor handle the situation; she is encouraged to use the more appropriate assertive response and to select some modeled behaviors that she herself would like to repeat in the next round of role play. In the discussion that follows and in succeeding role plays her effective responses are encouraged and given positive reinforcement by the leader, who is careful to give positive feedback before any criticisms. Slowly, the new, more assertive behavior pattern is shaped and perfected.

THE BORN LOSER   by Art Sansom

It's time I taught you the facts-of-business-life! You tremble around that office like a whipped puppy!...

Get tough! Assert yourself! Project! ...And don't forget my mother is coming for dinner!

I am eating out tonight!

Sometimes a little education can be a dangerous thing!

Given our previous discussion of how new responses are learned, the question that naturally comes to mind is, Does assertiveness training really work? Can training that is of relatively short duration extinguish habits—in this instance, ways of communicating—that have been reinforced over long periods of time? And can these new, more assertive patterns of behavior be maintained once a person leaves the class or the workshop in assertiveness training? It will be some time before we have scientific studies of the long-term effects of assertiveness training. We do know, however, that the effectiveness of such training will depend to a great degree on the relative strength of the reinforcers for nonassertive communication and how these stack up against those for assertive communication. One very important reinforcer for all nonassertive behavior is the avoidance of conflict, anxiety, and disapproval. It can be upsetting to stand up to your parents, to insist that you deserve a raise when you get a promotion, to repeat that you will not pay for damaged merchandise and that you must speak with the store manager. On the other hand, the increased self-esteem and the satisfaction of individual needs that are often the results of a more assertive communication style are powerful reinforcers. But different things are reinforcing for different people. It is likely that for some the avoidance of conflict will be such a strong reinforcer that it will far outweigh the many gains to be made through more assertive behavior. As always, a reinforcer has to be defined in terms of the individual. Moreover, a reinforcer must also be defined in terms of a given culture. A distinctly assertive communication style would not be acceptable in all countries or, for that matter, in all minority cultures.

Much of our scientific knowledge about how social behaviors are learned is still elementary. We have seen, however, that the social learning process has a great many implications for the study of interpersonal communication. Before exploring these further we take note of a social phenomenon that affects how well behaviors will be performed.

Social Facilitation

Have you ever been in an auditorium where only a few people were scattered throughout all the seats? How do the responses in such an audience differ from those in an audience whose members are seated close to one another? Have you ever noticed how a few people in an audience beginning to laugh or applaud start almost everyone doing the same thing? This shows how others influence our behavior. A special case of this type of influence is known as **social facilitation**—*the enhancing effect of the presence of others on a person's performance.*

The earliest study of this phenomenon was conducted by Triplett (1897). He found that people who were required to turn a fishing reel 150 times did better when they competed in the presence of others than in isolation. The research of Triplett and others led Allport (1924) to introduce the term "social facilitation." Later research has shown that social facilitation occurs only under certain conditions. For example, students who are required to give talks before a communication class and who have decided not to prepare often do rather poorly. They are also more likely to experience speech anxiety. Conversely, well-prepared students feel greater self-confidence, and their performance is usually enhanced by their high arousal level, which is stimulated by the presence of an audience. In other words, the presence of others generally inhibits your ability to learn or perform new responses (solving a new mathematics problem at the board, for example), but it enhances your ability to perform well-learned responses.

FEEDBACK AS A REINFORCER

In writing about feedback systems in computers and other machines, Norbert Wiener, the founder of cybernetics, observes that when "the information which proceeds backward from the performance is able to change the general method and pattern of performance, we have a process which may well be called learning" (1967, p. 84). When we examine feedback solely in interpersonal terms, we can be more specific and say that feedback reinforces some behaviors and extinguishes others. For example, one story has it that a psychology instructor who had been teaching the principles of instrumental learning was actually conditioned by his own class. The students decided to give him reinforcement by taking lots of notes, looking attentive, and asking questions whenever he moved to his right. Whenever he moved to his left, they tried to extinguish this behavior by not taking notes, being inattentive, and not asking questions. He was just about teaching from the right front corner of the room when he realized what was happening.

Influencing Through Feedback

Interpersonal feedback can influence the outcome of interaction in some rather subtle ways. For example, an interviewer's biases or even his or her characteristics can affect the responses of the person being interviewed. Thus Cantril (1944) found that Democrat interviewers received more pro-Democrat responses than Republican interviewers, who in turn obtained more pro-Republican responses than Democrat interviewers. It has also been shown that blue-collar interviewers receive more favorable responses on labor questions than white-collar interviewers (Katz, 1942). There is a strong possibility that feedback from the interviewer accounts for these findings.

We can find considerable evidence to justify the generalization that just about any verbal behavior can be reinforced through the use of "Good" or "Mmm-hmm." One team of researchers even found that during an interview a simple head nod was enough of a reinforcer to encourage the respondent to talk more. The results of their experiment lend support to the view that nonverbal as well as verbal feedback can have a sustained effect on the receiver's subsequent communication behavior.

In an attempt to determine the precise operations of head nodding and vocal reinforcers in less structured, face-to-face communication, Dittmann and Llewellyn (1968) seated pairs of subjects five feet apart and facing each other at a slight angle (a seating arrangement normally adopted by strangers). They were asked to converse with each other for two separate time periods of two minutes each on any subject that interested them. During the first period one person was to do most of the speaking and the other the listening; during the second they were to reverse the speaking and listening roles. Several consistent patterns of behavior emerged:

1. Head nod or vocal response is usually followed by some comment. This cue seems to be used as an indication to the first speaker that the other person now wants to speak.
2. Head nods and vocal responses frequently occur together and in

that order, and they are far more likely to occur when the first speaker drops his or her voice, indicating the completion of an idea.
3. In approaching the end of a statement, the speaker tends to look at a listener; in beginning a statement, the speaker tends to look away. The person listening gives better eye contact than the person speaking, so that when the speaker looks at the listener while ending a statement, the look may serve as a cue that the speaker is now ready to listen.
4. "You know" is used by a speaker to ask the listener for some feedback on how he or she is being received.

Dittmann and Llewellyn's study emphasizes a concept we spoke of in Chapter 1 and developed in Chapter 2: the interdependence of the participants in the communication process. It is significant for two reasons. First, it describes a relatively normal conversation rather than a rigged encounter. Second, it reminds us of the wealth of cues exchanged at specific points in a conversation in which one person relinquishes the role of message sender and the other person, who was listening, assumes it. Research has shown that as communicators we expect such responses from others and find them reinforcing. If we do not receive them, we tend to evaluate the other person negatively (Ellsworth and Carlsmith, 1968). The implications for the student are obvious. Providing feedback is an essential aspect of all two-way communication, and it influences all the five outcomes we discussed in Chapter 1. "Sending feedback," writes Barker, "is a learned behavior. If you can overcome sending feedback that is not perceivable or that is undesirable when perceived, you can learn to become a more effective responder" (1971, p. 122). In other words, as receivers we should not only be providing some kind of feedback, but we should be aware of the other person's response to that feedback.

Students often say that they do not like to talk if they are just agreeing with or adding to what someone else has already said. They feel that their comments will be repetitious and have no value. Yet there is considerable evidence that showing agreement or clarifying what someone else has said is functional behavior that elicits greater participation from other communicators. Scheidel and Crowell (1966) found that in small groups a full 35 percent of the discussion was devoted to feedback, most of it consisting of statements that either supported or clarified what had already been said. The experimenters suggest that one possible explanation for the substantial amount of feedback is "the reinforcing effect of the agreement comments which occur in the feedback process" (1966, p. 277). They also show that the tendency to give feedback is characteristic of highly task-oriented people, not just those who seek social approval. In fact, task-oriented group members seem to use feedback primarily as a tool for accomplishing the group goal more effectively.

The Information Value of Feedback

In addition to its task functions, feedback is also an important source of information about the self. Your **self-concept,** *your relatively stable impressions of yourself,* develops in part out of the feedback you receive from those around you. In fact, some psychiatrists take the position that we evaluate ourselves primarily on the basis of how we think others evaluate us. For example, the so-called black sheep of the family may come to think of himself or herself in those terms if parents, relatives, and neighbors all seem to perceive the person in this light.

It is known that feedback has a direct effect on level of self-esteem, one of the chief measures of self-concept. When people are asked to predict their own performance on a test—whether of their social, intellectual, or physical competence—and are later given feedback on how well they scored, they revise their predictions for the next experimental task in the direction of that feedback. This is true regardless of whether the feedback is accurate or not.

From a survey of more than fifty studies of speech communication feedback, Gardiner concluded that "Sources who receive positive audience response will develop more favorable attitudes toward themselves and toward the audience than sources who receive negative audience response" (1971, p. 31). He also found strong evidence that negative feedback can inhibit the delivery of the message sender and that this effect is reflected in fluency, rate of speech, voice loudness, nervousness, stage fright, eye contact, and body movement.

Even negative reactions can sometimes be valuable in improving communication skills. In a speech class designed to correct voice and diction problems, the instructor paired off the students. Each time one member of a team exhibited a "poor" communication habit, the other immediately called it to his attention. Most students found it a frustrating but rewarding experience (Tubbs and Tubbs, 1972, p. 23). Jenkins suggests a related value of feedback when he writes about prediction in face-to-face communication:

> Accuracy in predicting responses to communicative efforts tends to improve if an awareness of the results of one's attempts accompanies experience. For example, one learns what kind of behavior will be rewarded or accepted and what kind of behavior will result in punishment or rejection. . . . only through a set of experiences in a variety of groups can one learn that he must adjust his behavior and his predictions to the particular body with which he is associating. (Some, never learning this, have

SOCIAL BEHAVIOR AND MOTIVATION

Feedback is essential to all contexts of communication.

unvarying habits of communication.) As a person gains this insight, he becomes able to communicate appropriately and readily (Jenkins, 1961, p. 134).

REWARDS AND MOTIVATIONS

There are no absolute rewards in human interaction. Several studies have shown that people with similar attitudes or other perceived similarities are more capable of reinforcing each other than people who are dissimilar. One communication scholar sums up the point, *"Reward has to be defined in terms of the receiver"* (Berlo, 1960, p. 89).

Analyzing human interaction in terms of rewards and costs, Thibaut and Kelley offer an excellent theoretical framework from which to view these differences. For each of us the outcome, or consequences, of any interpersonal encounter will simply be the rewards we receive from interacting with a given person minus the costs we incur. **Re-**

wards are defined as *"the pleasures, satisfactions, and gratifications"* we enjoy, including the fulfillment of any of our needs. **Costs** are *"any factors that operate to inhibit or deter the performance of a sequence of behavior"* (Thibaut and Kelley, 1959, p. 12; italics added). Costs include not only negative feelings, but the fatigue and stress resulting from interaction.

Thibaut and Kelley assume that in all our interactions we actively seek positive outcomes from others and that we are constantly comparing the outcomes that different people provide for us. In fact, each of us has a standard for evaluating the rewards and costs of a relationship according to what we feel we "deserve." This standard is our **comparison level** (CL), or *minimum level for positive outcomes,* and it is in great part determined by the quality of our previous outcomes. A high-powered person who is self-confident and outgoing usually has a relatively high CL.

Your CL is your criterion for judging a relationship at a given moment. You also have a **comparison level for alternatives** (CL_{alt}), which is your *criterion for deciding whether to continue or terminate any relationship.* Obviously involvement in any human relationship automatically reduces to some extent the ability to form others. CL_{alt} is the lowest level of outcomes we find acceptable in a relationship as measured against all other opportunities. The greater the rewards a person can produce for himself or herself, the higher his or her CL_{alt}. We are constantly comparing each of our relationships with possible alternatives, and when the outcomes we receive drop below CL_{alt}, we terminate the relationship. Some time ago a television commercial made the point quite bluntly. The scene opens with a rather plain couple parked on a beach in a flashy new car. Then along comes a terrific-looking girl in a bikini. She asks the fellow if the car is his, and he invites her to sit in it. As the commercial ends we see the plain girl standing alone on the beach, shouting at the other two as they drive off. In this example the young man's alternatives suddenly improved with the acquisition of a new car—and his choice of dates changed rather abruptly.

We have seen how social learning influences and shapes our subsequent behavior patterns. To a large extent, this shaping determines our needs and expectations—our comparison levels, if you will. Early in their work Thibaut and Kelley emphasize the relationship between rewards and need satisfaction. To some degree it is the strength of one's various needs that determines what is rewarding. Therefore if we know more about motivation, we can make some predictions about differences in communication behaviors. In the following pages we shall look at four dimensions along which some of these differences can be measured.

The Need for Affiliation

One variable that has a great influence on communication behavior is **need for affiliation** (N Aff), or *the need to be with others*. Most of the rewards for people rated high in need for affiliation come directly from human companionship. Therefore they tend to be friendly and avoid disagreements. Their communication behaviors contrast sharply with those of low affiliaters. For example, high affiliaters seat themselves closer to other persons; they smile more often; they nod more often to indicate agreement or gain approval; they use more arm and hand gestures (Rosenfeld, 1966). In general high affiliaters give a great deal of supportive nonverbal feedback. And if they are relatively self-confident, they also tend to be more verbally supportive and affectionate to others.

Whether the need to affiliate is innate or learned is an issue still unresolved. We do know that a correlation exists between affiliative need and birth order, with only children and first-borns ranking highest in their need to be with others (Schachter, 1959). And as we shall see in Chapter 5, anxiety-producing situations intensify this need.

The Need for Achievement

A second motive that bears on communication style is **need for achievement** (N ach) —that is, *the need to demonstrate competence and to gain recognition for accomplishments*. Like the rewards of the person with strong affiliative needs, those of the high achiever are, at least to some degree, social. High achievers want to excel, to attain some high standard, whether it is in business, sports, or academic life, but they are also concerned with how others will respond to their accomplishments. Their communication is characterized by relatively frequent attempts to build up their confidence and to establish dominance over others while at the same time attracting attention to themselves. We also expect the high achiever to talk more than others, especially in situations where there is an objective to be reached (that is, task-oriented situations).

McClelland, who has done some of the most outstanding research on achievement motivation, pokes fun at the high achiever when he writes:

> Some psychologists think that because I've done so much on N ach I must like the kind of people who have a strong need for achievement. I don't. I find them bores. They are not artistically sensitive. They're entrepreneurs, kind of driven—always trying to improve themselves and find

a shorter route to the office or a faster way of reading their mail. . . . Yes, it's an efficiency kind of thing, but it also includes taking personal responsibility to solve problems and achieve moderate goals at calculated risks—in situations that provide real feedback. You can see why most innovative businessmen score high on N ach. (McClelland, 1971, p. 36)

One study of speech anxiety in college males linked need for achievement to level of self-confidence (Giffin and Gilham, 1971). It was found that high achievers were more self-confident as well as less likely to experience speech anxiety. Low achievers tended to have less self-confidence and to have more anxiety about speaking before others.

Most of our generalizations about achievement motive are based on data obtained from male subjects. The data on women are strangely different. For example, women who have a strong need for achievement, particularly very intelligent women, also tend to rate very high on measures of anxiety. This discrepancy has usually been interpreted as evidence that women do not have the competitive needs that men do—that, in fact, they have a will to fail. Not content with this explanation, Horner (1969) pursued the question by examining what consequences women expect as a result of high achievement. She found that whereas men expect positive outcomes as a result of their accomplishments, women often link achievement with negative outcomes, such as social rejection and loss of femininity. Such expectations are not unreasonable. For example, the female business executive has often been criticized for her supposed lack of femininity. A popular list of pointers titled "How To Tell a Businessman from a Businesswoman" gives us some interesting examples of the double standard that often applies in the business world:

> A businessman is aggressive; a businesswoman is pushy.
> A businessman is good on details; she's picky.
> He follows through; she doesn't know when to quit.
> He's confident; she's conceited.
> He is firm; she's hard.
> He is a man of the world; she's been around.
> He drinks because of excessive job pressure; she's a lush.
> He exercises authority; she's power mad.
> He's close-mouthed; she's secretive.
> He's a stern taskmaster; she's hard to work for.

In a more serious vein, two interesting comparisons have been made between high affiliaters and high achievers. A study of small groups (Aronoff and Messé, 1971) found that high achievers give more suggestions about procedures, offer more opinions, draw attention to themselves more often, and integrate past communication more than high affiliaters. Earlier evidence of the more task-oriented approach of high achievers comes from a study by French (1956). Subjects had to choose between a work partner who was a competent stranger and one who was a less competent friend. High achievers made their choices on the basis of competence; high affiliaters chose on the basis of friendship.

Dogmatism

As we communicate, we are continually evaluating ideas, people, and authority. On the basis of his intensive study of open- and closed-mindedness, Rokeach (1960) proposes that the way in which a person accepts or rejects ideas, people, and authority all go together. According to this view, each person has a belief-disbelief system, the sum total of his or her beliefs and disbeliefs about the physical and social world. The highly dogmatic (or closed-minded) person is one who has a relatively closed set of beliefs and disbeliefs structured around a more basic set of beliefs about absolute authority. It is this central set of beliefs that is the framework for various patterns of intolerance. **Dogmatism** is a measure of *how* we believe, not *what* we believe. The content of any given belief is irrelevant. It is *overreliance on authority* that makes a person dogmatic. The atheist can be as dogmatic as the religious zealot. A liberal Democrat can be more dogmatic than a conservative Republican.

What makes some people so much more dogmatic than others? The strong correlation between dogmatism in parents and their children (Rebhun, 1967) suggests that dogmatism is learned from parental attitudes. But open- and closed-mindedness are extremes along a continuum, and ratings of this dimension can change. For example, a number of studies confirm that during college young people tend to become more open-minded than they were previously (Lehmann, 1963).

The essence of the open- and closed-mindedness dimension is "the capacity to distinguish information from source of information and to evaluate each on its own merits" (Rokeach, 1960, p. 396). According to Rokeach, all the information (the input, in our terms) we receive has a dual nature. It gives us information about the subject of the communication and it also gives us information about the source of the communication (the communicator, his or her competence, reliability, and so on). For the highly dogmatic person it will be very difficult to judge the two kinds of information independently. This person's acceptance of authority is so complete that he or she will evaluate input in terms of the source it comes from rather than its content. That authority varies with the individual receiver. It might be the Catholic Church, *Time* magazine, the American Medical Association, César Chavez, the Reverend Sun Myung Moon, or even the Democratic party.

Very dogmatic people have difficulty not only in evaluating opposing beliefs but in simply tolerating them. Beliefs discrepant with their own are too threatening to their belief systems to be judged on the basis of merit or given serious consideration. Let us consider a hypothetical case—suppose we call him Howard Morgan. Morgan is deeply committed to the Republican party and supported Richard Nixon during both elections. Imagine then his reactions to the disclosures about the Nixon administration after the Watergate break-in. At the time information about Watergate first begins to surface, Morgan is able to dismiss it as completely unfounded. Even as more and more evidence accumulates—and many of his friends begin to condemn Nixon—it is extremely difficult for Morgan to reconcile new information with his firm beliefs about Nixon and the Republican party. Morgan becomes quite selective in what he reads and listens to. For example, he reads a newspaper that plays down any emphasis on Republican misconduct. As long as Republican leaders continue to support Nixon and Nixon himself claims no knowledge either of a break-in or a cover-up, Morgan remains extremely resistant to changing any of his beliefs. In fact, he interprets the increasing number of disclosures as an attempt by the Democratic party to discredit Nixon. Only when leaders of the Republican party begin to pressure Nixon to step down does Morgan consider modifying any of his original beliefs. And then it is only because these leaders represent part of the authority he accepts as absolute.

The resistance to change that characterizes dogmatic people and the great difficulty they have in assimilating new information discrepant with their beliefs have been demonstrated in several studies (for example, Ehrlich and Lee, 1969). It is this resistance to new information along with an inability to tolerate opposing beliefs that makes it so difficult to communicate with a dogmatic receiver—particularly if a desired outcome is attitude influence. Even an outcome as essential as understanding is jeopardized. For a major source of interference will be within the receiver, and it will be ongoing. It will affect the receiver's responses to others not only on a one-to-one basis but in a small group.

Machiavellianism

A fourth variable that affects communication behavior is the degree to which a person will manipulate other human beings as he or she interacts with them. The study of this dimension of personality began with the construction of a questionnaire in which people were asked to comment on a series of statements about human nature. Here are some sample items:

> Barnum was very wrong when he said there's a sucker born every minute.
> It is safest to assume that all people have a vicious streak and it will come out when they are given a chance.
> There is no excuse for lying to someone else.
> Most men forget more easily the death of their father than the loss of their property.
> Anyone who completely trusts anyone else is asking for trouble. (Christie and Geis, 1970, pp. 17–18)

The questionnaire was the first of a series of scales designed to measure **Machiavellianism,** *manipulative behavior in interpersonal relationships.* In the laboratory so-called high Machs and low Machs have been brought together in a number of ingenious games and situations involving bargaining, changing attitudes, and social influence. A basic difference between the two types seems to be that the high Mach, while not unconcerned about the success of his or her behavior, shows greater emotional detachment. For example, the high Mach does not assume that a partner in a game will be loyal or feel betrayed when the other partner is not. And if the stakes are high enough, the high Mach has little difficulty in advocating a position that is contrary to what he or she believes (Burgoon, Miller, and Tubbs, 1972). The high Mach manipulates more, wins more, persuades others more, and is less frequently persuaded. His or her first concern is the task at hand. Christie and Geis call the high-Mach pattern of behavior the "cool syndrome" (1970, p. 338).

The low Mach, on the other hand, is characterized as the "soft touch." The low Mach is first of all more susceptible to social influence. He or she frequently complies with the requests of others, changes opinions, and becomes emotionally involved (a possible reason low Machs lose to the high Machs as much as they do). The low Mach's orientation is generally social; the high Mach is task-oriented.

Machiavellianism is a personality dimension particularly relevant to our study of communication because high Machs perform most differently from low Machs when there is face-to-face encounter and the situation is loosely structured. Machiavelli's critics labeled him an "opportunist"; his admirers, a "realist." Whatever our personal feelings about a manipulative approach to human relations, it is clear that the high Mach is very effective in face-to-face encounters—especially those that require bargaining, improvising, or persuasion. Thus he or she is especially successful in producing two of the five communication outcomes discussed in Chapter 1: attitude influence and action.

The high Mach's talent for improvisation is apparent in the superior ability to think quickly when other people are present. We have already discussed the phenomenon of social facilitation: unlike most people, the high Mach is adept at learning or performing new responses in the presence of others. And in speech communication courses (though not in public speaking courses), it is the high Mach who tends to get the higher grade—presumably because these courses are more loosely structured and allow for a great many face-to-face exchanges between students (Burgoon, 1971).

Differences between high and low Machs seem to be the result of a complex social learning process, though Christie and Geis believe that parental modeling is not a major influence. They suggest that "some manipulative behaviors are learned at an early age by being rewarded unintentionally by parents and by early exposure to nonfamilial socializing agents such as peers and mass media" (1970, p. 338).

Who are the high Machs in our society? The research findings (Widgery and Tubbs, 1972) seem to reverse our expectations. It has been shown, for example, that college students have higher Mach scores than businessmen or Washington lobbyists and that younger people generally have higher scores than older ones. Furthermore, the Machiavellian orientation seems to be on the upswing. We leave you wondering whether you yourself are a high Mach or a low Mach—and how you got to be that way.

Summary

Each of us brings to a communication event certain characteristic ways of responding. In this chapter we have tried to show that these are largely shaped by learning experiences and that some behaviors can be modified by new learning experiences.

Our study of how we learn to communicate began with a review of some basic principles of classical conditioning and instrumental learning. Reinforcement, extinction, generalization, and discrimination were all discussed in terms of their relationship to communication. We then turned to social learning, a broader-based theory of how behavior is acquired. According to this school of thought, socially accepted or adaptive behavior is also acquired through modeling and vicarious reinforcement. Both these concepts were examined. The question of sex-typed communication behaviors was also explored, particularly with respect to assertiveness. Following a brief discussion of assertiveness training and social facilitation, we examined the reinforcing effects of both verbal and nonverbal feedback and suggested that feedback can also influence self-concept.

In the final section we explored the relationship between reward and motivation and considered some ways in which four variables—need for affiliation, need for achievement, dogmatism, and Machiavellianism—affect communication style.

Review Questions

1. How do classical conditioning, instrumental learning, and social learning differ?
2. Discuss the difference between generalization and discrimination in learning. What application do these concepts have to learning to communicate more effectively?
3. Discuss the influence of modeling and vicarious reinforcement on communication style. Give an example.
4. Describe two techniques used to teach more assertive behavior.
5. What is social facilitation? Give two examples of how social facilitation affects behavior.
6. How do the concepts of reinforcement and feedback operate in face-to-face communication? Why is feedback considered a reinforcer? What effect does feedback have on subsequent behavior?
7. What are comparison level and comparison level for alternatives? Provide an example of each in a hypothetical situation where young lovers are about to break up.
8. In what ways might need for affiliation, need for achievement, dogmatism, and Machiavellianism influence communication style?

Exercises

1. Refer to the model constructed for exercise 1, Chapter 2. Describe the principles of classical conditioning, instrumental learning, and social learning and provide examples of how they apply to (a) the four types of communicative stimuli (see objective 6, Chapter 2), and (b) five of the possible outcomes of communication (see objective 5, Chapter 1).
2. During an informal conversation with someone, select a particular word or phrase she uses and reinforce her (for example, smile, nod, or say "good") each time she uses it. Determine the extent to which the frequency of its use increases.
3. Look at the personal log you began for exercise 1 in Chapter 1. Which of your comments illustrate the effects of social reinforcement or extinction on communication behaviors? What stimuli were used as reinforcers? Who used them? What were the results?
4. Make a list of three people whose friendship you value. Evaluate the effectiveness of their communication with you and the part it plays in your relationship. What is it that sustains your attraction to each of them? Does this attraction have anything to do with social reinforcement, and if so, how?

Suggested Readings

Bandura, Albert, and Walters, Richard. *Social Learning and Personality Development*. New York: Holt, Rinehart and Winston, 1963. This fascinating little book contains an excellent summary of research in social learning. The effects of reward and punishment of behavior are discussed in terms of such topics as childhood violence as it relates to television viewing; spoiling children by rewarding temper tantrums; and overcoming one's fear of snakes.

Barker, Larry L. *Listening Behavior*. Englewood Cliffs, N.J.: Prentice-Hall, 1971. For those interested in developing their ability to listen, this book will be invaluable. The author combines theoretical discussion (including some observations about listening and learning) with practical discussions about identifying listening problems and improving listening behavior. An entire chapter is devoted to the subject of listening to biased communication.

Mann, Harriet et al. "Four Types of Personality and Four Ways of Perceiving Time." *Psychology Today* (December 1972), 6:76–84. Despite a ponderous title, this is an easily read article in which Mann defines four personality types and their ways of seeing reality.

Ruch, Floyd L. "Personality—Public or Private." *Psychology Today* (October 1967), 1:46–47, 58–60. This is a thoughtful examination of the invasion-of-privacy issue as it relates to personality testing of job applicants. Based on his own studies and research in previous experiments, Ruch states that testing for sociability is essential for filling executive positions. A good discussion-starter.

Chapter 4 Person Perception

OBJECTIVES

After reading this chapter the student should be able to:
1. Define the term "psychological set" and give at least two examples.
2. Describe two ways in which person perception differs from object perception and explain what implications these differences have for communication.
3. Explain the primacy effect and how it might influence communication.
4. Distinguish between personal generalizations and stereotypes.
5. Give two examples of how stereotypes can influence intercultural communication.
6. State three generalizations from research studies about individual ability to judge people.
7. Identify four characteristics associated with the ability to form accurate perceptions of others.
8. List two ways in which person perception and communication effectiveness can be improved.

4

One winter day in New York, a smartly dressed woman walked into Tiffany and asked to see some diamond rings. The salesman obliged, and she went through the tray, removing her own diamond to try on one ring after another. But she could find nothing to her satisfaction and so she thanked the salesman and left. A block away, at Harry Winston (a major competitor of Tiffany's), she did the same thing, but again left without making a purchase. It was more than an hour later that the Tiffany salesman discovered that a ring with a large diamond was missing from one of the trays; in its place was a ring with a much smaller diamond. And then he remembered the smartly dressed woman. It wasn't very long before the salesman at Harry Winston made a similar discovery—but his loss turned out to be more unfortunate. The ring was the missing diamond from Tiffany and had to be returned to that store.

The woman who carried through these unusual daylight robberies must have been very confident of the impression she would create. No doubt wearing a diamond ring helped. Yet the impression she created was based not only on her clothing or her jewelry; handsomely dressed women are a common sight in places such as Tiffany. How did she do it?

This incident really happened. It interests us here because it dramatizes how deceptive impressions of others can be—even when other people share our impressions. As communicators we depend on our perceptions of other human beings in almost every aspect of our daily life. The way we perceive others determines the kind of communication that takes place between us; in some cases it even determines whether communication takes place at all. In this chapter we shall examine in some detail what happens when we make a judgment about another person. Let us begin with a look at the process of perception itself.

PERCEIVING PEOPLE AND OBJECTS: A COMPARISON

Our total awareness of the world comes to us through our senses. Thus our perceptions—whether of tables and chairs or coffee cups or other human beings—have a common basis. Yet, curiously, two people will often disagree in their judgments about a third. Anyone who has tried to arrange a blind date for a friend can testify to that. Sometimes it is even difficult to recommend your own doctor or dentist to someone else. The reasons for such differences of opinion become clearer when we consider the ways in which interpersonal perception and perception in general are similar.

As we know from our discussion of selective attention in Chapter 2, we perceive only part of the available stimuli while filtering out other stimuli. There are two kinds of filters through which all input or sensation will pass. First, the inherent structures of our sense organs—our perceptual filters—limit our capacity to perceive. These limitations exist whether we are experiencing an object or a person. Although we all have these limitations, they vary considerably from one individual to another. Some of us have keener vision than others, some better hearing, and so on. We all see the world a bit differently, and no one sees it completely.

Second, our past experiences influence what we select and the way we perceive it. For example, quickly read the words in Figure 4.1. Do

Figure 4.1

```
      /\
     /  \
    / A  \
   / walk \
  / in the \
 / the park \
/_____\
```

you notice anything unusual? Readers often overlook the extra word "the" in the triangle because of their past reading experiences. We are so accustomed to seeing words in groups that we often do not perceive single words. Similarly, we often judge a person by the group in which we meet him or her; we generalize about that person on the basis of earlier experiences that seem comparable.

We know that expectations, or psychological sets, have a profound effect on our perceptions of objects. Given an ambiguous stimulus, a hungry man is more likely to perceive food objects, for example, than is a person who has just eaten. Psychological set also affects our perception of people. A defensive person is more apt to perceive strangers as hostile than a self-confident person. Before you read any further, take a look at the picture of the young woman in Figure 4.2. Do you see a young woman? Do you also see an old woman? The phrase "the picture of the young woman in Figure 4.2" led you to perceive the illustration in one way first, but after a while you should be able to see both a young woman and an old one. Try showing this

Figure 4.2

A TEST OF PSYCHOLOGICAL SET

Source: C. M. Mooney and G. A. Ferguson. "A New Closure Test," *Canadian Journal of Psychology,* 5 (1951), 129–133.

illustration to friends. Tell them that it is a picture of an old woman, and see whether your statement affects their perceptions. Actually, some people see the hat as a large rat facing toward the right and do not see a woman at all. So the perception is also influenced by the use of the word "woman."

Figure 4.2 is a deliberately ambiguous illustration. Psychologists have made good use of such ambiguous stimuli in testing personality. One such test, the Thematic Apperception Test (TAT), consists of a set of twenty pictures. As each picture is shown, the person being tested is asked to make up a story about it. The degree to which that story reveals past experiences and expectations can be striking. For example, a simple illustration of an elderly woman opening the door to a room was shown to a young man who had formerly been a bombardier in the air force. He responded as follows:

> She has prepared this room for someone's arrival and is opening the door for a last general look over the room. She is probably expecting her son home. She tries to place everything as it was when he left. She seems like a very tyrannical character. She led her son's life for him and is going to

take over again as soon as he gets back. This is merely the beginning of her rule, and the son is definitely cowed by this overbearing attitude of hers and will slip back into her well-ordered way of life. He will go through life plodding down the tracks she has laid for him. All this represents her complete domination of his life until she dies. (Arnold, 1949, p. 100)

At the time the young man was tested, he was undergoing psychological treatment. Facts that were later brought to light confirmed that his story clearly reflected his personal problems and that his relationship with his mother strongly resembled the one he had described. The stimulus that elicited his story, however, could evoke a virtually infinite number of interpretations. Each of us has a story for that picture.

Early philosophers, among them John Locke, compared the human mind to a *tabula rasa,* a "blank tablet," on which impressions were made. Today we know that perception is not a passive state in which stimuli are received and automatically registered. On the contrary, perception is an active process in which the perceiver selects, organizes, and interprets what he or she experiences.

Like object perception, person perception may be thought of in terms of three elements: the perceiver, the object of perception, and the context within which the object (in this instance, another human being) is viewed. The perceiver, who shall be referred to as P, is of course influenced by his or her own attributes as well as by those of O, the person who is being perceived. The cues that P gets from O are often called **proximal stimuli;** these are *the attributes of a person as seen through the eyes of the perceiver.* The context, or setting, within which the process of interpersonal perception occurs is both physical and psychological, as we shall see.

How far can we go in saying that the perception of people resembles the perception of objects? Theorists do not agree. Tagiuri points out an important respect in which the two acts of observation differ:

> Person perception is special . . . in that the similarity between perceiver and perceived is greater than in any other instance. Banal as this may seem, it has far-reaching consequences. The most obvious one of these is that the perceiver is probably maximally inclined and able to use his own experience in perceiving or judging or inferring another's state or intentions. Perceived and perceiver, in general, react similarly to events. This may be viewed as empathy or projection or whatnot. (Tagiuri and Petrullo, 1958, p. xi)

In other words, to some degree, however slight, we assume that the other person shares some of our characteristics, that he or she resembles us in some ways. We are—or so we think—familiar with some of that person's experience. Such assumptions may help us perceive more accurately. For example, if I know that you have just returned from a funeral, on the basis of my own experience I will probably interpret your silence as depression rather than indifference. On the other hand, we often misinterpret what we perceive precisely because we assume other people are like us. If I assume that your taste in music is like mine, when I offer to play some rock music, I may interpret your remark "Oh, great!" as genuinely enthusiastic though it is clear to most people from your facial expression that your reply was sarcastic.

SHORT RIBS by Frank Hill

Another way in which perceiving people differs from perceiving objects is that our perceptions and misperceptions influence and keep on influencing our interactions with others—because they keep responding to these perceptions. Sometimes people correct our misperceptions. But occasionally one misinterpretation leads to another, and we get further and further afield. Even if an initial misperception is corrected, it may persist because of the psychological sets we have about other people. Vine Deloria, an American Indian who was director of the National Congress of Americans, recalls his visit to the home of a congressman whose wife wanted to meet some Indians. With him were Helen Schierback (a Lumbee) and Imelda Schreiner (a Cheyenne River Sioux). Throughout the afternoon, the congressman's wife repeatedly asked them their names when she addressed them. When they left, she asked them again for their names so that she could say goodbye. "As we went out the door," writes Deloria, "she thanked us for coming and profusely apologized for not remembering our names. 'Indian names,' she said, 'are so peculiar and hard to remember.' It had completely escaped her that we all had European names" (Deloria, 1970, p. 27).

Person perception then is a special form of perception, and it will require some specific attention and study. Our concern in this chapter will be with how communicators form their impressions of others and with the accuracy of those impressions. We shall also give some attention to person perception as it relates to intercultural communication.

FORMING IMPRESSIONS OF OTHERS

Most people form impressions of others quite easily; yet they would find it difficult to explain how they do so. In fact, many feel that they make their judgments intuitively. Tagiuri describes the process of personality assessment well when he writes, "Regardless of the degree of skill which an adult may have in appraising others, he engages in the process most of the time without paying much attention to how he does it" (Tagiuri and Petrullo, 1958, p. ix).

We are accustomed to using the word "impression" about our judgments. We speak of being "under the impression" or of someone making a "lasting impression," a "false impression," or a "good impression." Even our legal system reflects the degree to which we rely on snap judgments. Before a trial begins prospective jurors are screened by the defense and the prosecution. In addition to raising specific objections to certain candidates for the jury, both the defense and the prosecuting attorney have several peremptory challenges; that is, they are each allowed to reject a certain number of would-be jurors without stating their reasons. Attorneys often make their decisions rapidly, though they are complex ones and are probably based on several considerations. They will probably take into account their perception of the potential juror and the client, and the impression they feel that the client will make upon that juror. And, of course, the attorney for one side might be more than willing to accept a juror whom opposing counsel found objectionable.

Attorneys usually seem to be rather skilled perceivers, accustomed to formulating judgments about others very quickly. But think of the members of the jury. They will be meeting and evaluating many people for the first time—and presumably doing this entirely on their own. If the case is a controversial or sensational one, the jurors may be kept apart from other people until the time they make their decision. They will be instructed not to discuss any aspects of the trial outside the courtroom, even with friends or family. In a short time each juror will probably have formed an impression of most if not all of those involved in the case—including the witnesses, the defense attorney, the prosecuting attorney, and even the judge.

Because a juror's final judgment about the person on trial can have dramatic consequences, it is important to consider how he or she forms initial impressions and whether those impressions will have any effect on later perceptions. Our own evaluations of people also have important if less dramatic consequences, so we might all benefit from looking more closely at how an impression of another person is formed.

A Private Theory of Personality

As we have seen, the attributes of each communicator influence not only what he or she sees but how he or she interprets what is seen. Many people are quite confident of their perceptions about others, and some even like to think of themselves as amateur psychologists.

Actually, each of us seems to hold what has been described as a "private theory of personality":

> One factor that determines the content we tend to select (in order to fill in a sketchy impression) is our general notion of "what goes with what" in people. This notion in fact constitutes a private theory of personality that each of us has and that determines, to a considerable extent, how we judge others. This private theory is almost never stated or examined and is therefore referred to by psychologists as an "implicit theory of personality" (Krech, Crutchfield, and Livson, 1969, p. 801).

You can see private personality theory at work in many shorthand attempts to size up people. For example, you might be asked, Is a glass with water to its midpoint half-full or half-empty? This question is a layman's way of finding out whether your view of life is optimistic (half-full glass) or pessimistic (half-empty glass). The layman is using your answer as a basis from which to generalize about your personality and to predict something about your future behavior. One of the major uses of personality evaluation is to explain and predict behavior on the basis of very limited information.

The First Impression

In our model of communication, time is seen as one of the most significant variables. It seems natural therefore to ask what effect, if any, the first impression will have on our future perceptions of another communicator. Ideally, as we learn more about a person, we come to perceive that person in the light of this new information so that our impressions are revised and refined. But is this true? Does a first impression enhance or interfere with later knowledge, or does it have no effect at all? There have been many studies of impression formation, and those of Luchins are among the most important.

In one of Luchins' experiments, the subjects were divided into two groups: the E-I group and the I-E group. Members of the E-I group were first asked to read this description of a young man named Jim:

> Jim left the house to get some stationery. He walked out into the sun-filled street with two of his friends, basking in the sun as he walked. Jim entered the stationery store which was full of people. Jim talked with an acquaintance while he waited for the clerk to catch his eye. On his way out, he stopped to chat with a school friend who was just coming into the store. Leaving the store, he walked toward school. On his way out he met the girl to whom he had been introduced the night before. They talked for a short while, and then Jim left for school.

They then read a second paragraph:

> After school Jim left the classroom alone. Leaving the school, he started on his long walk home. The street was brilliantly filled with sunshine.

Jim walked down the street on the shady side. Coming down the street toward him, he saw the pretty girl whom he had met on the previous evening. Jim crossed the street and entered a candy store. The store was crowded with students, and he noticed a few familiar faces. Jim waited quietly until the counterman caught his eye and then gave his order. Taking a drink he sat down at a side table. When he had finished the drink he went home. (Luchins, in Hovland et al., 1957, pp. 35–36)

Members of the second group, I-E, read the same material about Jim, but the paragraphs were given to them in reverse order. After reading the descriptions members of both groups were asked to write a personality sketch of Jim and to predict how Jim would behave under various circumstances not described in the paragraphs.

Luchins had arranged the material so that the first paragraph given to group E-I described a predominantly extroverted person whereas the second described someone who could be characterized as introverted. He wanted to find out whether the order in which the paragraphs were read would influence the conception of personality. The results of his experiment confirmed that this was indeed so: most E-I members described Jim as an extrovert; most I-E members described him as an introvert. Yet both groups read the same paragraphs; it was only their order that varied.

You might have guessed that if paragraph order were at all influential, the information in the paragraph read most recently would be decisive. (And indeed, there are times when a recency effect occurs.) But once we know that in Luchins' experiment a **primacy effect** exists, that *the information presented first is the most decisive,* it is tempting to look back and speculate about how this might work. Try reading the paragraphs above in reverse order—as they were read by the I-E group. Perhaps now you can see how such divergent interpretations of the same information could be given.

It is disturbing to think that first impressions can have such dramatic effects on judgment. We all know how often first impressions can be mistaken ones, and we also know how often decisions depend on first impressions. Imagine, for example, that you are being interviewed for membership in the fraternity you prefer or for your first job in your chosen profession and that you look very nervous and were very late for the interview. What is likely to be the outcome in these circumstances?

But the situation is not as alarming as it might seem. Luchins found that if people were warned not to make snap judgments before they read the descriptions of Jim, or if they were given simple arithmetic problems to do before reading the second paragraph, the primacy effect was reversed or eliminated completely. Several other studies of primacy and recency confirm Luchins' finding that the primacy effect is not inevitable.

In most situations we are forming first impressions of people on a one-to-one basis.

There are many times, however, when a primacy effect prevails, and we must examine more closely its influence on communication. If you look once more at the model in Figure 2.1, you will see that each communicator should be receiving input and feedback. Yet the primacy effect blocks both. It is, in our terms, a source of technical interference. To illustrate, if *P* is confident that he or she has judged *O* accurately, *P* is of course much less interested in receiving feedback about his or her impression of *O;* in other words, *P* is not receptive to feedback. Most of you have been in *O*'s place more than once. In a sense, it is as if you were invisible. No matter what you do or say, the other person does not seem to respond; you cannot affect his or her judgment about you. The frustration of being in such a position is summed up in the statement, "It's like talking to a wall."

Demonstrating this situation in terms of Luchins' experiment, let us say that a participant in group E-I—call her Roberta—has completed her impression of Jim after reading the first paragraph. Rightly or wrongly, Roberta feels confident that Jim is an extrovert. Confidence of this sort is interesting. In his analysis of Luchins' experiments, Brown points out that almost all the subjects were quite willing to answer questions about Jim's behavior that were totally unrelated to the information they had read about him; for example, "Is he: (a) shy; (b) more shy than forward; (c) more forward than shy; (d) forward; (e) none of these?" (Brown, 1965, p. 618). Only a few subjects asked how they were supposed to know such things.

Most of Luchins' subjects freely answered questions about Jim because they felt they knew him. Given information about some of his behavior, they inferred several other things about him and confidently predicted how he would behave in other social situations.

Now imagine Luchins' test in reverse—suppose you are given the following list of words describing Jim and asked to write a personality sketch of him:

energetic	ironical
assured	inquisitive
talkative	persuasive
cold	

Several years before Luchins' experiment, Asch (1946) used this list to learn more about how impressions of others are formed. He read each of the seven adjectives to a group of students and asked them to write a full impression of the person described. There were two important findings from the Asch experiment.

First, the students were able to organize the scanty information they received and to create a consistent, unified impression, though there is a great deal of variation in their personality sketches, and they all go beyond the terms of the original description. Here are two samples:

> He seems to be the kind of person who would make a great impression upon others at a first meeting. However as time went by, his acquaintances would easily come to see through the mask. Underneath would be revealed his arrogance and selfishness.

> Possibly he does not have any deep feeling. He would tend to be an opportunist. Likely to succeed in things he intends to do. He has perhaps married a wife who would help him in his purpose. He tends to be skeptical. (Asch, 1946, p. 261)

Second, Asch found that certain trait names are more influential than others in forming the personality sketches. When one of the adjectives on the list was substituted for its opposite, the personality descriptions were radically different. Can you guess which of the seven adjectives was the crucial one in this experiment? It was the word "cold." Half the students were read the list with the trait name "warm" substituted for "cold." When in another experiment Asch substituted the pair "polite-blunt" for "warm-cold," he found that these traits had a relatively small effect on the way personality impressions were formed. To most of his subjects, whether a person is warm or cold was more important than whether he is blunt or polite. Thus we can say that in the minds of most people, some traits are more central or more heavily weighted than others.

Trait Associations

Since 1946 several studies have been made of how people believe traits are linked together. Students in an economics course at the Massachusetts Institute of Technology were unwitting participants in one such experiment by Kelley (1950). They were told that their instructor was out of town and that the department was interested in evaluating a new lecturer. All the students were given a brief biographical note about the lecturer on the pretext that they would later be asked to fill out forms about him. What they did not know was that the biographical notes differed. Half the students received the following biographical note:

> People who know him consider him to be a rather warm person, industrious, critical, practical and determined.

The other half received the same note but with a single word changed:

> People who know him consider him to be a rather cold person, industrious, critical, practical and determined. (Kelley, 1950, p. 433)

After the lecturer had finished speaking and left the classroom, the students were asked to describe him and to rate him on fifteen different characteristics. Those who had read the "warm" biographical note usually described the lecturer as social, popular, and informal. Those given the "cold" description felt he was neither sociable nor popular; they thought of him as formal and self-centered.

Indirectly, experiments such as those of Asch and Kelley tell us that certain traits influence our judgments more than others. For a long time most theorists believed that impressions of others were often interpreted on the basis of what they called the "halo effect," the tendency to extend a favorable impression of one trait to other traits—in other words, a tendency for the perceiver to exaggerate the uniformity of personality. You might think of a friend as honest and polite, for example, just because you consider him or her intelligent. And if your first impression of a person is unfavorable, you might attribute many other undesirable traits to that person. This explanation sounds reasonable, but we know now that the concept is too simple to account completely for the way we interpret our perceptions. Certain traits are clearly more decisive in, or central to, our judgments than others. We are still learning about **trait associations,** and it will be some time before we can isolate all the traits critical to the process of person perception.

Personal Generalizations and Stereotypes

One's private theory of personality is in large part based on generalizations, many of which are derived from personal experience. If Jane favors boys of fraternity XYZ, for example, then she may be attracted to Phil simply because he is a member. Similarly, if she thinks math students are creeps, then she may refuse a first date with one regardless of whether he fits her personal definition of math students. If your luggage is stolen while you are traveling in Italy, you may come to feel that Italians are dishonest. If you have seen several Swedish films starring beautiful actresses, perhaps you have come to believe that all Swedish women are beautiful.

In saner moments we realize that generalizations based on limited personal experience can be inaccurate and misleading. Jane may find that the next member of fraternity XYZ she dates is a creep. You may get to know members of a wonderful Italian family who practically take you into their home. The first Swedish girl you actually meet may be unattractive.

But how we perceive other human beings also depends on generalizations derived from our shared experience as members of a given culture or society. In discussing the Müller-Lyer illusion (p. 27), we observed that culture was a determinant of visual perception. It is even more significant from the standpoint of human communication that culture can be a determinant of person perception.

The influence of a culture on the person perception of its members is most directly seen in its sterotypes. A **stereotype** is *a generalization about a class of people, objects, or events that is widely held by a given culture*. We cannot say categorically that all stereotypes are false. According to one hypothesis, there is a kernel of truth in all of them. Thus we can at least acknowledge that some are accurate enough to provide a very limited basis for making judgments about groups of people we hardly know. But when applied to a specific individual, most stereotypes are highly inaccurate—and many are false. Relying on stereotypes rather than on direct perceptions can result in embarrassing social situations. The story is told, for example, of an elderly club member who was attending a distinguished public dinner in London:

> [He] was disconcerted to find himself seated next to a silent Chinese. Wanting to be courteous, however, he leaned toward him and asked, tentatively, "Likee soupee?" The Chinese looked at him briefly, nodded, but said nothing, and conversation lapsed. However, it appeared that the Chinese was a foreign guest of some note, for as coffee was served he was called upon to say a few words. He rose, bowed, and made a fifteen minute speech in impeccable English about the sociological significance

"The cabby."

of the European Common Market. Amid polite applause, he then sat down, turned to his abashed English neighbor, and, after the briefest of pauses, asked softly: "Likee speechee?" (Bloodworth, 1967, p. 6)

There can be no doubt that race membership affects our perceptions of others. Malpass and Kravitz (1969) found, for example, that people of one race (both black and white were studied) were better able to recognize pictures of members of their own race than pictures of members of another. A more light-hearted illustration of this phenomenon is depicted in a popular cartoon. The setting is a Chinese restaurant in the United States. All the waiters are Chinese; all the customers are Americans. In the foreground a waiter holding a tray with a covered dish on it is conferring with several other waiters. "I can't remember which customer ordered this," he says. "They all look alike."

In their research on interracial stereotypes, Ogawa and Rich (Rich, 1974) studied the communication stereotypes held by white Americans about black, chicano, and Japanese Americans, and those held by blacks about white, chicano, and Japanese Americans. Each group was asked to specify the communication behaviors typical of members of the other racial groups. Among white Americans the most positive stereotype was that of the Japanese American. And despite the increasing demands of Mexican Americans on the white community, it was the black Americans whom whites perceived as most threatening. Black Americans felt the same way about whites. Comparing black perceptions of whites and white perceptions of blacks makes for interesting reading:

The Twelve Most Frequent Communicative Traits*

Traits Checked (Rank Order)	Percent	Traits Checked (Rank Order)	Percent
White Perceptions of Black Americans		Black Perceptions of White Americans	
Argumentative	40	Evasive	41
Emotional	35	Critical	26
Aggressive	32	Conservative	24
Straightforward	26	Ignorant	24
Critical	26	Boastful	23
Sensitive	20	Aggressive	22
Ostentatious	19	Arrogant	21
Defiant	17	Ostentatious	21
Hostile	17	Concealing	19
Open	17	Emotional	18
Responsive	17	Individualistic	15
Intelligent	17	Nonmilitant	15

* Table adapted from Rich, 1974, pp. 54, 58.

Notice that four of the same traits—"emotional," "critical," "aggressive," and "ostentatious"—appear on both lists in the table. Rich points out that although none of the four terms has a necessarily negative connotation, "taken together they seem to describe the existence of a mutual contempt between the black and white communicators" (Rich, 1974, p. 59). That whites and blacks continue to perceive each other in such negative ways is a major obstacle to the effectiveness of their communication.

Even positive stereotypes can have damaging effects on intercultural communication. In this country, Asian Americans have generally been singled out as America's most "successful" minority. As we said, in the Ogawa and Rich studies the most positive stereotype was that of the Japanese Americans and this group was also stereotyped most strongly by all the other groups studied. (Chinese Americans were not subjects in this research, but they are also strongly stereotyped.) During the 1960s, when black groups were becoming increasingly vocal, the mass media seemed to be giving special emphasis to the "success story" of Asian Americans. "Intelligent," "hard-working," "quiet," "soft-spoken," "well-mannered"—these were some of the all too predictable terms for describing this racial group. Amy Tachiki's introduction to *Roots: An Asian American Reader* gives us the other side of the success story:

> Like all stereotypes, there is some factual support for the success image of Asian Americans, if success is to be defined along economic, materialistic parameters. A sizable number of Chinese and Japanese Americans have attained higher educational, employment, and income levels—that is, compared to other *non*white groups in the United States. What the mass media selectively overlooks in Asian success are such factors as middle management ranks, de facto segregation, delayed promotion in jobs, and other subtleties of institutional subordination. In addition, the success stereotype does not consider the psychological and cultural costs which have been the price of Asian American success. (Tachiki et al., 1971, p. 1)

Since the late 1960s many younger Asian Americans have begun to express their frustration and anger with the way in which they are so frequently perceived by members of other racial or ethnic groups. They object in particular to the notion that they are passive, conforming people. This incident from a biographical sketch by a Chinese American student illustrates the very damaging effect stereotyping can have on communication between people of different ethnic or racial backgrounds:

> During the latter part of my senior year I was selected to go to Washington, D.C. to attend a Presidential Scholars program. At the conference I was the only Asian, there were also only four Blacks. One night we were allowed to rap all night. During our rap session I sat and listened. There were many southern whites at the conference. One of them started coming down on the Black movement. He said that the Blacks wanted too much too soon. I just sat there at first because I couldn't relate. Then the whitey pointed at me and said, "Look at him, he's not complaining and demanding, look how well off the Orientals are!" This blew my mind completely. (Low, in Tachiki et al., 1971, p. 108)

Stereotypes extend further than just to social and ethnic groups. They can refer, for example, to physical attributes. Think of the long-standing American stereotype concerning the advantages of being blonde. Advertising for hair dye makes use of it in such slogans as "Is it true Blondes have more fun?" and "If I've only one life . . . Let me live it as a Blonde." The length of one's hair has also become the source of stereotypes. A few decades ago a "longhair" referred to someone (particularly a man) who was devoted to the arts, especially to classical music. Today a young person with long hair might be pegged as a "freak"—or, in some contexts, a "radical."

Physical attributes have considerable influence on our first impressions of others. One study showed that pictures of people can be separated into groups of attractive or unattractive on the basis of facial features. And it is significant that in our culture attractive people are judged to have better character than unattractive people (Widgery and Webster, 1969).

Citing earlier studies, Secord (1958) points out that in addition to stressing physical attributes, each culture emphasizes certain facial cues. Several decades ago in our own culture, he notes, the amount of lipstick a woman wore was "more important than the shape of her ears." And people are usually perceived as more intelligent, reliable, and industrious when they are wearing glasses (Secord, in Tagiuri and Petrullo, 1958, pp. 308, 313). No doubt you have seen people who are aware of the power of this stereotype and exploit it to create an impression. Politicians and moderators of talk shows seem inclined to do this.

Conversely, status differences can affect our perception of physical attributes. In one study (Wilson, 1968) a speaker named Mr. England was introduced to each of five different college classes by a different title:

Class 1   A student from Cambridge
Class 2   A demonstrator in psychology from Cambridge
Class 3   A lecturer in psychology from Cambridge
Class 4   Dr. England, senior lecturer from Cambridge
Class 5   Professor England from Cambridge

When students were asked to estimate Mr. England's height, it was found that the mean estimate given by each class increased from class 1 to class 5; that is, the class 2 estimate was greater than the class 1, the class 3 greater than the class 2, and so forth. In other words, the higher Mr. England's status, the taller the students thought he was.

In each of the examples of stereotyping discussed, a person is considered to have attributes generally ascribed to the group of which he or she is a member. That person is not perceived as a unique human being, but as a member of a certain category of human beings. In a sense, the person is judged in terms of context. Although some generalizations about categories are valuable to us in daily experience, generalizations about human beings tend to distort our perceptions and to interfere with our ability to make accurate judgments.

Unlike the primacy effect, however, personal generalizations or stereotypes cannot be eliminated simply by alerting the perceiver to their dangers. Crockett and Meidinger (1956) have found, for example, that people who are authoritarian and closed-minded seem to do more stereotyping than those who are not. But one cannot simply tell a person to be less authoritarian. Writing about intercultural communication, Barna observes:

> Unfortunately, we cannot "cure" the stereotype by demonstrating the "truth" in order to teach a lesson of tolerance or cultural relativity. Stereotypes persist because they sometimes rationalize prejudices or are firmly established as myths or truisms by one's own national culture. They are also sustained and fed by the tendency to perceive selectively only those pieces of new information (even contrary evidence) corresponding with the image. (Barna, in Samovar and Porter, 1972, p. 243)

CHARACTERISTICS OF ACCURATE PERCEIVERS

But granted the selective quality of human perception, we can still ask whether certain types of people are generally more accurate in their perceptions of others. Certainly, we all know people who feel their perceptions to be extremely accurate. Therefore, the first issue we shall raise is whether there is a relationship between self-confidence and accuracy of person perception. Does self-confidence about our ability to judge others make a difference in how we see them?

There are some social situations in which self-confidence can make a difference. Consider people who expect to be rejected by others. Perceiving others as hostile or unfriendly, they often act defensive or overly superior, and their behavior may very well help produce the rejection they fear. On the other hand, people who expect to be accepted by others, who perceive them as friendly, are often outgoing and congenial, and their behavior will account in good measure for their popularity. These people help confirm their own expectations. In such situations a favorable self-concept may lead to success and an unfavorable self-concept to failure. This phenomenon is called the "self-fulfilling prophecy." In terms of our communication model, we might say that a person who begs the question receives no feedback. Although his or her beliefs about the other communicator are confirmed, we cannot say that these judgments are based on accurate perceptions.

Crockett and Meidinger (1956) tried to find out what made the difference between people who have confidence in their perceptions of others and those who lack this confidence. Were the more confident people also more accurate in their evaluations of others? No. The researchers found that there was not necessarily a correlation between accuracy of perception and confidence in that perception.

If self-confidence is no measure of accuracy, what is? Surely, you might say, some people are more skilled or astute in evaluating others. Perhaps you even consider yourself a "good judge of character." For a long time psychologists have tried to determine whether some people are indeed better judges than others. Although the problem seems clear-cut, research findings are contradictory. Only one study (Cline and Richards, 1960) supports the view that there is a general ability to judge people. Other studies do not confirm this finding. On the contrary, they suggest that (1) some people are easier to judge than others (perhaps because they are more open or straightforward), (2) some traits are easier to judge than others, and (3) people are better at judging those who resemble themselves.

From what we know at present, it seems likely that judging ability may be quite specific to context. Psychologists have also found this to be true for other traits. Although it is assumed, for example, that a person who tells the truth in one situation will not lie in others, an early study of children by Hugh Hartshorne and Mark Arthur May (1928–1930) shows that this is a questionable assumption; an individual's interpretation of moral conduct will vary from situation to situation. Other traits vary with context. The late Igor Stravinsky, one of the foremost composers of the twentieth century, was known for his self-assurance and commanding intellect. Stravinsky was unafraid; he openly referred to music critics as "pests" and once announced that his music was "not to be discussed or criticized." Yet this formidable man "was so nervous when performing in public that he thrice forgot his own piano concerto" (*The New York Times,* 1971, p. 48).

Our ability to judge other people seems to vary just as much as other traits. One thing that affects our judgment is whether we are alone or in the presence of other people when we are perceiving someone. In one study (Tubbs, 1969) female college students were asked to view a person bargaining in two different situations. The bargainer was very cooperative in the first situation and very competitive in the second. All the subjects were able to distinguish between the two types of bargaining behaviors quite easily. When a subject was one of a group of four observers, however, and the answers of the other three were rigged to disagree with hers, in every case she was influenced by group opinion. Later the subjects filled out questionnaires designed to measure their perception of the bargainer; their answers showed that group influence had been so strong that when their perceptions did not correspond with those of the group, the subjects denied what they had seen with their own eyes. In fact, they believed the opposite of what they had seen.

Majority or group opinion is just one instance in which context— the third element of perception—exerts its subtle influence on person perception. Yet despite the fact that accurate person perception varies from one situation to another, theorists generally agree that certain characteristics seem to be associated with sound perceptions of others.

First, intelligence is a prime factor. Second, the ability to draw inferences about people from their behavior seems related to accurate perception. Third, people who score low on tests of authoritarianism tend to be better judges of others. They are less rigid in their expectations, judging more from what they know about the person and assuming less that he or she is like themselves. (Jacoby [1971] reports that people who score low on tests of dogmatism are more accurate in perceiving dogmatism in others.) And fourth, those with a high degree of objectivity about themselves tend to have insight into the behavior of others. Openness and awareness of one's own shortcomings seem to play a part in this process.

How does this information relate to improving our effectiveness as communicators? We certainly cannot improve our intelligence directly—and the ability to draw valid inferences about people from their behavior probably depends in part on intelligence. Nor can we simply tell ourselves to be less rigid or authoritarian. Research has demonstrated that attitudes are rarely changed so easily. The one thing we can do is become conscious of, and less defensive about, our own limitations. As we shall see in Chapter 6, this fourth characteristic is one of the most important for our purposes.

IMPROVING PERCEPTION AND COMMUNICATION

Failures in communication frequently occur because (1) people have inaccurate perceptions of each other and (2) they are unaware that their perceptions are inaccurate. The Kelley experiment described in a previous section provides us with some information on this subject. Among students given the description of the lecturer as "warm," 56 percent participated in the classroom discussion; among those informed that he was "cold," only 32 percent engaged in any classroom discussion. This trend is borne out in everyday experience. If you are told, for example, that a girl you know only casually is snobbish or stand-offish, you are not likely to ask her out on a date. If you feel that a particular instructor is stubborn and somewhat hostile, you probably won't consider questioning him about why he gave you such a low grade on the last exam. Kelley's experiment confirms that our perceptions of others can determine not only the kind of communication that takes place but whether or not we attempt to communicate at all.

It would seem then an easy matter to facilitate more effective communication by simply improving the accuracy of our perceptions. Yet the three elements of perception—the perceiver, the object of perception, and the context within which the perception occurs—are so interwoven that one cannot be analyzed apart from the others. The most important thing the perceiver can do is take into account the need to make perceptual adjustments as any of these three components varies.

The second source of misunderstanding—lack of awareness that one's perceptions may be inaccurate—is closely linked to the first. Improved perception and improved communication can occur only after we realize that our perceptions are personal, subjective, and therefore subject to error. One of the authors remembers a conversation in which two people disagreed about their perceptions of a third. When one was asked whether she was sure of what she was saying, she replied, "Would I say it if it weren't true?" Her statement shows an obvious lack of awareness that human perceptions are subject to error. As long as she was unwilling to admit that possibility, there was little chance that an effective exchange of viewpoints could take place.

It would be utopian to say that more accurate person perception always makes for more effective communication. Nevertheless, communication in both long-term and short-term relationships is often enhanced when the participants perceive each other accurately. For example, if a husband knows his wife, he can react to her more effectively in many situations. Notice the difference between these two conversations:

Conversation 1

Wife: Would you help me with the shopping today?
Husband: No, I want to watch a ball game on television.
Wife: You never want to do anything with me any more.
Husband: Oh, that's not true.
Wife: (*Becoming upset.*) I sometimes wonder if you love me any more.

Conversation 2

Wife: Would you help me with the shopping today?
Husband: Well, I did want to watch a ball game on television. Could you wait until after the game? It's not that I don't want to go. I just don't want to miss the game.
Wife: Well, I think it will be too late to go after the game.

The husband in conversation 1 reacts only to the most obvious content of his wife's message. The husband in conversation 2 knows from past experience that sometimes if his wife asks him to accompany her she also wants to know whether he values simply being with her. He is sensitive to the more subtle relationship aspects of his wife's requests and tries to respond to her total message.

We need not be speaking of marital communication; the same principles apply to dating relationships and to many less intense interpersonal encounters. For example, the interview relies heavily on accurate person perception even though it usually involves a relatively short-term relationship. Here is a situation in which two or more people meet to exchange information—ordinarily about a subject that has been decided on beforehand—and to formulate impressions of one another. In a selection or job interview, it is each person's intention to size up the other's attributes. Person perception is one of the prime objectives. In an evaluative interview an employee's work is appraised by a supervisor, and guidelines for improved job performance are discussed. Several studies have shown that two of the most important objectives of evaluative interviews are that the employee perceive the supervisor as helpful and constructive rather than critical, and that the supervisor and employee perceive effective job performance in a similar way.

We have tried to suggest that interpersonal sensitivity is a requirement in both long- and short-term encounters. Later in this book we shall discuss some differences between perception of the self and perception of others as well as some methods of increasing one's awareness of self and others (Chapter 6). In the chapter that follows, we shall see that although early impressions depend to a great extent on the perceiver's preconceptions and stereotypes and on the other person's physical appearance, as contact with a person continues, the content of his or her messages (both verbal and nonverbal) plays a greater role in modifying our perception of that person.

Summary

In the present chapter it has been our intention to demonstrate that person perception is an active process in which communicators select, organize, and interpret what they experience. It has also been our aim to show how person perception affects intercultural communication.

After suggesting some parallels and distinctions between person and object perception, we focused on how our impressions of other human beings are formed. We spoke of private personality theory, primacy and recency effects, trait centrality and trait associations, and personal generalizations and stereotypes.

We saw that our impressions, while formed with relative ease, are not necessarily accurate. Some characteristics of accurate perceivers were mentioned, but judging ability itself was seen as specific to context. In concluding we discussed inaccurate perception as a source of communication failures and illustrated how improved perception contributes to effective communication.

Review Questions

1. What is psychological set? Give two examples.
2. Discuss two ways in which person perception is different from ob-

ject perception. What are the implications of these differences for communication?
3. What is the primacy effect? How might it influence communication?
4. How do personal generalizations and stereotypes differ?
5. Discuss two ways in which stereotypes influence intercultural communication.
6. What three generalizations can you make from the research studies cited here about individual ability to judge people?
7. Discuss four characteristics associated with accurate perception of others.
8. What are two ways in which person perception and communcation effectiveness can be improved?

Exercises

1. Select one of the case problems listed in the Appendix. Ask five people to read the same case problem and each write a short paper supporting a solution to the problem. Examine the solutions offered in terms of differences and similarities in person perception. How do the following concepts relate to the similarities and differences:

   a. psychological set
   b. psychological filter (see objective 5, Chapter 2)
   c. primacy effect
   d. stereotype perceptions

2. Write down some of the perceptions you have of your classmates. Then refer to your earlier comments in your personal log. Have you changed or confirmed some of your original impressions?

3. Reread your descriptions (in exercise 2) of people who really impressed you at first. Write a list of words describing each person. Then try to identify the specific verbal and nonverbal behaviors that led you to draw up each list. Now that you know each of these people better, what additional experiences have shaped your perception of each of them?

4. Write a paragraph describing someone you think is an effective communicator. List all the attributes that seem to contribute to this effectiveness. Now think of a poor communicator. What characteristics seem to cause the ineffectiveness? What characteristics do you possess that affect how you perceive these two people?

5. Have the class split up into groups of five. Your instructor will give you copies of the "Preliminary Scale of Interpersonal Perceptions." Fill out these forms, giving your perceptions of each of the other members in your group. Do not put your own name on the forms. When everyone has filled out all the forms, exchange them so that each person has a rating from every other group member. Then

look at the ratings you received from the rest of the group. You might want to discuss these with others in the group to gain additional feedback.
6. Interview a person who does a lot of interviewing. Discuss communication and person perception with that person. Have the interviewer elaborate on how he or she perceives interviewees and selects cues in assessing them.

Suggested Readings

Deloria, Vine. *We Talk, You Listen.* New York: Macmillan, 1970. In Chapter 2, the author, an American Indian, gives a frank, very personal account of the effects of stereotyping minority groups.

Fabun, Don. *Communications: The Transfer of Meaning.* Beverly Hills, Calif.: Glencoe Press, 1968. This colorfully illustrated and highly readable booklet serves as an excellent, entertaining primer on communication. It indicates several practical applications of communication theory and relates perception to communication.

Hastorf, Albert, Schneider, David, and Polefka, Judith. *Person Perception.* Reading, Mass.: Addison-Wesley, 1970. This is a brief paperback introducing the subject of interpersonal perception. The authors discuss basic issues and numerous research findings concerning impression formation, attribution theory, and interpersonal behavior.

Rosenthal, Robert. "Self-Fulfilling Prophecy." *Psychology Today* (September 1968), 2:44–51. The author proves that experimenters influence their subjects. Time after time, no matter what the conditions, whether the subjects were human or not, the group that was expected to do better on the tests *did* do better—even when the positive correlation existed only in the experimenter's mind.

Chapter 5: Bases of Human Attraction

OBJECTIVES

After reading this chapter the student should be able to:
1. Describe two ways in which proximity affects interpersonal relationships.
2. State three theories about the effects of proximity on attraction.
3. Suggest how proximity might affect intercultural communication.
4. Describe the relationship between attraction and similarity.
5. Explain the basic assumption of cognitive consistency theories.
6. Draw two diagrams, one depicting a balanced state and one depicting an unbalanced state.
7. Describe three alternative strategies that one might employ to balance an unbalanced state.
8. Discuss three variables that qualify generalizations about attitude similarity.
9. Contrast the theory of complementary needs with the research findings on the relationship between perceived similarity and attraction.
10. Describe three situations that influence communicator choice and give an example of how each affects attraction.
11. List three advantages of the sociometric test.
12. Identify at least two attributes of persons generally perceived as providing consistent positive reinforcement.
13. Identify at least four attributes shared by persons who are generally disliked.

5

In an offhand way we notice who is popular and who is not—who, so to speak, gets chosen. We also notice that we tend to communicate with some people more frequently than we do with others. But beyond saying that we seek the company of A or that we turn the corner every time we see B coming, we find the patterns of likes and dislikes within a group of people difficult to account for. We express our preferences when we choose our friends, our school leaders, our roommates, our dates, and—most important—our marriage partners; yet it often seems that the choices we make are random. How, if at all, are the choices we make as communicators related? And why are we attracted to some people and put off by others?

These are the themes of this chapter, and they will lead us back quite directly to the study of communication: "To know the lines of attraction and avoidance within a social system," writes Barnlund, "is to be able to predict where messages will originate, to whom they will flow, and much about how they will be received" (1968, p. 71). As we examine the determinants of human attraction, some consistent patterns of communicator choice should begin to emerge.

PROXIMITY

The most obvious determinant of attraction is **proximity,** or *geographic closeness*. We can state the principle simply: Other things being equal, the more closely two people are located geographically, the more likely they are to be attracted to one another.

The effects of proximity are seen in a number of ways. If you are not within a reasonable distance of another person, your chances of meeting and becoming friends are quite slim. How many friends do you have who live more than 3,000 miles away from you? Probably very few, unless you formerly lived in another country or people from another region spent some time in yours. In support of the notion that proximity fosters attraction, researchers have found that you are far more likely to marry a person who is geographically close to your home or school than someone living or studying far away (Gouldner and Gouldner, 1963).

Proximity in a work setting.

Once we get to know people, proximity also affects whether our relationships will continue. A great number of friendships and courtships are damaged by the effects of physical separation. A Frenchwoman living in the United States commented to one of the authors on how easily she could get to know Americans. Then she added with some hesitation that if these new acquaintances moved or returned to another part of the country, she never heard from them again. One thing she may not have considered is the vastness of this country compared with France. The drive from northern to southern France can be made in a day—certainly an easier distance over which to maintain a friendship than the distance between Maine and Florida. Perhaps the old saying "Out of sight, out of mind" has some validity simply because of the effort it takes to sustain relationships across many miles. Relationships that do continue despite this obstacle are maintained by the intensity of the rewards derived from them. In other words, the rewards outweigh the additional costs.

These conclusions about proximity are obvious, but what about the effect of much smaller distances on attraction? Are you more inclined to become friends with people who live next door than with those two blocks away? What about students who live on the same floor

BASES OF HUMAN ATTRACTION

in your dormitory as opposed to those who live two floors beneath you? In their classic study of the Westgate and Westgate West housing projects, Festinger, Schachter, and Back (1950) asked residents, "What three people in Westgate or Westgate West do you see most of socially?" The greatest percentage of residents chose their next-door neighbors; the next most frequent choice was the neighbors who lived two doors away; and, in general, percentages dropped as a function of distance so that those who lived at opposite ends of a single floor chose each other least. Yet a look at the relationship between sociometric choice and distance on a single floor of a Westgate West building is startling: apartments are about twenty-two feet apart, and the greatest distance between apartments, those at opposite ends of the floor, is only eighty-eight feet.

Theories About the Effects of Proximity

Why should a few feet make any difference in how friendships are formed, and why, in general, should proximity tend to foster attraction? A number of different explanations have been proposed.

One theory is that *if we know we are going to be in very close proximity* to someone—living next door or working side by side over a long period of time—*we tend to minimize or even overlook that person's less desirable traits.* For example, it becomes more politic to emphasize the positive qualities of the family next door than to be in constant conflict, especially if children from the two families play together. In effect, this is an aspect of the selective attention process referred to in Chapter 2. As receivers we tend to process the more desirable stimuli while filtering out those that offend us. In one highrise apartment building, a middle-aged couple took an apartment on the fifteenth floor. Susan, their next-door neighbor, was an aspiring young actress who thought she could sing. It wasn't too long before the couple got to know Susan, and since both of them liked her, they soon adjusted to her screeching to the music of show tunes. In the apartment directly below them, on the other hand, lived a tenant who was sometimes home during the day and was fond of playing the piano. The couple developed a running feud with their piano-playing neighbor, whom they rarely met except in the elevator, and they frequently complained about her playing to the building superintendent.

A second theory about why proximity tends to intensify liking is that the *opportunities for communication clearly increase as a function of proximity.* For example, in a large organization people who work on the same floor are more likely to share coffee breaks and gossip, go out to lunch together, or even meet after work. This is especially true if the people are members of the same department. The more two people see each other, the more probable it is that they will spend leisure time together, exchange confidences (see Chapter 6 on self-disclosure), and offer support in difficult times. In other words, the opportunities for communication increase, and liking is often a result of the increased frequency of interaction.

We shall discuss similarity at some length, but we touch on it here because there seems to be some relationship between *similarity* and proximity. People with a common geographic location often have other things in common even before they interact. Two families living on the same block in the inner city tend to be closer in socioeconomic level than either would be to a family living in a high-rise apartment in another section of the city. As such people interact they tend to share information and ideas and to influence one another. We expect, for example, that the views of a Kansas farmer will be more similar to those of another Kansas farmer than to those of a resident of New York or San Francisco.

Another theory about the relationship between proximity and attraction is based on research findings about *familiarity*. Zajonc (1968) has found a definite correlation between liking and familiarity. When he showed photographs of human faces to his subjects, he observed that the more often a subject saw a particular face—the number of exposures varied from one to twenty-five—the more he or she liked it. This experiment and others conducted by Zajonc, including some on language, suggest that familiarity in and of itself may increase liking. And proximity, of course, increases the frequency of interaction and thus the degree of familiarity.

Proximity has a second aspect, however. The familiarity that often reinforces feelings of attraction can, under different circumstances, reinforce hostile feelings instead. For example, from the records of police departments we know that the majority of violent assaults take place between family members, neighbors, and acquaintances. But let's take a less dramatic situation. The boy in your class who always borrows your notes and old themes may become very familiar—too familiar! If your initial contacts with him have been irritating, every new encounter may simply intensify your dislike. And suppose that feeling becomes mutual. One day you announce that you're sick of doing his work for him. Dislike ripens into hostility and after that each time the two of you meet, the experience is an unpleasant one. So instead of intensifying positive feelings, proximity and the increased communication it facilitates can also intensify hostile feelings.

Proximity and Intercultural Communication

But how does the proximity of people from different cultures affect the quality of their interaction? If black, white, and chicano families who have never known each other all come to live in the same housing development, will their prejudices about each other dissipate or intensify with their increased interaction? Although there is some research indicating that integration on a short-term basis may have some negative effects (Kramer, 1950), there is persuasive evidence that for people of different races integrated housing or increased contact in work settings or classrooms results in less racial prejudice, antagonism, and stereotyping (see Mann, 1959; Works, 1961). There is other evidence that some though not all of our stereotypes about people of other cultures are modified as a result of direct experience. For example, Americans tend to perceive Greeks as lazy, inefficient, and unsystematic, and this stereotype is not altered by actual contact with Greek people. On the other hand, Greeks are initially perceived by Americans as overly inquisitive about personal affairs (such intimacy and personal involvement is very characteristic of Greek culture), but after increased contact with Greeks, Americans will use words such as "witty," "charming," and "obliging" to describe them. In this case, increased contact has resulted in stereotypes that are "more differentiated and more ambivalent" (Triandis, 1971, p. 105).

Writing about communication between people of different races, Smith emphasizes the importance of proximity:

> Reading the history of a race is not talking face to face with a member of that race. Availability is putting yourself where there can be contact. . . . Proximity, of course, requires willingness. Transracial communication increases in more meaningful ways as the interaction among whites and minority groups increases as a result of open housing and openmindedness. (Smith, in Samovar and Porter, 1972, p. 294)

But lest we paint too rosy a picture, let us mention a few of the conditions under which the increased contact of people from different cultures results in increased hostility. The violent response to busing in Boston, Massachusetts, is a case in point. When people who are hostile toward one another to begin with are forced together more often, there are more opportunities for conflict and more prolonged hostility that reinforces initial attitudes. Nor does proximity seem to foster liking when members of one culture are clearly of lower status than the other. If we want evidence of this we have only to recall the resistance of affluent suburbanites to any proposals for low-income minority housing within their communities.

But even when people in proximity are of equal status and start off without negative attitudes toward one another, we cannot predict which people will become friends. Given physical proximity we still favor some people and reject others. In short, proximity is often a precondition of liking, but there are other bases for attraction.

SIMILARITY

Suppose that you and your roommate have a lot of different kinds of friends, and you've decided to give a small party. Would you invite people who were similar in their tastes, values, and attitudes or people who appeared to be very different from each other? And what sort of communication would take place at that party? According to one theory (Rogers and Shoemaker, 1971), within certain limits the more similar the communicators are, the more effective their communication will be. One limiting condition, say Rogers and Shoemaker, is that if the similarities between people are so pervasive that they have the same attitudes and beliefs about every subject, there is no need for communication. For example, the conversation might be deadly at a party in which every person was in agreement about every subject from movies to politics. On the other hand, people who are dissimilar in almost every respect lack a common ground, a base from which to share experiences and exchange ideas. According to this theory, the ideal situation is one in which people have many similarities but are dissimilar enough in their attitudes about the subject at hand to interact and perhaps to influence one another's attitudes. Similarity clearly prevails, however. After all, the goal of attitude influence is to change the other person's attitude so that it more closely resembles your own.

Observation, research, and theory all bear out the statement that we like people who appear to be similar to us. Almost a hundred years ago Disraeli remarked, "An agreeable person is a person who agrees with me." A more contemporary writer puts it this way, "we tend to like people who have the same beliefs and attitudes we have, and when we like people we want them to have the same attitudes we have" (Heider, 1958, p. 195). In addition, personality, style of dressing, socioeconomic level, religion, age, status, and so forth will affect our feelings toward others. We tend to attract and be attracted to people who are like us and, conversely, we tend to dislike and be disliked by those who differ from us.

If this is the case, then given adequate knowledge of people's attitudes, interests, values, and backgrounds, it should be possible to predict which members of a group will become friends. In a now classic study of the acquaintance process, Newcomb (1961) had a unique opportunity to pursue exactly this line of reasoning. His subjects were male students, all strangers to each other, who transferred to the University of Michigan. In exchange for participating in the study through periodic testing, they were allowed to live rent free in a dormitory on campus for one semester. Before they came to the dormitory, Newcomb tested the students on their backgrounds, interests, values, and attitudes. He found that on a long-term basis, students who remained friends after college had shown many similarities in their test results. In one group of seventeen men, for example, three distinct cliques emerged. There was a group of five men who were all liberal in politics and religion, all intellectual, and all members of the arts college, and who all rated high on aesthetic, social, and theoretical values. There was a four-member group with one man classified as a "hanger-on," in which three of the four were engineering students; all had practical interests and had been rated high in economic and religious values. The third group consisted of three small-town midwestern Protestants, two of them engineering students; all three men had been rated low in theoretical values. In this group of seventeen, four of the remaining five were extremely isolated from the group, and the last appeared to be on the borderline between the first and second cliques.

But let us focus for a moment on the dynamics of attitude similarity and attraction in two-person communication. Suppose that two people who have never met before are to have a discussion on capital punishment and that each is told the other person will be very compatible in terms of personality traits. Or imagine that each is told the other will be incompatible. Brewer (1968), who designed an experiment based on these two situations, found that there was a high correlation between perceived similarity in attitudes and attraction. Following their discussions the pairs of subjects who expected to be attracted to one another tended to be more similar in their attitude toward capital punishment than discussion partners who expected to be incompatible. In other words, as we communicate with someone whom we think is similar to us, we are likely to become more similar to that person in our attitudes toward a given issue. In addition, the more we perceive that person to be similar to us in attitude, the more we tend to be attracted to him or her.

Here and elsewhere when we describe findings about similarity and attraction, we are speaking of *perceived* similarity. As was emphasized in Chapters 2 and 4, human perception is a selective process and not always an accurate one; often we are influenced by how we expect people to look or think or behave. For example, we expect people we like to agree with us on a wide range of topics, and we probably exaggerate the extent of this agreement. No doubt we also tend to overemphasize our differences with those we dislike.

Balance Theory

One explanation of the great appeal of perceived similariy is proposed by the **cognitive consistency theories,** *a group of related theories* *all based on the assumption that every human being has a strong psychological need for consistency.* People want their beliefs, attitudes, values, and feelings to fit together, and they try to maintain consistency and to create it where it does not exist. Each of the consistency theories has its own terminology: one calls this drive a need for "balance," another "congruity," and a third "consonance." We shall look principally at balance theory, the earliest and simplest of the three.

Balance theory was first presented by Heider, who formulated the basic concept on which all consistency theories are founded. According to this theory, it is the desire for consistency, or balance, that makes us want a person we like to have the same attitudes and beliefs we have. Conversely, it is more comfortable psychologically, more balanced, to believe that a person we dislike has very different attitudes and beliefs. A basic premise of balance theory is that imbalanced states or situations have a tendency to change in the direction of balanced ones.

Balance theory has a simple way of mapping out balanced and imbalanced states. The balance model starts with three basic elements: the person (P), the other person (O), and some object or idea (X).* These are shown in a triangle that has three links. Plus signs represent positive feelings between two of the links, minus signs represent negative feelings, and the direction of feeling is shown by an arrow. Any situation represented by an even number of minus signs or an absence of minus signs is balanced; if it is represented by an odd number of minus signs, it is imbalanced. With these simple elements we are ready to illustrate a number of balanced and imbalanced states.

Suppose that person P is John, person O is Nina, and X represents transcendental meditation, or TM. In Figure 5.1 we see four possible balanced states involving these three elements. The links in Triangle 1 are all positive. John likes Nina and approves of TM, as does Nina. In Triangle 2 John likes Nina and disapproves of TM; Nina shares his attitude. But don't be misled. One person doesn't have to like the other for a situation to be balanced. Look at Triangle 3, in which John dislikes Nina and doesn't like TM either. It's still a balanced situation, because Nina's attitude toward X—in this instance, TM—is positive. Balance also exists in Triangle 4. Here John dislikes Nina and favors TM, while Nina's attitude toward it is negative. Again their conflicting attitudes toward X are not disturbing to John because his feelings about Nina are negative. In fact, it's probably reassuring for him to think that not only does he dislike her, but he disagrees with her on this issue. There is no pressure for change in any of the four situations we have described. Looking again at Figure 5.1 you can

---

* O could also represent another concept or idea rather than a person, but this is an application of balance theory that we shall not discuss.

Figure 5.1

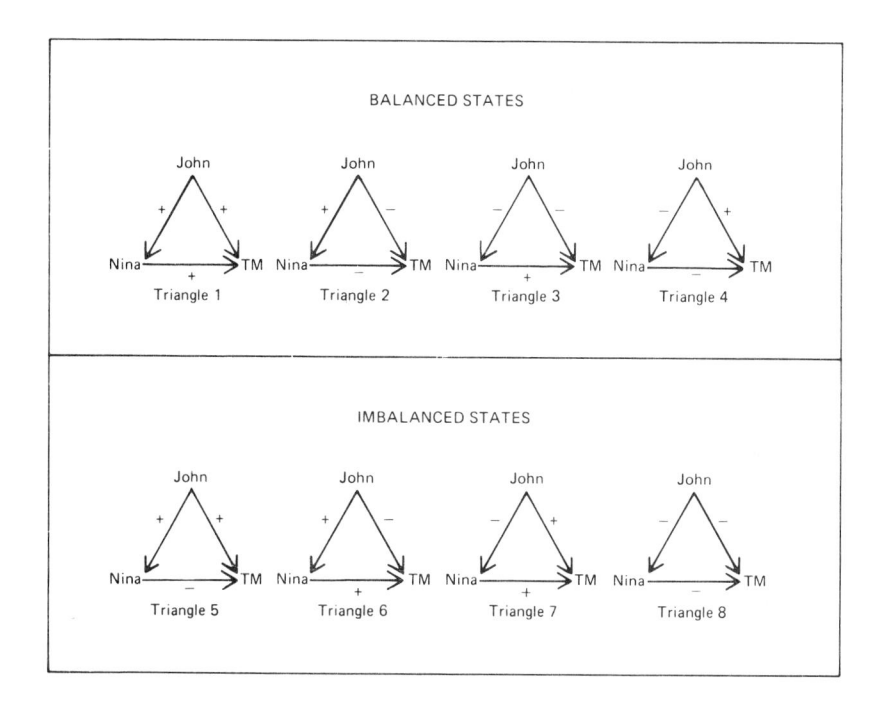

```
                    BALANCED STATES

       John           John           John           John
       /\             /\             /\             /\
      +  +           +  −           −  −           −  +
     /    \         /    \         /    \         /    \
  Nina──→TM      Nina──→TM      Nina──→TM      Nina──→TM
        +              −              +              −
    Triangle 1     Triangle 2     Triangle 3     Triangle 4

                    IMBALANCED STATES

       John           John           John           John
       /\             /\             /\             /\
      +  +           +  −           −  +           −  −
     /    \         /    \         /    \         /    \
  Nina──→TM      Nina──→TM      Nina──→TM      Nina──→TM
        −              +              +              −
    Triangle 5     Triangle 6     Triangle 7     Triangle 8
```

see that each of these balanced states is represented either by an even number of minus signs or an absence of minus signs.

But what makes a situation uncomfortable enough to motivate some change? Let's consider the same two people again. Look at Triangle 5. This time John likes Nina and thinks TM is great, but Nina thinks TM is a "rip-off." Since John likes Nina, he'd like her to agree with him. In Triangle 6 the situation is different, but also imbalanced. John likes Nina, but has no use for TM, whereas Nina thinks well of TM. Or perhaps, as in Triangle 7, John dislikes Nina, but both like TM. The situation in Triangle 8 is comparable to the one in Triangle 7. Again John's feelings for Nina are negative, but they both have similar attitudes—this time, negative ones—toward TM. It is easier, more comfortable, to disagree with someone you dislike. (Notice that in each of the four imbalanced situations we see an odd number of minus signs.)

Triangles 5 through 8 all represent states of imbalance. Keeping in mind Heider's prediction that imbalanced states will change in the direction of balanced states, let us consider how that might be accomplished. Take the state of imbalance represented by Triangle 5. John likes Nina and has a good opinion of TM, but Nina thinks TM is a rip-off. How much their difference in attitude bothers him will depend on the strength of his feelings about both Nina and TM. He might try to convince her that TM is really a worthwhile activity. If his efforts were successful, attitude influence would produce the balanced state given in Triangle 1. But perhaps Nina is very resistant to changing her attitude, so because he wants to maintain his friendship with her John starts to change *his* thinking about TM. In this case rationalizations about TM ("It's a waste of time," "It's probably a lot of bunk," and so on) might result in a negative evaluation on John's part, and we would then see the balanced situation described by Triangle 2. But perhaps John has a personal involvement in TM. Imagine, for example, that he is now part of a group that meets every Friday evening to learn the techniques of transcendental meditation and that he has paid $150 to join this group. All his efforts to convert Nina to his way of thinking have failed. Another way to restore balance is to change his evaluation of Nina. He may begin to rationalize that she's not very attractive anyway or that she's not very bright and that going out with her is getting to be a bore. If John's feelings about Nina really become negative, we have the balanced state shown in Triangle 4.

Applying the balance model to actual communication events has distinct limitations. The first is that this model indicates whether a feeling is negative or positive but does not represent differences in its intensity. I might think that *Jaws* was a terrific movie or that it was mildly entertaining, but in either case my feeling about it would be represented simply by a plus sign in the model. John might think that Nina was just a nice person or he might be in love with her, but again all we see is a plus sign. Another limitation of the balance model is that it can only represent two-person communication, and it can do this only with respect to a single attitude. So although balance theory gives us some insight into the dynamics of similarity and attraction, actual communication is too complex to be described by such a model. As we shall see, attitude similarity on one or five or even ten issues is no assurance of attraction between two people.

Qualifications of Similarity Predictions

Newcomb's study makes clear that it is not only similar attitudes but similar backgrounds, experiences, values, and so on that influence our attraction to another person. There are times, however, when similarities do not foster attraction. In competitive situations, for example, two people with identical goals often grow to dislike each other, primarily because of jealousy (Heider, 1958, p. 197). Two men vying for the same woman are unlikely to become friends. And two women who both want the same job probably will not like each other.

Therefore, that two people have some similar attitudes is not a sufficient basis on which to make predictions about whether they will like each other. We have to know something about other similarities. We also have to know something about three variables that affect attitude similarity: the proportion of issues on which two people agree, the salience of various attitudes, and whether reciprocity of liking is perceived.

Proportion of Issues. Our relationships with others are such that we rarely agree on all issues, even with our closest friends. Nevertheless we tend to agree with our friends on a greater **proportion of issues** than we do with those whom we dislike. Again this works two ways. We choose our friends because we agree on more issues, and we tend to agree on more issues because we are friends. Furthermore, no single issue may make or break a friendship, but the proportion of issues on which we agree is a good indicator of whether it will continue. When computer dating has been successful, the reason is probably that though people matched on any single issue are not that likely to be attracted to one another, people matched on a substantial number of issues will in all probability be compatible.

Salience. A related consideration is attitude **salience,** or importance. To put it simply, some of our attitudes are more firmly established, more central to us, than others. Changing a salient attitude in order to make a situation more balanced is usually more difficult than changing a nonsalient attitude. Therefore agreement on salient attitudes is often crucial in determining our relationships with others. Two roommates may differ over which one should clean up the room, but they may still be friends despite their disagreement. If they disagree about whether to use drugs in the room, however, this issue potentially has far greater importance and is more likely to affect their relationship.

One young married couple we know disagreed on several apparently minor questions (where they would live, whether to buy a car, and so on) and were able to weather the storm. But differences about whether to start a family (the wife wanted a child; the husband did not) became so crucial that the marriage ended in divorce. Marriages between people who are dissimilar in religion, race, education, or socioeconomic status are more likely to end in divorce than marriages between people who are similar in these respects. One reason for this is probably that attitudes toward these factors often have great salience in intimate relationships between people; another is that any of these issues (education, for example) may be highly salient for one marriage partner and unimportant for the other.

Thus although the number of similar attitudes is important, we cannot make a simple tally of agreements and disagreements; not all attitudes have the same weight. We tend to like people who agree with us on a substantial proportion of highly salient issues.

Reciprocal Liking. Another variable that affects our attraction to others is whether **perceived reciprocity of liking** exists—whether we feel that the people we like also like us. Certainly, we have all experienced situations in which our liking for a person is intensified by our feeling that he or she likes us too. When we like someone and our feeling is not reciprocated, we tend to lose interest in that person. This commonsense prediction is supported by research findings (Blake and Tesser, 1970).

Knowing that another person likes us is rewarding because it increases our self-esteem. Sometimes the effect of that knowledge on our own judgments can be transparent. We are reminded of an incident that took place at a university faculty meeting during which a candidate for a job as assistant professor in history was being evaluated. The candidate had previously expressed interest in sharing an office with one specific faculty member—let us call him Professor Jones. Each member of the history department was asked to rate the candidate on a scale from one to ten, with ten being the highest positive evaluation. Most of the evaluations were between five and eight. When Professor Jones' turn came, he announced, "In my humble opinion I'd rate him a 10!"

It is reassuring to find that we are not always this vulnerable to flattery. In a review of research, Berscheid and Walster qualify the reciprocity-of-liking rule by observing that though esteem produces reciprocal liking and acts as a positive reinforcer, "it is much more effective in producing liking when it is congruent with the subject's own evaluation of himself" (1969, p. 60). Flattery, it seems, does **not** get you everywhere.

Complementarity of Needs. Several years ago Walter Matthau and Jack Lemmon co-starred in the film *The Odd Couple,* a comedy about two men who decided to share an apartment. Matthau played a casual, shambling, very sloppy character who never picked up after himself and couldn't have cared less about his own appearance or that of his surroundings. Jack Lemmon played an extremely methodic and compulsively neat person who was constantly cleaning the apartment, replacing the cap on the toothpaste tube, picking up after Matthau, and complaining. The two were constantly at each other's throats. One partner was casual, messy, and totally indifferent to social appearances and the other partner was extraordinarily precise and obsessed by a need for order. At the end of the film, Lemmon, the compulsive, left the apartment, and the two went their separate ways. The viewer was left with the feeling, however, that each would soon become involved again in a similar relationship.

There are many actual relationships in which attraction seems to be based not on similarity but on complementarity. And many of these relationships seem mutually satisfying. Perhaps you can think of a couple you know who, despite great differences in personality, seem very compatible. "After all," you might ask, "aren't opposites supposed to attract?"

Winch (1958) proposes a **theory of complementary needs** that seems to contradict some of the findings about similarity that we have been discussing. According to this theory, *in selecting marriage partners and even friends we are attracted to people who are most likely to satisfy our needs*. Maximum gratification of needs occurs when two people have complementary rather than similar needs. For example, a woman with a strong need to be protective and a man with a strong need to be dependent might be very compatible. One friend might have a strong need to dominate a relationship, while the other was comfortable only in a submissive role. A restrained, low-keyed spouse might be the perfect foil for the extravert who dominates every party with funny stories and general clowning. Remember that Winch is speaking about complementary needs, not complementary attitudes, interests, or values. For example, two people might differ in the intensity of their needs for protection or dominance and still have many similarities.

Most research has not substantiated Winch's theory; yet the principle of complementarity has an intuitive appeal. We can all think of instances in which it seems valid: the perfectionist married to the easygoing person who has no difficulty in compromising; business partners, one doing all the wheeling and dealing, the other doing the paperwork. Even in instances where we look at two people and ask, "How did those two ever get together? They're like night and day," it's instructive to think about what each person is getting out of the relationship. If you cannot understand how a very aggressive woman could marry a very submissive man, ask yourself how long she might stay married to a man who was as aggressive as she.

Thibaut and Kelley offer the interesting speculation that some human relationships may be based primarily on similarity, whereas others may be based primarily on complementarity. Perhaps, as they suggest, similarity and complementarity both contribute to the rewards of interaction (Thibaut and Kelley, 1959, p. 47). It is also possible, as some research on mate selection has suggested (Kerckhoff and Davis, 1962), that in a short-term relationship agreement on values is critical and that complementary needs become significant only in long-term relationships.

SITUATION

We qualified our statement about the effect of proximity on attraction with the phrase "other things being equal." We could qualify statements about similarity and attraction in the same way. But other things rarely are equal; there are other conditions, many of which are specific to the communicator, that determine the rewards human beings receive from one another and, therefore, the choices they make. One of these is **situation**.

Experience and common sense tell us that in one situation we prefer to associate with some people and in another we reject them. In other words, the situation itself may alter the standards by which we pick receivers in our communication attempts. We shall look at three kinds of situations that have this effect.

Anxiety

Anxiety-producing situations affect our need to interact or affiliate with others. Schachter (1959, pp. 17–19) was able to study this by telling college women that they were to be subjects in an experiment on the effects of electric shock. One group was told that the shocks would be extremely painful; the other group was told that they would be mild and painless. A ten-minute "delay" was announced before the experiment, and the women were given the choice of waiting alone or with others. The choices they made were really what Schachter's experiment was all about. Schachter found that in the high-anxiety group (expecting painful shock), 63 percent of the women preferred to wait with others before the shock; in the low-anxiety group (expecting painless shock), only 33 percent of the women wanted company. The high-anxiety condition also produced a much more intense desire for affiliation than the low-anxiety. And though "misery loves company," it isn't just any company: anxious subjects preferred to wait with others who, presumably, were anxious, too.

Schachter's experiment demonstrates that anxiety-producing situations can increase our need to affiliate and also change our criteria for choosing companions. Apparently, the need to be comforted through sharing unpleasantness tends to supersede our other needs for associating with people. Boot camps and fraternity-pledging programs have long operated on this principle. People who share relatively unpleasant experiences often become more cohesive as a group—probably because together they find it easier to endure the hardships they are or will be experiencing.

Changes in Self-Esteem

A second situation that may influence communicator choice is a **change in the level of self-esteem**. Consider this example. Sam and Suzy have gone together for almost six months when suddenly she jilts him. Because he obviously is not good enough for Suzy, Sam's self-esteem is at an all-time low. Then along comes Valerie. Sam has never considered her as attractive or intelligent as Suzy, but she seems to be interested in him. Sam strikes up a romance on the rebound.

The rebound phenomenon, if we can call it that, illustrates what can happen to interpersonal choice as a result of a change in the level of one's self-esteem. An experiment by Walster (1965) explains something about how this works.

Walster "hired" female college students to participate in a study of personality. Before the testing began each student "accidentally" met a male student, actually a confederate of the experimenter. By a strange coincidence the male student was also looking for the experimenter. As the couple waited the boy made it clear that he had a romantic interest in the girl. He talked to her for fifteen minutes, trying to arrange a date. After the experimenter appeared, the girl was given some personality tests and then given results that were rigged to alter her level of self-esteem. Some girls heard themselves described as mature, original, and sensitive. Others were told that they were weak, immature, antisocial, and lacking in leadership abilities.

After receiving the results of the personality tests, each subject was asked to give her honest evaluation of five people, including the student who had asked her for a date. As Walster predicted, girls who received negative personality assessments were more responsive to the boy's advances than girls who received positive test results. Her data suggest that when self-esteem has recently been lowered, our need for affiliation increases, and we become more accepting of affection from others. Under these conditions, people we might have considered unappealing may now seem more desirable as companions.

Isolation

A third situation that influences our choice of receivers is **isolation from the rewards of others**. Although each of us has known occasional loneliness, brief isolation can sometimes be peaceful and pleasant. Prolonged isolation, however, is almost always unpleasant. Hence in prisons one of the severest forms of punishment is solitary confinement. Similarly, prisoner-of-war camps often use isolation to break a prisoner's spirit. And think of the numerous cartoons in which a man shipwrecked on a desert island inhabited only by lovely native women eagerly greets a fellow countryman as "someone to talk to."

Each of these circumstances illustrates that social isolation tends to be less pleasant than interaction with others. Some researchers have found that as we are deprived of the rewards possible from human interaction, we become more receptive to those rewards. Thus a third influence on our choice of receivers is the degree to which we have been isolated from contact with others. We would expect again that as we are deprived of social reinforcement, our strong need to interact with other human beings tends to override our standards for acceptable friends.

POPULAR AND UNPOPULAR PEOPLE

People with whom we associate on a continuing basis reward us in ways that make those associations worthwhile. Yet even when we are forced to communicate with people we ourselves have not chosen—classmates, fellow employees, or some neighbors, for example—we prefer some people to others. One means to determine the pattern of preferences and rejections within a group of people is through the sociometric test.

The Sociogram

The **sociometric test,** which was first developed by Moreno (1953), is a simple one. In private, group members specify those persons with whom they would like to participate in a given activity; in many versions of the test, they also indicate those with whom they would not care to participate. Obviously, test choices vary as the situation changes. Consider the criteria you would use to answer these questions:

1. With whom would you most like to discuss a problem?
2. Whom would you pick to represent the class as a good communicator?
3. With whom would you like to work on a project?

The sociometric test has several advantages. First, it is easy to administer: it has been used with children and even adapted to study the communication patterns within an entire community. Second, it is easy to score. And third, its results can be set out in tables, statistics, or diagrams. The diagram—or **sociogram,** as it has come to be called—is especially popular because of its visual power. It uses geometric figures

BASES OF HUMAN ATTRACTION

to represent the group members and lines to represent their choices and rejections.

Figures 5.2 and 5.3 are sociograms drawn up from data obtained in a sensitivity training group. Figure 5.2 illustrates the answers to the question, "Whom would you like to have as a leader?" The question behind Figure 5.3 was, "With whom would you like to be better friends?" You can see from the two sociograms that when the choice criterion was changed, the results were distinctly altered. Power and popularity are often distinct qualities. Although Dan and Pete are most frequently chosen as leaders, Don is the person most frequently chosen as a potential friend. In Moreno's terms Dan and Pete are the **overchosen members** of the group in Figure 5.2; Don is the overchosen member in Figure 5.3. Sociograms also identify **isolates,** those who are not chosen by anyone. The isolates in Figure 5.2 are Doug, Jim, Bob, Arnie, Crell, and Charlie; in Figure 5.3 they are Bob, Charlie, Arnie, and Nick. **Cliques,** or *subgroups,* are also reflected in sociograms; see Jim, Doug, and Allen in Figure 5.3, for example. Thus a sociogram summarizes information about interpersonal preferences among mem-

Figure 5.2

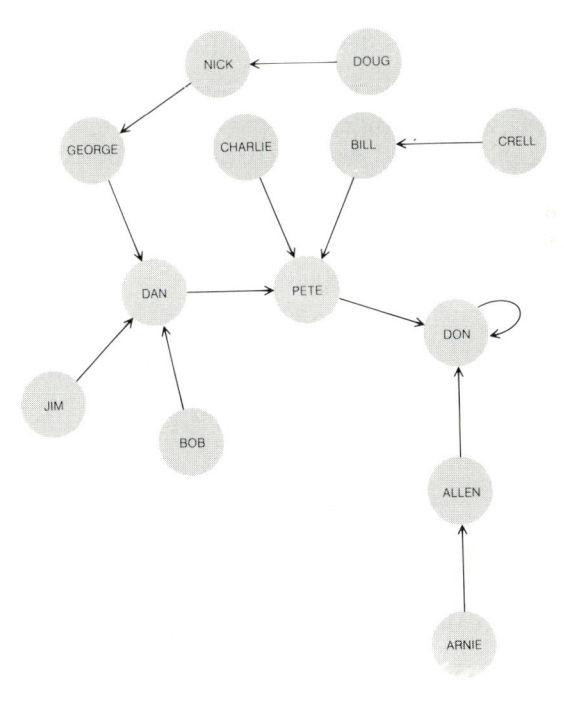

WHOM WOULD YOU LIKE TO HAVE AS A LEADER?

INTERPERSONAL COMMUNICATION

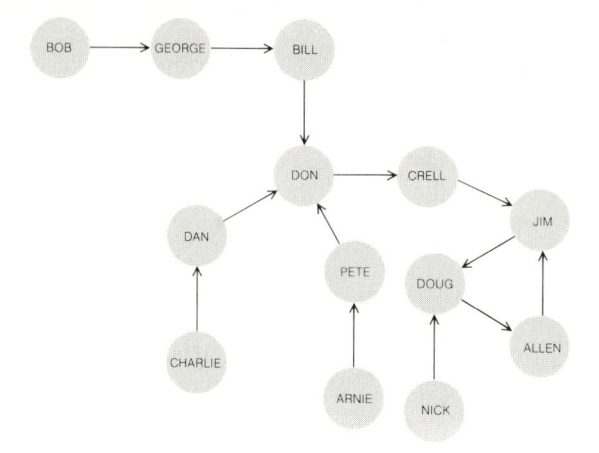

Figure 5.3

```
BOB → GEORGE → BILL
                 ↓
      DON → CRELL
                    → JIM
DAN              ↗   ↑
 ↑      PETE  DOUG
              ↑    ↘ ALLEN
CHARLIE  ↑    ↑
       ARNIE  NICK
```

WITH WHOM WOULD YOU LIKE TO BE BETTER FRIENDS?

bers of a given group and also identifies a number of communication links within it.

Overchosen People and Isolates

The overchosen people in sociograms provide us, to use Thibaut and Kelley's term, with positive outcomes. No doubt this sometimes results from actual or perceived similarities or from other determinants of attraction. Nevertheless, the question remains: Are certain types of people more reinforcing than others?

In spite of some contradictory findings, the answer appears to be that there are some people who consistently provide positive outcomes for others. Think of someone you know who is exceptionally popular and try to pinpoint what it is that makes him or her that way.

One of this person's attributes may be *physical attractiveness*. Generally speaking, we are attracted to good-looking people. In general, we tend to associate high attractiveness with positive personality characteristics and low attractiveness with negative personality traits (Miller, 1970). The effect of a person's physical appearance on our evaluation of him or her is usually greatest in the initial stages of our contact and diminishes as we become familiar with his or her other qualities.

Aside from liking physically attractive people because they are good to look at, we sometimes like them because we feel that by being seen with them, we will enhance our own image. The college man who consistently dates beautiful women is very likely to improve his own image among both his male friends and his prospective female acquaintances. The coed who dates handsome men is also increasing her self-esteem.

In addition to physical attributes, certain *behaviors* also appear to be more reinforcing than others. In more than one study, people who were seen as generous, enthusiastic, and affectionate were better liked than those described as stingy, apathetic, and cold. A summary of research (Barnlund, 1968, p. 79) tells us that popular people tend to be better-adjusted and more sociable, mature, and stable, whereas less popular people tend to be more "aggressive-egocentric" or "withdrawn-shy." It seems then that we can identify some behaviors that are generally more rewarding than others. Differences in situation will certainly exist, but given a set of behaviors, we may still be able to make some predictions about our choices as communicators.

Our interest in developing more effective patterns of communication naturally leads us to the question: Are there some behaviors that are disliked by almost everyone? Or to use another frame of reference: Are there any relatively stable traits by which we can describe the isolate, the person who is rejected by others?

Delia (1971) approached this issue by asking each of his subjects to write a profile of a person he or she disliked. Three types of descriptions appeared over and over again in his data, and all three were consistently disliked by a high percentage of the subjects.

In the first profile the person described is self-centered, arrogant, and conceited. Such people are unrewarding to deal with because they think significantly more of themselves than they do of anyone else. Interacting with them makes you aware of their lack of interest in your opinions and ideas and consequently diminishes your feeling of self-esteem.

The second profile is closely related to the first; it describes someone who is dogmatic, obnoxious, and pushy. Here is a person less concerned with the feelings and viewpoints of other people than with imposing his or her will on them. You usually respond in one of three ways. You fight fire with fire by imitating the offensive behavior: if he or she pushes you around, you push back; if he or she insists on a particular point, you are equally insistent in stating your opinion. Or you offer passive resistance: "Just because you have silenced a man does not mean you have convinced him" is the slogan of one contemporary poster. Your third alternative is to submit; but despite your response your attitude is again likely to be negative.

The third type of disliked person is someone who is two-faced, or insincere. Other studies confirm the high value we place on a person's intentions. Anderson (1968) found that in rating likable personality traits, his subjects valued sincerity above all others. We also know that overheard conversations are more persuasive than direct ones—we are likely to believe completely in a speaker's sincerity if we think he or she does not know we are listening (Walster and Festinger, 1962). And apparently we are more susceptible to persuasion if we perceive a speaker's arguments as sincerely motivated.

Unfortunately, few of us recognize our own portraits. We may be aware that we are acting insincerely, but we do not think of ourselves as obnoxious or domineering. We reserve those terms for others. One graduate student we know continually cuts into conversations with comments such as "Listen to me—I have the facts!" and "I hate to interrupt you with the facts." Yet he does not see himself as dogmatic. Nor does he see people roll their eyes when he starts to talk.

Delia seems to have hit upon three types of inherently unrewarding behavior. No doubt there are others. The specific behaviors are less important, however, than the concept that some people repeatedly provide negative outcomes and that they become the people least chosen by others.

Summary

Our study of communicator choice began with a discussion of proximity, or geographic closeness. We found that other things being equal, the closer two people are geographically, the more likely they are to be attracted to each other. Several explanations of this phenomenon were presented, and there was some discussion of how proximity affects intercultural communication.

We saw that although proximity is usually a precondition of attraction, we tend to attract and be attracted to people who we perceive to be similar to us, and, conversely, we tend to dislike and be disliked by those we differ from. Many similarities—attitudes, background, values, socioeconomic status, and so on—were seen to be reinforcing and to increase attraction. To explain the relationship between attraction and similarity (particularly attitude similarity), we turned to a discussion of balance theory. Statements about the principles of attraction were qualified with a discussion of need complementarity and other variables—anxiety, changes in self-esteem, and isolation.

We concluded with a discussion of the sociogram and the types of people who consistently provide either positive or negative outcomes for others.

Review Questions

1. How is proximity related to attraction? Give two examples.
2. Discuss three explanations for the relationship between proximity and attraction.
3. In what way might proximity influence communication between people of different cultures?

BASES OF HUMAN ATTRACTION

4. How is similarity related to attraction? Discuss three variables that qualify generalizations about attitude similarity.
5. What is the basic premise underlying all cognitive consistency theories?
6. How does the theory of complementary needs compare with the research findings on the relationship between perceived similarity and attraction?
7. Discuss three situations that influence our choice of communicators. Give an example of how each affects attraction.
8. What are three advantages of the sociometric test?
9. What are two attributes of people generally perceived as providing consistent positive reinforcement? What are four attributes of people who are generally disliked by others?

Exercises

1. Examine the following diagram of an apartment house. Using the concept of proximity as it relates to attraction, discuss the probable relationships between the residents of each apartment (for example, which residents probably would engage most often in conversations).

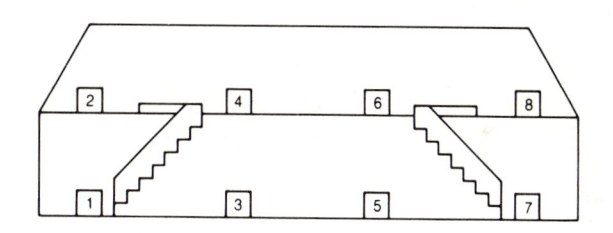

2. John is a motorcycle freak. Sally, John's girl friend, does not like motorcycles because she thinks they are dangerous.
   a. Using balance theory, draw a diagram depicting this relationship.
   b. List the alternatives available to Sally for balancing the situation and make a diagram for each alternative.
3. Describe a situation in which you entered into a relationship on the rebound. Analyze the positive and negative aspects of that relationship. If you were to encounter a similar situation, what, if anything, would you do differently?
4. Have some friends rate a number of topics on a scale such as the one shown here. Then create two paragraphs, one agreeing with the general attitude of the class on each issue—legalizing marijuana, for example—and one disagreeing. Put a byline on each of the two paragraphs, using fictitious names. Then have your friends indicate the extent of their attraction to the authors. See whether they pre-

fer the person whom they perceive as holding an attitude similar to their own. This would validate the theory that perceived attitude similarity yields attraction.

Strongly agree	Agree	Neither agree nor disagree	Disagree	Strongly disagree
5	4	3	2	1

5. Create a composite description of the kinds of people you are attracted to. What does this composite tell you about yourself?
6. Conduct a sociometric analysis in class or among a group of your friends. Choose several criteria, such as the ones on which Figure 5.2 and 5.3 are based, that seem relevant for different reasons. Go over the results of the sociogram by yourself, and try to determine the reasons that some people are overchosen and others are isolates.
7. Go back to the early entries in your personal log for this class and identify some specific behaviors or events that caused you to like or dislike certain members. Interpret your findings in the light of the cost-reward framework discussed in Chapter 3.

Suggested Readings

Aronson, Elliot. "Who Likes Whom and Why." *Psychology Today* (August 1970), 4:48–51, 74. Experiments conducted by the author and three associates are the basis for theories on why people like (or do not like) one another. Some of the results are surprising. This is a well-written, easily understood article, good both as entertaining reading and for group discussion.

Berscheid, Ellen, and Walster, Elaine. *Interpersonal Attraction*. Reading, Mass.: Addison-Wesley, 1969. This short book offers a highly compact introduction to the subject of interpersonal attraction. Included are such topics as why certain people are attracted to each other; the effects of stress, loneliness, or insecurity on one's need to be liked; the effect of geographic proximity on our choice of friends and marriage partners; why we like those whom we think like us; and how we choose a partner in romance.

Chapman, A. H. *Put-Offs and Come-Ons: Psychological Maneuvers and Stratagems*. New York: Berkley, 1968. A psychiatrist has put together an insightful and entertaining inventory of interaction "maneuvers and stratagems" that people use on other people. He discusses come-on forces, which explain behaviors that attract people to one another, and put-off forces, which do the opposite. His inventory includes "Whine and Decline," "Temper Tantrum," "Love Will Come Later," and "Garbage Like Me."

Chapter 6
Self and Others: Relationship Aspects of Communication

OBJECTIVES

After reading this chapter the student should be able to:
1. Distinguish between the content and relationship aspects of communication.
2. Distinguish between confirming and disconfirming response styles.
3. State the most important implication of research on behavior attribution for students of communication.
4. Describe the four levels of awareness illustrated by the Johari Window.
5. Define metacommunication.
6. Describe the dyadic effect and give at least two examples of it.
7. List five characteristics of appropriate self-disclosure.
8. Distinguish between supportive and defensive climates of communication.
9. State the relationship between trust, accuracy, and effectiveness in human communication.
10. Identify four different types of listening.
11. Describe three communication contexts in which the most appropriate kind of listening would be empathic listening.

6

"One way to understand communication," writes Gibb, "is to view it as a people process rather than as a language process" (1961, p. 141). And certainly in studying interpersonal communication we must make a distinction between *message content* and the *relationship between communicators*. Communication is the vehicle through which we develop, maintain, and improve human relationships. At times it becomes the vehicle through which human relationships are undermined or even destroyed.

It seems obvious that every message has content, whether the information is correct or incorrect, valid or invalid, or even undeterminable. It is less apparent, however, that every message also defines how it is to be interpreted and consequently something about the relationship between the people involved. (A mother who cautions her exuberant son by saying, "Please don't run around when we're in a department store," defines her relationship with her child quite differently from the mother who says, "Be sure to run around a lot here so that I get good and angry.") Even the most casual message exists on this second level. Thus Ruesch and Bateson have observed that "every courtesy term between persons, every inflection of voice denoting respect or contempt, condescension or dependency, is a statement about the relationship between the two persons" (1968, p. 213).* It is the relationship aspect of communication that concerns us in the present chapter.

CONFIRMATION AND DISCONFIRMATION

As we communicate we expect more than a simple exchange of verbal and nonverbal information. Each person conveys messages that tell how he or she perceives the other and their relationship, and each expects to receive responses in kind. Perhaps the most satisfying interpersonal response we can hope to receive is total **confirmation,** or as

---

* For an extensive discussion of content and relationship levels of communication, see Watzlawick, Beavin, and Jackson (1967, pp. 51–54).

INTERPERSONAL COMMUNICATION

Sieburg and Larson define it, *"any behavior that causes another person to value himself more"* (1971, p. 1, italics added). Buber writes: "In human society, at all its levels, persons confirm one another in a practical way, to some extent or other, in their personal qualities and capacities, and a society may be termed human in the measure to which its members confirm one another" (1957, p. 101).

Drawing by Charles M. Schulz. © 1972 United Feature Syndicate, Inc.

Let us illustrate what we are talking about by imagining a dialogue between two well-known sportscasters, Howard Cosell and Frank Gifford. Cosell makes the comment, "That was some touchdown drive. Wasn't it a dandy, Frank?" "That it was, Howard," replies Gifford. "Beautiful execution." Gifford responds to Cosell and also agrees with the content of his statement, thus confirming Cosell's very existence as a person. Suppose instead that Gifford answers, "Well, *you* might think so, but I've seen better drives by the ninth-graders in my neighborhood." Gifford responds, but in a way that rejects the content of Cosell's statement and by implication rejects Cosell himself. This limited recognition of Cosell is confirming on one level but disconfirming on another. A third response is possible. Imagine that Gifford ignores Cosell's question entirely by commenting, "The Rams will now be kicking off into a fifteen-mile-per-hour wind." This remark has the same impact as would a fourth possibility: complete silence. Both are totally **disconfirming,** or to paraphrase Sieburg and Larson (1971), they are *behaviors that cause people to value themselves less;* they reject both the speaker and what he or she has to say.

The painful experience of being disconfirmed time after time, especially by someone important to us, is expressed in a letter that the novelist Franz Kafka once wrote (and never sent) to his father:

> Maddening also were those rebukes in which one was treated as a third person, in other words, considered not worthy even to be spoken to angrily; that is to say, when you would speak ostensibly to Mother but actually to me, who was sitting right there. For instance: "Of course, that's too much to expect of our worthy son," and the like. (Kafka, 1966, pp. 37, 39)

Disconfirmation seems to be one of the most damaging interpersonal responses. The psychotherapeutic literature suggests that people who are continually disconfirmed by others may even come to question their own identity. Even discussions of pathological communication have some bearing on everyday transactions between people:

> There can be little doubt that such a situation [being completely unnoticed by others] would lead to "loss of self," which is but a translation of the term "alienation." Disconfirmation, as we find it in pathological communication, is no longer concerned with the truth or falsity . . . of P's definition of himself, but rather negates the reality of P as the source. . . . In other words, while rejection amounts to the message "you are wrong," disconfirmation says in effect "you do not exist." (Watzlawick, Beavin, and Jackson, 1967, p. 86)

Given some awareness of the confirming-disconfirming dimension of human relationships, we must still ask the practical question: What kinds of responses are most confirming or disconfirming? We find part of the answer in the Sieburg and Larson study whose definitions we have already noted. Appropriately enough, the subjects were members of the International Communication Association. They were asked to describe the behaviors of the persons with whom they most enjoyed and least enjoyed communicating. As we look at the results of this survey, two distinct response styles emerge.

If we list the responses considered most confirming, describing

Confirmation can be nonverbal as well as verbal.

them briefly in order of rank, first comes *direct acknowledgment.* The other person acknowledges what you have said and gives you a direct verbal response. Next is the expression of *positive feeling.* He or she conveys his or her own positive feeling about what you have just said. Then comes *the clarifying response.* Here the other person tries to get you to clarify the content of your message ("Could you expand on that a bit?"). When a person gives an *agreeing response,* he or she reinforces or affirms what you have already said. *The supportive response* offers comfort, understanding, or reassurance ("I know just how you feel").

It seems that the response people find most disconfirming is *the tangential response.* Here the other person acknowledges your previous comment but quickly shifts the direction of the conversation ("Did he cover a lot in class today?" "Not much. Does this skirt look too long?"). Next in unpopularity comes *the impersonal response,* marked by intellectualized speech and avoidance of the first person ("One often finds oneself getting angry"). *An impervious response* disregards you completely, offering neither verbal nor nonverbal recognition. When the other person gives *an irrelevant response,* he or she changes the subject as would be the case with a tangential response, but this time the person makes no attempt to relate that response to your previous comment ("I had a lousy day. I'm really ready to quit." "I wonder why Ann hasn't called. Do you think she forgot?"). *An interrupting response* cuts you off before you have made your point and does not let you finish. A person makes *an incoherent response* if he or she consistently speaks in sentences that are rambling, disorganized, or incomplete. *The incongruous response* gives you conflicting verbal and nonverbal messages ("Of course you are the one who should decide. It's up to you," said in an exasperated tone of voice).

These lists of behaviors are by no means exhaustive. Nevertheless, they highlight the differences between a confirming response style, which generally acknowledges, supports, and accepts other human beings, and a disconfirming response style, which denies and undermines their personal sense of worth.

The research of Sieburg and Larson no longer stands alone. A review of studies conducted at the University of Denver during the past five years suggests that "confirmation/disconfirmation may be the most pervasive and important aspect of interpersonal communication" (Cissna, 1976, p. 1). Certainly, this is a dimension of human relationships with potential for influencing a range of communication outcomes.

Yet to counsel that all our responses to others be totally confirming would be unrealistic. There are times when we want to or must reject the communication of others, at least at the content level. Even in taking issue with others, however, we can keep in mind the importance of maintaining a confirming response style.

AWARENESS OF SELF AND OTHERS

We spoke in Chapter 3 of self-concept, the relatively enduring impressions of oneself, developed in part from the feedback we received from those around us. Then in Chapter 4 we went on to stress inaccurate perception of other human beings as both a symptom and a cause of communication difficulties. It now seems likely that at least one qualitative difference exists between the perception of self and the perception of others, and that it may compound the problem. A recent series of studies suggests that we see our own behavior as responses to the demands of a given *situation,* but we view the same behavior in others as generated by their *disposition,* that is, stable traits and needs.

Even when we know others well, we seem to interpret their motivations in different terms. In one experiment (Nisbett et al., 1973) male college students were asked to write a brief explanation of why they liked the girl they dated most regularly and another of why they had chosen their major. Each also wrote explanations of his best friend's choices of girl friend and college major. While subjects tended to explain their own choices in terms of situation ("She's a relaxing person"; "Chemistry is a high-paying field"), they frequently saw the behavior of their friends in terms of personality traits or needs. ("He needs someone he can relax with"; "He wants to make a lot of money").

Two reasons for these perceptual differences have been proposed. First, the information available to the actor (the one who performs the action) and the observer may be different. The observer sees the actor at a particular point in time. Generally, he or she does not—cannot—know firsthand the actor's history, experiences, motives, or present emotional state; these can only be inferred. Thus if we see a person overreact to a mildly critical remark, as observers we may not know what events preceding this episode made it the straw that broke the camel's back. A second possibility is that even when the same information is available to both actor and observer, they process it differently because different aspects of it are salient to each of them.

Storms (1973) suggests that these information differences may exist in actor and observer because their points of view are literally quite different. You do not see yourself acting; under ordinary circumstances you cannot be an observer of your own behavior. And while as an actor you watch the situation in which you find yourself, the other person spends most of his or her time observing you, not the situation.

But suppose we reverse the viewpoints of actor and observer. Storms found that he could change the orientation of actor and observer by showing them videotapes of their own interaction. Videotape offered the actor a new perspective, that of an observer, and often changed his or her inferences about why he or she had behaved in a particular way. After seeing ourselves on tape, we are much more likely to explain our behavior as a reflection of personal disposition than as a response to the environment.

While a change in visual orientation seems to heighten self-awareness, the prospect of viewing videotapes of all our behavior is neither appealing nor feasible. Nor is it perhaps desirable. Storms mentions, for example, that when videotape is used in therapy, patients sometimes take undue responsibility on themselves for their behavior, overlooking genuine elements in the environment that have influenced their actions. Videotape is not the answer. What is needed is a more balanced view of oneself and of others, a view that enables us to interpret behavior in terms of both disposition and environment.

Research on behavior attribution has several implications. The most important for our purposes is that by combining information about ourselves that is available only to us with an awareness of how other human beings perceive us, we may begin to see ourselves in sharper perspective.

The Johari Window

One of the most provocative models for conceptualizing levels of awareness in human behavior is the **Johari Window** (Luft, 1959). ("Johari" derives from the first names of the two psychologists who developed it, Joseph Luft and Harry Ingham.) Essentially, the model offers a way of looking at the interdependence of intrapersonal and interpersonal affairs. The illustration in Figure 6.1 represents you as you relate to other human beings by four quadrants—in effect, four panes of a single window. The size of each quadrant or pane is determined by awareness—by yourself and by others—of your behavior, feelings, and motivations. Unlike most windowpanes, those of the Johari Window sometimes change in size.

Each of you may be described by a Johari Window. Quadrant 1, the *open quadrant,* will reflect your general openness to the world, your willingness to be known. It comprises all aspects of yourself known to you and to others. This quadrant is the basis for most two-person communication.

By contrast, quadrant 2, the *blind quadrant,* consists of all the things about yourself that other people perceive but that are not accessible to you. Perhaps you tend to monopolize conversation unwittingly, or you think of yourself as quite a wit but your friends find

Figure 6.1

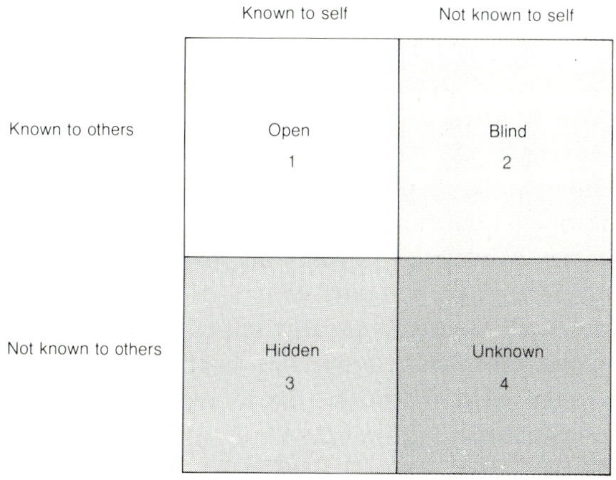

	Known to self	Not known to self
Known to others	Open 1	Blind 2
Not known to others	Hidden 3	Unknown 4

THE JOHARI WINDOW

SOURCE: Reprinted from *Of Human Interaction* by Joseph Luft by permission of National Press Books. Copyright © 1969 by National Press Books.

your humor heavy-handed. Then again you might feel quite confident and yet have several nervous mannerisms that others are aware of but you are not. The blind quadrant could contain any of the unintentional communicative stimuli mentioned in Chapter 2.

In quadrant 3, the *hidden quadrant,* you are the one who exercises discretion. This quadrant is made up of all the things you prefer not to disclose to someone else, whether they concern yourself or other people: your salary, your parents' divorce, your feelings about your roommate's closest friend, your overdue bills, and so on. In short, this quadrant represents your attempts to limit input or communicative stimuli concerning yourself.

The last pane, quadrant 4, is the *unknown quadrant.* The blind quadrant is unknown to you though known to others. The hidden quadrant is unknown to others but known to you. Quadrant 4 is completely unknown. It represents everything about yourself that has never been explored, either by you or by other people. It contains all your untapped resources, all your potential for personal growth. You can only infer that it exists or confirm its existence in retrospect.

The four quadrants of the Johari Window are interdependent: a change in one quadrant will affect others. As you reveal something from the hidden quadrant, for example, you make it part of the open quadrant, thus enlarging it and reducing the size of the hidden quadrant. Should friends tell you about your nervous mannerisms, this information becomes part of the open quadrant, with a corresponding shrinkage of the blind quadrant. Such change is not always desirable. Sometimes, for example, telling a person that he or she seems nervous only makes him or her more ill at ease. Because inappropriate disclosure of a feeling or perception about another can be damaging, your friends will need to use some discretion in communicating with you about quadrant 2.

Basically, however, Luft proposes that it is rewarding and satisfying to enlarge the open quadrant—that is, not only to learn more about yourself but to reveal yourself to some degree so that others will know you better too. It is also his belief that greater knowledge of self in relation to others will result in greater self-esteem and self-acceptance. If you can learn more about yourself and others, you can change the shape of your own Johari Window. An improved window might look something like the one in Figure 6.2.

Metacommunication

One way to learn more about yourself and others is through **metacommunication**—that is, *communication about communication*. This is a concept closely linked to the relationship level of human encounters. For example, if you say to your mother, "Tell him to mind his own damned business," and she replies, "I wish you wouldn't swear so much. You do it more and more, and I don't like it," she is responding not to the content of your remark but to your method of getting your

Figure 6.2

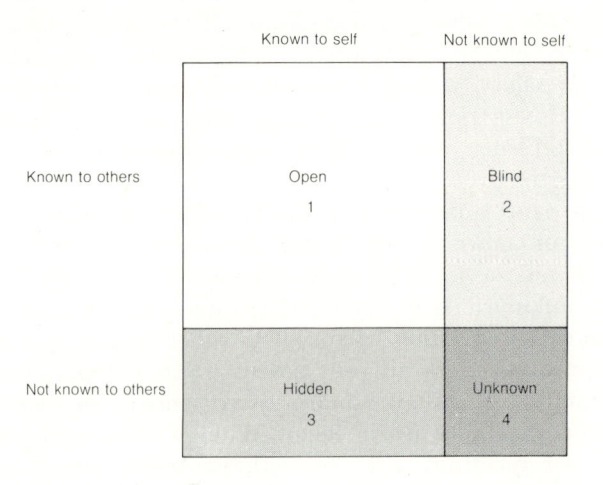

	Known to self	Not known to self
Known to others	Open 1	Blind 2
Not known to others	Hidden 3	Unknown 4

AN IMPROVED JOHARI WINDOW

point across. The content of her communication is communication itself.

Any comment directed at the way in which a person communicates is an example of metacommunication. For years the procedure in public speaking classes has been for students to give practice speeches and then have the instructor and class members give their reactions to the speaker and the speech. Comments such as "I thought you had excellent examples," "You could have brought out your central idea more explicitly," and "Try to be a little more enthusiastic" are all instances of metacommunication.

Metacommunication is not always so explicit. Sometimes discussions that begin at the content level become forms of metacommunication. We can best illustrate with an anecdote. A young man and woman, dressed for a night on the town, have just stepped out of a cab. As they stand at the corner waiting for the light to change, they rapidly become involved in a heated argument:

Wife: Next time try to get home earlier so we can be on time.
Husband: It's only a party. Next time tell me beforehand if you think it's so important to be there at eight sharp. And don't sound so annoyed.
Wife: But you're always late.
Husband: I'm not *always* late. Don't generalize like that.
Wife: Well, you're late a lot of the time. Why do you always put me down when I say something about you?
Husband: I don't "always" put you down. There you go again, generalizing.

Although they may well remember it simply as a quarrel about lateness, this couple is arguing about how they communicate with each other. The husband tells the wife not to sound so annoyed, the husband informs her that she makes too many generalizations, she counters that he puts her down, and so on. As they make these disclosures, they bring information from the blind quadrant into the open quadrant. But disclosures about the blind quadrant have to be made with some discretion. Moreover, because these disclosures take place in a defensive atmosphere, there is little chance that they will improve the relationship between husband and wife.

In a more supportive situation, the use of metacommunication might help people become aware of ways in which their communication practices are ineffective. For example, one teen-age girl finally confided to her mother that she was embarrassed when the mother tried to sound "hip" in front of the daughter's teen-age friends. It is sometimes awkward to provide such feedback. When it is given in a kind rather than a hostile way, however, it can serve as a valuable impetus to self-improvement.

Self-Disclosure

Some years ago Lewin (1948), a German-born psychologist, made a comparison between the personality structures of Americans and Germans. Americans, he observed, start conversations more easily, are more willing to help strangers, and form friendships more readily than Germans. Superficially, Americans are less resistant to communicating than Germans, but their openness is restricted to the more peripheral aspects of personality. While Germans seem more aloof in casual encounters, Lewin felt, once they make friends they are more open about the central, or core, levels of their personalities, and the friendships they do form tend to be deeper and last longer.

Whatever the reasons for these differences, in Johari terms the Americans seem to suffer by comparison because they interact on a relatively shallow level, leaving the most central areas of their personality inaccessible to others. We can be more specific about American patterns of self-disclosure if we look at the work of Jourard (1971) and his associates.

They find, for example, that married people typically disclose themselves more to their spouses than to anyone else. Unmarried college students usually reveal more to their best friend of the same sex than to any friend of the opposite sex; they also reveal less to their fathers than to people in any of their other close relationships. Females are more open about themselves than males, and Jewish college males disclose significantly more about themselves than do Catholics, Methodists, or Baptists. Self-disclosure also decreases with advancing age. And as we might expect, certain categories of personal information are disclosed more readily than others: people seem to be much freer in talking about their tastes and interests, attitudes, and opinions than they are in answering questions about money, personality, or anything to do with their bodies (Jourard, 1971, p. 105). (See Appendix for an exercise in self-disclosure.)

Jourard's work with the mentally disturbed has led him to the conclusion that we often expend a great deal of energy trying to keep others from knowing us for fear that if our true selves were known we would be rejected. He believes that this very act of concealment keeps us from sustaining healthy human relationships:

> Self-disclosure, or should I say "real" self-disclosure, is both a symptom of personality health . . . and at the same time a means of ultimately achieving healthy personality. . . . I have known people who would rather die than become known. . . . When I say that self-disclosure is a symptom of personality health, what I mean really is that a person who displays many of the other characteristics that betoken healthy personality

. . . will also display the ability to make himself fully known to at least one other significant human being. (Jourard, 1964, p. 24)

Jourard is not suggesting indiscriminate self-disclosure. He acknowledges that efforts at revelation can be damaging or even faintly comic. In the movie *Bob and Carol and Ted and Alice,* Natalie Wood played the part of a young woman who could not turn off the openness she had learned to express in an encounter group. When a waiter in a restaurant asked her how she was, she replied in some detail. Then she asked the waiter how he was, and he replied—briefly. Not satisfied with his response, she left her dinner companions and followed him into the kitchen, saying emphatically that she really did want to know how he was. The waiter was very embarrassed by her behavior.

Self-disclosure is an attempt to let authenticity enter our social relationships. At times it is an attempt to emphasize how we enact our roles rather than how others expect us to enact them. It may even be an attempt to step out of a role entirely. When does it work? When does it improve human relationships? Luft describes several characteristics of appropriate self-disclosure, five of the most salient being these (Luft, 1969, pp. 132–133):

1. It is a function of the ongoing relationship.
2. It occurs reciprocally.
3. It is timed to fit what is happening.
4. It concerns what is going on within and between persons present.
5. It moves by small increments.

Apply these standards to the restaurant scene just described or to any of your own attempts at self-disclosure that didn't come off and you may be able to determine what went wrong.

Appropriate self-disclosure is not one-sided. It is an exchange process that can and often does prompt greater disclosure from the other person. It also results in more positive feelings between two people. The work of Jourard confirms this sequence of behavior: when one person discloses something about himself or herself to another, he or she tends to elicit a reciprocal level of openness from the second person. Jourard refers to this pattern as the **dyadic effect.** He goes even further when on the basis of his experience as a therapist he suggests that "the capacity to disclose authentically, *in response* that is appropriate to the setting, to the authentic disclosure of the other person in a dyad [two-person group] is probably one of the best indicants of healthy personality" (Jourard, 1964, p. 179).

There is a tendency to assume that in long-term relationships, self-disclosure is an ongoing process in which each person's knowledge about the other is increasing. But as we pointed out in Chapter 2, the effect of time on communication is not always constructive. In one study at the Merrill-Palmer Institute, married couples were given a sentence completion test that included such items as "Trouble between us would not have arisen if . . ." and "Personal habits of mine which annoy my mate most are . . ." Each person completed the list of statements for himself or herself and then as he or she felt his or her spouse would respond. The many discrepancies between the answers of husbands and their wives indicated that married couples often have a very limited understanding of each other—a research finding that is borne out by a number of other studies (O'Neill and O'Neill, 1972, pp. 109–110).

Self-disclosure, then, is not that easily achieved, for to reveal yourself to another person implies more than the mere transfer of new information. It requires, first of all, an increased level of self-awareness —of your motives or your own self-concept or the intensity of your feelings, for example. And it requires a high level of trust, a dimension of human relationships that we shall discuss in the section which follows.

TRUST

The story is told of two Russian businessmen who accidentally met in a Moscow railroad station. "My dear Ivan, where are you off to?" asks the first. "Minsk," replies Ivan only to hear the retort, "What a liar you are, Ivan. You're just saying that you are going to Minsk because you want me to think you are going to Pinsk, but I know that you are

Trust is an important dimension of all human encounters—political as well as social.

going to Minsk." There seems to be a variant of this anecdote for almost every national group. In the Austrian version, for example, the second man is on his way to Budapest (Luft, 1969, pp. 52–53).

Implicit in all jokes of this kind is the recognition that what two people say to each other and how each interprets what is said depends to a great extent on the level of **trust** between them. Although the term has been used in a number of ways, Rotter sums up the important issues when he defines trust as *"an expectancy . . . that the word, promise, verbal (oral) or written statement of another individual can be relied on"* (Rotter, 1971, p. 444).

Game Behavior

Frivolous as it may seem, we approach the subject of trust by looking at game behavior. The strategies people choose when they play games or have observed others playing games give us some opportunity to examine the effects of varying levels of trust on face-to-face communication. Game theory distinguishes between zero-sum games, in which players must compete, and non–zero-sum games, in which players may either compete or cooperate and increase their total gains. Researchers who have attempted to quantify data about levels of trust have been most interested in non-zero-sum games. Among the most popular of these is Prisoner's Dilemma (Rapoport and Chammah, 1965, pp. 24–25).

To understand how Prisoner's Dilemma works, imagine that two prisoners, Nick and Pete, are being held incommunicado. Charged with the same crime, they are put in separate rooms so that one cannot know how the other will respond to the accusations leveled against them. Nick and Pete are each aware that they can be convicted only if one of them confesses. Each then has two alternatives, shown in Figure 6.3, to confess or not to confess. But their situation is not that clear-cut. There are other conditions. If both confess they will both be convicted (—1 designates the payoff). If only one confesses, he is freed for turning state's evidence and also given a reward (2 designates the payoff); in this case the prisoner who holds out receives a more severe sentence than he would if he also confessed (—2). If neither prisoner confesses, both are acquitted (1).

While it is in the interest of each partner to confess to whatever the other does, it is in their collective interest to hold out. Yet if Nick wants to hold out but distrusts Pete—that is, thinks he will confess—it seems to be in Nick's interest to act competitively by betraying him. If Nick thinks that Pete will not confess, Nick's confession can earn him his freedom as well as a reward—another competitive strategy. If Nick and Pete trust one another completely, they can both hold out and gain their freedom—a cooperative strategy.

What makes the game so compelling is that it places each player in

Figure 6.3

	Pete Not confess	Pete Confess
Nick Not confess	1,1*	-2,2
Nick Confess	2,-2	-1,-1

PAYOFF MATRIX FOR PRISONER'S DILEMMA*

SOURCE: Anatol Rapoport and Albert Chammah, *Prisoner's Dilemma: A Study in Conflict and Cooperation* (Ann Arbor, Mich.: University of Michigan Press, 1965), p. 9. Copyright © 1965 by The University of Michigan Press. Reprinted by permission.

a mixed-motive situation: should he cooperate with his partner (not confess and face a possible prison term) or compete for his own gain (confess, get the reward, and let his partner take the rap)? Although games such as Prisoner's Dilemma seem contrived, we face mixed-motive situations quite frequently. Should you study alone or with a friend who needs help in the subject when you know that helping the friend may slow you down but may also help you learn the material better. Should you share your notes with a student who missed class when you know that the next exam will be marked on a curve and each lower grade raises your own?

Tubbs (1971) used Prisoner's Dilemma to study the influence of competitive and cooperative strategies on the choices of a third party observing the game. The subjects were sixty undergraduate women enrolled in a psychology course at the University of Kansas. Seated alone in a viewing room, each subject observed a sequence of ten Prisoner's Dilemma games. Only one of the players—a confederate of the experimenter—was visible, and she had been instructed to play the games in a predetermined sequence. After the games were over, each subject was asked to rate the players on a questionnaire and to indicate how she would have played the game against the player she

* The first digit in each box represents Nick's payoff; the second represents Pete's payoff.

had just observed. Results showed that the observation of cooperative (trust-producing) strategies prompted cooperative choices from viewers and that of competitive (distrusting) strategies produced competitive choices.

The study illustrates a frequently found phenomenon—that a given type of behavior by one person tends to elicit a similar response from the other. We have already seen this pattern with respect to the dyadic effect, the high correlation between disclosure output to a given person and disclosure input from that person.

Other findings from the observation experiment suggest that there may be a significant difference between trust in an interpersonal relationship and trust in other communication contexts. In this study, trust-inducing behavior was perceived as evidence of good character, but competitive, defense-inducing behavior was seen as evidence of expertness. This is validated outside the laboratory. For example, a young woman who brags about herself and is highly competitive may threaten others so much that they run down her character, but her behavior may still increase their respect for her abilities. On the other hand, research on public communication indicates that the receiver's willingness to trust the source will depend on the receiver's perception of both character and expertness.

There is some evidence that in playing non-zero-sum games such as Prisoner's Dilemma, people tend to compete even when it is to their advantage to cooperate. Remember, though, that in the version of Prisoner's Dilemma we described, the two players were not allowed to communicate. This is the procedure in many non-zero-sum games. When communication between players is permitted, we see a significant increase in the number of cooperative choices (Deutsch, 1960; Deutsch and Krauss, 1960). It seems then that, other things being equal, communication in and of itself sometimes raises the level of trust between people.

Some Effects of Distrust

A study of small-group interaction conducted by Leathers (1970) gives us some insight into the effects of distrust. Through cooperative game playing and other reinforcing behaviors, a member of the group (actually a confederate of Leathers) developed a high level of trust in one of the subjects. Suddenly during a group discussion, he started to give the subject negative reinforcement by inserting these statements into the conversation (Leathers, 1970, p. 184):

1. That's a ridiculous statement. I disagree.
2. Are you serious in taking such an absurd position?
3. You are wrong. Dead wrong.

4. I don't understand why I ever agreed with you.
5. That's downright foolish.

This succession of trust-destroying responses had three pronounced effects. First, the subject became tense: he kept rubbing his hands vigorously and opened his eyes very wide, and his neck muscles became constricted. (Other members of the group began to squirm in their seats and avert their eyes.) Second, he became inflexible: he held rigidly to his beliefs and would not allow himself to be swayed. Third, his comments became more personal, and they were often insulting. ("Man, are you a strange cat. Oh wow, you can't be real. Are you kidding me. You are nothing but a white racist.") While it remains to be seen whether lack of trust between members of a group affects their ability to achieve group goals (consensus, for example), it had some disastrous effects on their interaction.

All the defensive responses we have just described can be thought of as forms of interference that exist within the communicator. For example, communication scholars and psychologists have known for some time that the more uneasy the psychological climate between two people, the more distortions and misinterpretations will occur. As a case in point, one of the greatest obstacles in intercultural communication is high anxiety. Barna gives us the example of a foreign student who, suddenly placed in a new environment, must adapt to a strange culture with a different tempo, other norms and values—and perhaps to a new language he has studied but never spoken before. "His self-esteem is often intolerably undermined unless he employs such defenses as withdrawal to his own reference group or into himself, screening out or misperceiving stimuli, rationalizing, overcompensating, even hostility—none of which leads to effective communication" (Barna, in Samovar and Porter, 1972, p. 244).

In addition to functioning as a source of interference, defensive behaviors tend to be circular—that is, they tend to generate defensiveness on the part of other communicators and often to cancel out some of the major outcomes of effective communication. Thus Mellinger (1956) has shown that when two people distrust each other, each tries to distort the other's perception of his or her thoughts and feelings. He observes: "a primary goal of communication with a distrusted person becomes the reduction of one's own anxiety, rather than the accurate transmission of ideas" (Mellinger, 1956, p. 304). Defensive behaviors not only distort understanding, they take away from the pleasurable aspects of communication by creating tension. They may even interfere with efforts to introduce attitude change or motivate action.

Reducing Defensiveness

How do we break down a person's defensiveness? Not, as you might think, by attacking his or her system of defenses. In encounter groups, for example, an attempt is made to create a psychological atmosphere that is supportive rather than threatening, an atmosphere in which differences of all sorts—in attitude, dress, behavior, life style—are tolerated. Harrison explains why this new environment is necessary:

> the destruction of defenses does not serve learning; instead, it increases the anxiety of the person that he will lose the more or less effective conceptual systems he has with which to understand and relate to the world, and he drops back to an even more desperate and perhaps unrealistic defense than the one destroyed. (Harrison, in Golembiewski and Blumberg, 1970, p. 85)

The application to all face-to-face communication is clear. Abruptly stripping someone of all defenses only increases his or her distance from other people. We can be supportive in all our interpersonal relationships if we know more about the behaviors that reduce or arouse defensiveness.

In his highly influential article on interpersonal trust, Gibb contrasted two atmospheres that could be established through communication. He called them **supportive** and **defensive climates,** and he described them in terms of six sets of categories (Gibb, 1961, p. 147):

Supportive Climates	*Defensive Climates*
1. Description	1. Evaluation
2. Problem Orientation	2. Control
3. Spontaneity	3. Strategy
4. Empathy	4. Neutrality
5. Equality	5. Superiority
6. Provisionalism	6. Certainty

At first glance categories 1 and 4 in the defensive climate seem contradictory: evaluative, or judgmental, behavior arouses defensiveness, but so does complete neutrality. We can reconcile this apparent contradiction if we recall that complete neutrality is disconfirming because it communicates a lack of concern. Gibb points out, for example, that attempts to reassure a troubled person by saying that he or she is overanxious or should not feel bad may be interpreted as a lack of acceptance. It can be highly supportive, however, to show empathy with the person's emotions without trying to change him or her. Pearce and Newton, who consider it "the basic mode of significant communication between adults," define **empathy** as "perception and communication by resonance, by identification, by *experiencing in ourselves some reflection of the emotional tone that is being experienced by the other person*" (1963, p. 52; italics added).

From his survey Gibb concluded that when trust increases, efficiency and accuracy in communication also increase. To this we might add that while a supportive climate is important even in short-term relationships, in more permanent relationships (in marriage or on the job, for example) it has even greater possibilities for influencing all five communication outcomes. As we suggested in Chapter 1, the better the relationship between people, the more likely it is that the other outcomes of effective communication will also occur.

Empathic Listening

Let us reexamine for a moment the concept of empathy. The term comes from the German *"einfülung,"* which is translated literally as "feeling into"—extending ourselves to the point that we share some part of the other communicator's experience. One of the most effective and direct ways in which we can communicate empathy for another human being is in the way we listen to that person.

As was emphasized in Chapter 2, hearing and listening are far from synonymous. Moreover, human beings listen differently at different times. As an adult, much of your communication involves **pleasurable listening**, the aim of which is enjoyment. A second type of listening is **discriminative listening**, with the primary purpose of understanding and remembering. This is the kind of listening you do when you work, attend class, or receive instructions. Other situations require **critical listening**—listening to discern whether intentionally or unintentionally the sender is distorting information for his or her own purposes. But when your intention is to improve your relationship with the sender you need **empathic listening**—in which *the receiver listens to understand the entire message that the sender may be trying to convey and is willing to withhold judgment and criticism.*

Empathic listening implies sensitivity to nonverbal as well as verbal communicative stimuli. One writer refers to it as "listening between the lines" (see Nichols and Stevens, 1957, pp. 56–60). The well-known psychoanalyst Theodore Reik spoke of "listening with the third ear":

> The analyst hears not only what is in the words; he hears also what the words do not say. . . . In psychoanalysis . . . what is spoken is not the most important thing. It appears to us more important to recognize what speech conceals and what silence reveals. (Reik, 1948, p. 125)

Empathic listening involves two skills. In addition to developing one's sensitivity to the total message (or "listening between the lines"), it involves the ability to suspend judgment. The psychologist Carl Rogers has written "that the major barrier to mutual interpersonal communication is our very natural tendency to judge, to evaluate, to approve or disapprove the statement of the other person, or the group" (1961, p. 330). This is a tendency that we must overcome if we are to listen empathically. To suspend judgment is not to voice agreement. It implies only that we hear the other person out, and in doing so we confirm him or her as a human being.

Nikki Giovanni and Margaret Walker, two American writers of very different generations, spoke about the effects of nonevaluative listening in a very personal terms:

> G ... I do know that I need to know things, and one reason that we can sit through this conversation is that you can give a lot to me and I can take it in. Which doesn't mean that I'll just say, well, you know, goddamn, you're right.
> W We don't always agree, but we can listen, anyway.
> G Not only do that, but I've found in my few years on earth that if you listen, even when you disagree, it changes you: if you just *hear* the person. Because you have to respect somebody else. I think that the writers of my generation have one terrific problem in terms of a lot of other people. It's a typical young people's problem and I don't consider myself young on that level. It's that we do not invest integrity into the people around us, into the people before us, and therefore we cannot think of ourselves as possessing integrity. If you cannot give integrity to someone it is because you do not think of yourself as possessing it. (Giovanni and Walker, 1974, p. 58)

Clearly, empathic listening is often an important aspect of any relationship between a client and a counselor—whether that counselor be a lawyer, a psychiatrist, or even the student adviser in a large university. Consider the value of empathic listening in the organizational setting of a managerial consulting interview:

> If a person tells me ... that his desk is too small, I do not try to convince him that the size of his desk is sufficient for his purposes; I am thinking of the social setting in which desks appear in his work situation. What human relationship does the desk symbolize for him? It may be that in his organization the higher in the business structure the person goes, the bigger the desk becomes. It may be that the person who is talking to me is a college man with a burning desire to succeed.... When he complains that the desk is too small, he may really be telling me about his dissatisfaction with his advancement in the company. If so, I get him to talk about that. (Roethlisberger, 1955, p. 95)

But empathic listening is no less important between neighbors, college roommates, friends, married couples, or parents and children. For example, a friend of yours who has just split up with her boyfriend may just want someone to talk to. No statements of sympathy, no friendly advice. Just someone who is there and who listens.

It is also possible that through empathic listening we can sometimes gain information that we could not have acquired in other ways.

Drawing by Charles M. Schulz. © 1974 United Feature Syndicate, Inc.

One reason for this is that empathic listening can foster self-disclosure. This was certainly true for Hedrick Smith, who recently wrote a best-seller called *The Russians* (1976). The book is based on his experiences in Russia, where for three years he was a foreign correspondent. Smith was able to learn a great deal about the Soviet way of life from his casual meetings with Russians while shopping, dining, and traveling. In an interview (Groh, 1976) Smith explained that he made it a point never to ask direct questions about a subject or to criticize the Soviet system, but he did express his interest in the people he met. Once when Smith was traveling by train with his four children, a Russian woman commented on the size of his family. She had one child and explained that although she would have liked to have three or four children, she and her husband both had to work and did not like the idea of putting children in a day-care center. And because of the housing shortage, they would not be able to find an apartment large enough to accommodate four children. In describing this incident Smith observed, "I could never have obtained, from any official source, so much information about housing conditions, the role of women or Russian day care centers" (Groh, 1976).

We listen differently at different times. When we want to reduce defensiveness and provide a supportive atmosphere in which trust increases and self-disclosure is possible, we need the skills of empathic listening.

Summary

In Chapters 1 and 6 we have identified improvement of human relationships as one possible outcome of interpersonal communication. We proposed then that the more satisfying the relationship between two communicators, the more likely it was that the other outcomes of effective communication would occur. As we discussed the relationship aspects of communication, we tried to demonstrate why this should be the case. We spoke of the differences between confirming and disconfirming response styles and of the specific behaviors that increase or diminish self-esteem.

Awareness of self, as the next section demonstrated, differs from awareness of others because the perspectives of the actor and the observer differ. We then turned to the Johari Window model for a way of conceptualizing the effects of various levels of awareness on human interaction. Metacommunication and self-disclosure were discussed as means of improving the Johari Window.

We approached our third subject, trust as a dimension of human relationships, by looking at how people behave when they play games or observe others playing games (particularly in mixed-motive situations). We looked at some of the effects of trust destroying behavior and discussed the supportive and defensive climates that could be established through communication. In conclusion, we examined the two skills involved in empathic listening.

Review Questions

1. How do the content and relationship aspects of communication differ? Provide examples of each.
2. What are some major differences between confirming and disconfirming response styles? Give examples of each.
3. State the most important implication of research on behavior attribution for students of communication.
4. What are the four levels of awareness exemplified by the Johari Window? How do these different levels affect human communication?
5. What is metacommunication? Give some examples.
6. What is the dyadic effect? Give at least two examples.
7. What are five characteristics of appropriate self-disclosure? How does self-disclosure relate to communication?
8. How do supportive and defensive climates of communication differ?
9. What is the relationship between trust, accuracy, and effectiveness in human communication?
10. Name four different types of listening.
11. Specify three contexts of communication in which empathic listening would be the most appropriate form of listening.

Exercises

1. The next time you observe a disagreement between two people, try to determine whether they are disagreeing on the content level, the relationship level, or both. Relate your observations to two other disagreements that you have experienced, and analyze those disagreements in the same way.
2. In a small group—five people or so—have each person attempt to increase his or her awareness of self and others by telling each of the others one positive and one negative impression he or she has formed about that person. If time permits, have a free discussion

in which group members go into greater depth, asking for and giving further impressions.
3. Write a paragraph describing someone whom you trust very much. Then write a description of someone you do not trust. Finally, elaborate on the behaviors that you want to develop and avoid in building a trusting relationship with someone in the future.
4. Observe five communication events that illustrate five different outcomes of communication (see Chapter 1). Analyze the events in terms of the following questions:
   a. What were the relative frequencies of confirming and disconfirming response styles for each communication event? Does there appear to be any relationship between the type of communication outcome and the predominant response style? If so, why do you think this is the case and what implications does this have for your own communication behavior?
   b. In which communication events were trust and self-disclosure most apparent? Why do you think this was so?

Suggested Readings

Johnson, David. *Reaching Out: Interpersonal Effectiveness and Self-Actualization.* Englewood Cliffs, N.J.: Prentice-Hall, 1972. This book offers an insight into the relationship between interpersonal communication skills and actualizing one's potential. It will complement the study of such topics as listening, constructive confrontation, modeling, and reinforcing interpersonal skills.

Kelly, Charles M. "Empathic Listening," in R. Cathcart and L. Samovar (Eds.). *Small Group Communication: A Reader.* Dubuque. Iowa: Wm. C. Brown, 1975, pp. 340–348. The author makes the distinction between empathic and deliberative listening, and presents the differences between them as primarily motivational.

Luft, Joseph. *Of Human Interaction.* Palo Alto, Calif.: National Press, 1969. This book elaborates on the rationale behind the Johari Window model as well as its application. It also explains more fully the value of self-disclosure. The author's treatment will be of interest to undergraduate and graduate students alike.

O'Neill, Nena, and O'Neill, George. *Open Marriage: A New Life Style for Couples.* New York: Evans, 1972, pp. 109–127. The authors, who incidentally are husband and wife, present a very practical and vividly written analysis of problems in marital communication. Much of the discussion centers on how we listen—or don't listen.

Tubbs, Stewart L., and Baird, John W. *The Open Person . . . Self-Disclosure and Personal Growth.* Columbus, Ohio: Charles E. Merrill,

1976. This book examines the literature on self-disclosure and attempts to show that a high level of self-disclosure is not always appropriate. Seven methods for personal and interpersonal growth are discussed: transcendental meditation, biofeedback, body and sensory awareness, Gestalt therapy, general semantics, encounter groups, and transactional analysis. The seven methods are then applied to communication with acquaintances, work associates, and marriage partners.

Chapter 7: The Verbal Message

OBJECTIVES

After reading this chapter the student should be able to:
1. Explain what is intended by the statement "The word is not the thing."
2. Distinguish between denotation and connotation.
3. Describe the Semantic Differential and give an example of a differential.
4. Distinguish between private and shared meanings.
5. Explain the concept of overlapping codes and its relevance to intercultural communication.
6. Distinguish between egocentric speech and socialized speech.
7. Distinguish between a restricted code and an elaborated code.
8. Discuss the theory of verbal deprivation.
9. Explain the term "black English vernacular (BEV)."
10. State the Whorfian hypothesis.
11. Describe two ways in which language and thought are related.
12. Discuss four imprecise uses of language and give examples of how each affects communication.
13. Identify two sources of confusion about words or phrases and give an example of each.
14. Discuss the influence of viewpoint or frame of reference on intercultural communication.

7

Suggestions for improving the relationship aspects of communication are not always warmly received—especially when they are associated with the term "human relations." Take Malcolm McNair's comment, which first appeared in the *Harvard Business Review:*

> in the effort to blow human relations up into a science and develop a technique of communication, some of the enthusiasts have worked up such standard conversational gambits as 'This is what I think I hear you saying,' or 'As I listen, this is what I think you mean.'
>
> No doubt there are times when a . . . reaction of this kind is appropriate, but if the human relations practitioner makes such phrases part of his conversational repertoire, there are times when these cute remarks may gain him a punch in the nose. Sometimes people damn well mean what they are saying and will rightly regard anything less than a man-to-man recognition of that fact as derogatory to their dignity. (McNair, 1957, p. 28)

If you were to take sides in the controversy, you might tend to agree with Mr. McNair's statement. Words, you might argue, have certain agreed-on meanings. This position seems obvious and quite reasonable. Yet McNair commits the common error of assuming that words are "containers" of meaning (in somewhat the same sense that cups may be containers of coffee). Instead, as we saw in Chapter 1, the communication process is highly complex: it involves sending communicative stimuli—in this instance, verbal communicative stimuli—from one person's nervous system to another's with the intent of *creating* a meaning that is similar to the one in the mind of the sender. So there are situations in which meanings are ambiguous, and we may have to say "This is what I think I hear you saying" or "This is what I think you mean." It is clear, then, that although McNair's reaction is not that uncommon, the term "human relations" has a very different meaning for him than it does for most advocates of human relations. Let us approach the question of meaning through a closer look at the nature of language itself.

WORDS AND MEANINGS

To linguists the basic elements of language are sounds or, more precisely, distinctive features, which are components of sounds. To students of interpersonal communication, the basic elements of language are words, and words, as we know, are symbols. When we write the words "United States" in a notebook, we are obviously using some marks on a piece of paper to represent a particular land mass. People who speak other languages use other symbols to represent the same land mass—the French, for example, use "Etats-Unis" and the Spanish, "Estados Unidos."

Symbols and Referents

A recent example of the arbitrary relationship between a word and the thing it symbolizes can be taken from the realm of science. The name of the space vehicle used to travel from the mother ship to the surface of the moon was originally "lunar excursion module"; later it was changed to "lunar module." In effect, we witnessed the words "lunar module" being created. Therefore, it is easy to recognize that the name was arbitrarily assigned to the vehicle so that it would be possible to communicate about it without pointing every time we referred to it.

In every branch of science, we have seen new words coined to keep pace with technological development—"antibiotic," "microwave," "photon," "DNA," are a few examples. There are 6,000 words just in the National Aeronautics and Space Administration's *Dictionary of Technical Terms for Aerospace Use*. And one writer comments that in the last twenty-five years, "advances in technology and communication media have produced a greater change in our language than in any similar period in history" (Long, 1969, p. 87).

Naming a space vehicle is a process somewhat similar to that of naming a newborn child. Initially, no association exists between a name and the person to be named. Similarly, we would agree to call a vehicle that lands on the moon a "moon landing vehicle" or even a "xog." In this context it seems clear that a **word** is merely *a symbol of the object it represents*. The term "lunar module" only represents the vehicle. The vehicle itself is the **referent,** *the object for which the symbol stands*. Clearly, the word is not the thing.

If words referred only to objects, no doubt our communication problems would be eased considerably. We could establish what referents we were speaking about with somewhat less difficulty. But words also refer to events, properties of things, actions, relationships, concepts, and so on. The referent of the term "Asian" seems clear. But suppose you are asked, "*Who* is an Asian, *what* is an *Asian,* and *what* does being an Asian mean to you?" These questions were addressed to a group of more than 200 authorities who were considered, and who considered themselves, Asians (Sithi-Amuai, 1968). There were many answers: Asia stands for a geographic concept, a political concept, an emotional concept, an ethnic theory, a fatalistic society, a kind of personality. In all, eighteen different interpretations of the word "Asian" emerged. If we cannot find agreement on the word "Asian," what about terms that represent higher levels of abstraction? What are the referents of terms such as "ethics," "freedom," and "professionalism"?

The relationship between meaning and reference becomes clearer to us when we encounter words in a foreign language. If we see "ἄνθρωπος" ("*ánthrōpos*"), the Greek word for "man," for the first time, we have no way of determining what concept that word represents simply by looking at the word itself. Even with new words in our own language, we have to learn what concepts they represent. Notice how we carefully avoided saying, "what the words mean." Meanings are not inherent in words. Words in and of themselves are meaningful only after we have associated them with some referents. It is human beings who assign meanings to words.

Suppose you and a friend disagree about the meaning of "word." You turn to the dictionary to settle your differences only to find this formidable list:

1. A unit of language that functions as a principal carrier of meaning
2. Speech or talk
3. A short talk or conversation: "to have a word with someone"
4. An expression or utterance: "a word of praise"
5. A warrant, assurance, or promise
6. News, tidings, or information
7. A verbal signal such as a password
8. An authoritative utterance or a command: "His word was law"
9. The Scriptures
10. A proverb or motto
11. A recommendation: "to put in a word for someone"
12. To express
13. An expression of astonishment: "My word!" (Adapted from *The Random House Dictionary of the English Language,* 1969, p. 1516.)

Meaning, it would seem, is not to be found in the dictionary. Instead the dictionary lists the uses or functions of language. "Dictionaries," one communication expert explains, "do not 'give meanings' or even definitions; they give more or less synonymous words or phases" (Cherry, 1966, p. 71).

Denotation and Connotation

In discussing meaning some students of language make the traditional distinction between "denotation" and "connotation." We have said that words are meaningful only after we have associated them with some referents. When we speak of **denotation,** we refer to *the primary associations a word has for most members of a given linguistic community.* When we speak of **connotation,** we refer to *other, secondary associations a word has for one or more members of that community.* Sometimes the connotations a word has are the same for nearly everyone; sometimes they relate solely to one individual's personal experience. For example, to a naturalist, a furrier, a chicken farmer, and a man who has just been bitten by a fox the word "fox" may have completely different connotations. And often a word will have very special connotations for an ethnic group within the broader linguistic community:

> The real hip thing about the "baby" term was that it was something that only colored cats could say the way it was supposed to be said. I'd heard gray boys trying it, but they couldn't really do it. Only colored cats could give it the meaning that we all knew it had without ever mentioning it—the meaning of black masculinity. (Brown, 1965, p. 171)

Because words can elicit powerful emotional reactions, they are often said to have negative or positive connotations for people. Today the word "housewife" has strong negative connotations for a great many women. Several years ago the editors of English language dictionaries were interviewed concerning the possibility of introducing a substitute term (Shenker, 1972). They commented that in the past "homemaker," "home manager," "household executive," "domestic engineer," and several other terms had been proposed and rejected. They predicted no immediate changes, and the term "housewife" is still very much in use. Nonetheless, we have seen several changes in the use of language in the last few years, some a result of the women's movement. For many women the words "chairperson" (rather than "chairman") and "Ms." (rather than "Miss" or "Mrs.") have more positive associations, and slowly these words have entered the English language.

As yet little research can be cited in the study of word connotations. One study (Arnold and Libby, 1970) investigated male and female responses to sex-related terms in an attempt to identify differences in response. Not surprisingly, it was found that women tended to respond much less favorably than men to the following words:

Wife swapping
Husband swapping
Prostitute
Whore

In another investigation (Crane et al., 1970) male and female subjects were exposed to various words on a tachistoscope, and their galvanic skin responses (GSR) were measured as an index of their reactions. Although there were nonsignificant differences between responses to "good" words ("beauty," "love," "kiss," and "friend," for example) and "aversive" words ("cancer," "hate," "liar," and "death," for example), some words caused significant reactions in both men and women. These were called "personal" words and included the subject's first name, last name, father's first name, mother's first name, major in school, year in school, and school name. In general, subjects were more physiologically aroused by the personal words than by either the good or the aversive words.

Some of the most influential research on the measurement of meaning has been conducted by Osgood and his associates (1957), who developed an instrument called the **Semantic Differential.** With the Semantic Differential, a researcher can *test a person's reactions to any concept or term*—sex, music, my mother, open enrollment, tree, ego, welfare, Jimmy Carter—and then compare them with those of other people. The test itself is a seven-interval scale whose limits are defined by sets of bipolar adjectives. In the accompanying scale, for example, we see a Semantic Differential for the concept of abortion. The subject rates the concept by checking the interval between each pair of adjectives that best describes it. The researcher draws a line connecting each of the points made by the subject and thus creates a profile of the subject's concept of abortion.

Abortion

Sharp	___:___:___:___:___:___:___	Dull
Courageous	___:___:___:___:___:___:___	Cowardly
Relaxed	___:___:___:___:___:___:___	Tense
Small	___:___:___:___:___:___:___	Large
Good	___:___:___:___:___:___:___	Bad
Hot	___:___:___:___:___:___:___	Cold
Powerful	___:___:___:___:___:___:___	Weak

Deceitful ___:___:___:___:___:___:___ Honest

Fast ___:___:___:___:___:___:___ Slow

Cruel ___:___:___:___:___:___:___ Kind

Active ___:___:___:___:___:___:___ Passive

Statistical analysis of the work of Osgood and his associates suggests that our judgments have three major dimensions: evaluation (E), potency (P), and activity (A). Thus we say that abortion is good or bad and cruel or kind (evaluation), that it is powerful or weak and small or large (potency), and that it is fast or slow and active or passive (activity).

The subjects of Osgood's early research were Americans, but he was intrigued by the possibility of cross-cultural studies and went on to explore the dimensions of affective meaning in twenty-six different language communities (Osgood, 1974a; 1974b). According to Osgood, the major dimensions of affective meaning in all these cultures were the same: evaluation, potency, and activity. "But why E, P, and A?" writes Osgood:

> One reason is that, humans being a kind of animal—just peruse any day's newspaper—the most important questions today, as in the day of the Neanderthal, about the sign of a thing are: first, *is it good or is it bad for me?* (is it a cute Neanderthal female or a sabertooth tiger?); second, *is it strong or is it weak with respect to me?* (is it a sabertooth tiger or a mouse?); third, *is it an active or a passive thing?* (is it a sabertooth tiger or merely a pool of quicksand that I can carefully skirt?). Survival of the species has depended upon answers to such questions. (Osgood, 1974a, p. 34)

From his cross-cultural research Osgood has been able to compile an *Atlas of Affective Meanings*. The 620 concepts in this atlas run the gamut from "Accepting things as they are," "Accident," "Marriage," and "Masculinity," to "Master," "Yesterday," "Youth," and "Zero." Although Osgood found certain definite cultural variations, many concepts were evaluated similarly by members of a great many different cultures. One such concept was THE DAYS OF THE WEEK. Monday was generally evaluated as the worst day in the week; things tended to improve after that, gathering momentum on Friday and reaching a peak on Sunday, the best day. For Iranians, on the other hand, the worst day was Saturday (comparable to our Monday), and Friday (the Moslem holy day) was the best. A closer look at a concept such as ADOLESCENCE yielded another interesting comparison between cultures. American teen-agers evaluated ADOLESCENCE as "slightly Bad and quite Weak, but very Active," whereas the Japanese teen-agers felt that ADOLESCENCE was "very Good, Strong, and Active" (Osgood, 1974b, p. 83).

The great appeal of the Semantic Differential is its flexibility. The procedure is so general that it can be precisely tailored to the needs and interests of the experimenter. And as one writer observed, though the technique was "intended to show how people *feel* about the concepts being rated . . . there is no reason in the world why it cannot be used to determine what people *think* are the important properties of those same concepts" (Deese, 1970, p. 106; italics added).

Private and Shared Meanings

In psychology and semantics much research is based on the distinction between denotation and connotation. The Semantic Differential, for example, is said to measure "connotative meaning." But when we examine it closely, the distinction between denotation and connotation seems to break down. All people who speak English are members of the same linguistic community; yet within that community certain groups exist for whom even the primary associations, or denotations, of a given word are different.

Take the case of the Americans and the British. In England you take a "lift," not an "elevator"; if you ask for the "second floor," you get the first. You take the "underground," not the "subway," and a "tram," not a "streetcar." You "queue up"; you don't "stand in line." You go to a "chemist's," not a "pharmacy." The list seems endless. Writing about diplomacy, Oliver (1962) observes that in England "compromise" has many positive associations and implies "joining together the best elements in two proposals," whereas in this country we associate "compromise" with "the surrender of good and the acceptance of evil—as is indicated in our saying that a girl's virtue or a man's honor may be compromised" (p. 67). Perhaps there is some truth in the remark that America and England are two allies separated only by an ocean and a common language.

For students of communication it may be more helpful to distinguish between private and shared meanings rather than denotation and connotation.

The concept of **private meaning** is epitomized by Humpty Dumpty's famous declaration to Alice in *Through the Looking Glass and What Alice Found There:* "When *I* use a word . . . it means just what I choose it to mean—neither more nor less" (Carroll, 1965, pp. 93–94). We can all use language in this way. We can assign meanings to words without agreement and in effect create a private language. We can decide, for example, to call trees "reds" or "glimps" or "haves." Schizophrenic speech is often idiosyncratic in this way, but

In many school settings student and teacher have overlapping linguistic codes.

schizophrenics are unaware that their use of language is private: they use the words they have re-created and expect to be understood. When one young patient was admitted to a hospital, she continually referred to her father, a lawyer by profession, as "the chauffeur." Everyone with whom she spoke found this reference bizarre. Only in treatment was it learned that when she called her father a "chauffeur," she meant that he did her mother's bidding—that he was completely under her domination.

Presumably, if we assign private meanings to words, we are aware that we can use them to communicate with someone only if we let that person know what the referents of these words are. **Shared meaning** requires some correspondence between the message as perceived by the sender and the receiver. As Deese has written, "In order for communication to take place between two or more individuals, meaning must be shared" (Deese, 1970, p. 126). Two friends, a husband and wife, an entire family, or a group of physicists may decide to use language in a way that makes little sense to others. Among themselves, however, they can communicate with no difficulty. The same phenomenon occurs among members of much larger social aggregations. For example, one article has described the extensive vocabulary associated with the San Francisco drug culture:

Glossary of San Francisco Drug Language (Adapted from Smith and Sturges, 1969, pp. 168–173)

This glossary was compiled from information collected during interviews conducted in San Francisco's Haight-Ashbury. We believe it is representative of contemporary San Francisco drug language. This listing is entirely descriptive, and while certain inconsistencies may prove to be disturbing, they are part of this new vocabulary.

Acapulco gold—Superior grade of marijuana, somewhat gold in color, supposedly grown near Acapulco, Mexico
Barbs—Barbiturates
Blow the vein—To use too much pressure on a weak vein, causing it to rupture
Bummer, bum trip—Adverse reaction to drugs
Candy—Cocaine
Cartwheel—Benzedrine time spansules
Columbus black—Marijuana of high potency grown in Central America that is black in color
Cunt—Best part of vein for injection
Ditch—Inside of the elbow (which has two large veins)
Doper—Drug user
Dust—Cocaine
Freak—Anyone addicted to drugs (often combined with acid-, meth-, etc.)
Head—User of drugs (often combined with acid-, meth-, etc.)
Heat—Police
Joint—Marijuana cigarette
Key—About 2.2 pounds of marijuana (one kilogram)
Magic mushroom—Psilocybin
Miss Emma—Morphine
Nárcos, narks—Narcotics agents
Panama red—Marijuana from southern Mexico and Central America
Phennies—Phenobarbital
Poppers—Amyl nitrite
Rig—Paraphernalia for injections
Roller—Vein that won't stay in position for injection
Rush—Intense orgasmlike euphoria experienced immediately after an intravenous injection
Shit—Heroin or sometimes marijuana

Silver bike—Syringe with chrome fittings
Smack—Heroin
Speed—Methamphetamine
Strung out—Condition from habitual use of a drug
Ticket agent—Dealer in hallucinogenic drugs
Uppers, ups—Stimulants, especially Benzedrine or Dexedrine

For the subgroup that uses this language, the meaning of "candy" or "ticket agent" or "smack" is clear. Members of the group will have no difficulty understanding one another when they use these terms because they share a code. Communication difficulties emerge only when they expect meaning to be shared by those outside the group. This is a recurring expectation, especially in a country such as the United States, where so many different ethnic groups coexist.

In intercultural communication, the sender and the receiver often have **overlapping codes,** *"codes which provide an area of commonality but which also contain areas of unshared codification"* (Smith, in Samovar and Porter, 1972, p. 291). Smith also points out that even if the code they use at home is very different, members of minority groups are usually compelled to learn and make some use of the language of the majority because in education, business, and politics this language dominates. For example, "except for peripheral relationships with maids, gardeners, and so on . . . most white communicators do not understand Black community language" (Smith, in Samovar and Porter, 1972, p. 291).

Before reading further test yourself on the vocabulary list below taken from black American street culture. Opposite each item is its accepted synonym in this subculture. Cover the items on the right before starting the test. Give yourself one point for each correct answer, and grade yourself according to the following scale: 50–40, A; 39–30, B; 29–20, C; 19–10, D; below 10, F.

1. Ax
2. Blow some jams
3. Boss
4. Busted
5. Close-knuckle drill
6. Come outa your act
7. Cooker
8. Cop
9. Cop out
10. Cut me loose
11. Doing a bit
12. Dropping beans
13. Dust
14. Flaky

1. Musical instrument
2. Play some records
3. The best
4. Caught by the police; fired
5. Fist fight
6. Be genuine
7. A real swinger
8. Buy; get; steal
9. Explain; squeal
10. Leave me alone
11. Doing jail or prison time
12. Taking pills to get high
13. Money
14. Not too smart; dumb

THE VERBAL MESSAGE

15. Flick
16. Fox
17. From the git go
18. Front
19. Funny changes
20. Gig
21. Grease
22. Grip
23. Hit on the broad
24. Hog
25. Hump; humping
26. Ice it
27. Joint
28. Joneses
29. Lame
30. Let's make it
31. Man (the)
32. Mellow
33. Not wired too heavy
34. Not wrapped too tight
35. On the humble
36. Peek your hole card
37. Piece
38. Pressed
39. Ride
40. Run it down
41. Run you through a thing
42. Running game
43. Shot a blank
44. Show
45. Split
46. Stomps
47. Stone fox
48. Stone trick
49. Tore down
50. Tore up

15. Movie; television
16. Good-looking woman
17. Beginning
18. Suit
19. Double-talk
20. Date; job
21. Eat
22. Car
23. Sweet-talk a woman
24. Cadillac
25. Working the job
26. Stop
27. Marijuana cigarette
28. Dope habit; hooked
29. Square
30. Let's leave
31. Policeman; white man in authority
32. Girl friend
33. Not too smart; dumb
34. Not too smart; dumb
35. Innocent
36. Find out your secrets
37. Hand gun
38. Dressed up
39. Car
40. Tell it like it is
41. Trick you
42. Doing something wrong
43. Sweet talk failed
44. Make an appearance
45. Leave; go
46. Shoes
47. Especially good-looking woman
48. Lied; didn't keep word
49. Drunk
50. High

Suppose many of these expressions are unfamiliar to you, and your test score is low. You would object violently if you were informed that this score is a measure of your intelligence. Unfortunately, many intelligence tests rely heavily on the assumption that test taker and test writer use language in much the same way, a problem we shall touch on in the discussion of encoding in the next section. Interpersonal communication is equally reliant on assumptions of shared meaning. It presupposes agreement between communicators concerning the symbols they exchange and therefore some consciousness not only of language but of one another. In discussing message encoding we hope to show that who is listening is no less important than who is speaking.

MESSAGE ENCODING

"You're lying," "I don't think you are telling the truth," "Fibber," "I don't believe you," "You liar"—these are alternate ways of formulating a single message, and there are many others. We use "Fibber" in one context, "You're lying" in another, and "I don't believe you" in a third, and we seem to make these distinctions without effort. Occasionally we wonder how to broach a delicate subject, but most of the time we speak without deliberation. Yet **encoding a message,** or *formulating it in words,* is a complex process, however straightforward the message may be:

> Coding requires the selection of appropriate verbal and nonverbal signs to express the internal state of the sender of the message. But to be effective, this must be accompanied by an imaginative interpretation of the probable meaning to be assigned to the cues by the receiver. Without the capacity to encode and the capacity to interpret from the vantage point of the receiver, the sender would not know what to put into a message. (Barnlund, 1968, p. 9)

In short, when we encode a message, we must have some awareness of the receiver if we want to be understood. (For an introduction to this subject from the psycholinguistic point of view, see Smith and Miller [1966].)

A look at how children use language gives us a better understanding of what takes place in the encoding process. Children astonish us with their verbal facility. The three-year-old can formulate sentences, repeat all sorts of long words and colloquial expressions, and use several tenses correctly. Some three-year-olds have a vocabulary of nearly 1,000 words. The five-year-old speaks in correct, finished sentences and even uses complex sentences with hypothetical and conditional clauses. At this age the structure and form of language are essentially complete.

To study the functions of language in children, the Swiss psychologist Jean Piaget (1955) made exhaustive observations and analyses of the way children speak both when they are alone and when they are in the company of other children. He also devised a series of experiments to determine how objective children try to be in communicating information. A typical Piaget experiment follows this pattern. A child is shown a diagram of a water tap—sometimes Piaget uses a diagram of a bicycle—and given a precise explanation of how it works. Once it has been established that the child understands the experimenter's explanation, he or she is asked to repeat it (with the aid of the diagram) to another child. In another variant of this procedure, the child is told a simple story and asked to repeat it to a second child. How do children perform these communication tasks? Apparently not very well. Piaget found that though a child fully understood an explanation or story, he or she was not necessarily successful in communicating it to another child.

Why should this be so? It is not that the child lacks the necessary vocabulary. Nor is he or she by any means inarticulate. Piaget's work has led him to the conclusion that in the child under age seven or eight, language has two distinct functions and that two kinds of speech exist: egocentric and socialized speech.

As Piaget describes patterns of **egocentric speech** in the child, he gives us a perfect example of a poor encoder:

> Although he talks almost incessantly to his neighbours, he rarely places himself at their point of view. He speaks to them for the most part as if he were thinking aloud. He speaks, therefore, in a language which disregards the precise shade of meaning in things and ignores the particular angle from which they are viewed, and which above all is always making assertions, even in argument, instead of justifying them. . . . In a word, the child hardly ever even asks himself whether he has been understood. For him, that goes without saying, for he does not think about others when he talks. (Piaget, 1955, p. 60)

Piaget believes that until a child is seven or eight, egocentric language constitutes almost half his or her spontaneous speech, and his book *The Language and Thought of the Child* is full of amusing "conversations" between children in which virtually no communication takes place:

> L.: "Thunder rolls."
> P.: "No, it doesn't roll."
> L.: "It's water."
> P.: "No, it doesn't roll."
> L.: "What is thunder?"
> P.: "Thunder is . . ." (*He doesn't go on.*) (Piaget, 1955, p. 44)

In contrast to egocentric speech, **socialized speech** involves adapting information to the receiver and in some sense adopting his or her point of view; it involves social rather than nonsocial encoding. Piaget goes beyond his findings about language to argue that the adult "thinks socially, even when he is alone, and . . . the child under 7 thinks egocentrically, even in the society of others" (Piaget, 1955, p. 60).

INTERPERSONAL COMMUNICATION

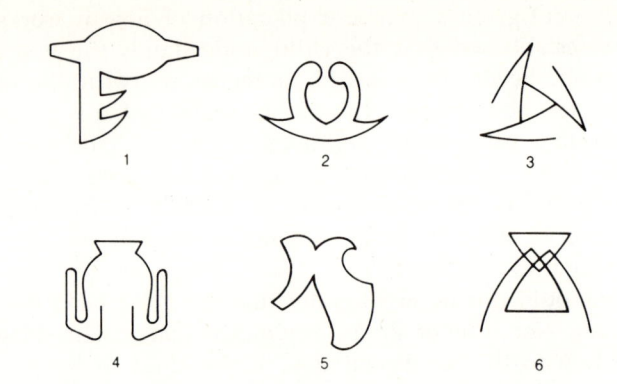

Figure 7.1

DESIGNS ON BLOCKS FOR A COMMUNICATION EXPERIMENT

Source: Sam Glucksberg, Robert M. Krauss, and Robert Weisberg, "Referential Communication in Nursery School Children: Method and Some Preliminary Findings," *Journal of Experimental Child Psychology*, 3 (1966), 335. Reprinted by permission.

One team of researchers went on to a further examination of this discrepancy between the communication skills of children and adults (Krauss, in Walcher, 1971). Their strategy was to create a communication problem in the form of a game called Stack the Blocks. Two children, one designated "speaker" and the other "listener," are seated opposite each other at a table. They are separated by an opaque screen so that they cannot see each other. Before each child is a wooden dowel and a set of six blocks. A hole has been drilled through each block so that it may be stacked on the dowel, and each block is imprinted with a different graphic design. As you can see from Figure 7.1, the designs have **low codability**—that is, they are *difficult to describe*. The speaker's blocks are in a dispenser, and he or she is instructed to remove them one at a time. While stacking each block on the dowel, the speaker must also describe it to the listener, who must put what he or she thinks is the same block on his or her dowel. Describing the design of the block so that the listener can identify it and stack his or her blocks in the same order is the communication problem.

In what terms does the speaker describe the novel design of each block to the listener? Here are the descriptions of design 3 given by five nursery school children:

Somebody running
Eagle
Throwing sticks
Strip-stripe
Wire

Their descriptions of design 4 are equally varied:

Daddy's shirt
Milk jug
Shoe hold
Coffee
Dog

There is little social encoding in these identifications. How, for example, is the listener expected to know what "strip-stripe" refers to or what "Daddy's shirt" looks like? In the role of speaker, some kindergartners and first-graders make comments such as "It goes like this," using one finger—which of course the listener cannot see—to trace the design in the air. In general, children tend to use private rather than socially shared images; as a result their messages are often idiosyncratic.

Variations of the Stack the Blocks experiment have been conducted with children of all grade levels as well as with adults. While nursery school children seem totally unable to complete this communication task, it has been found that effectiveness in communication clearly increases with age (as measured by grade level).

If we interpret these results literally, we expect all adults to have perfect encoding abilities. We know, however, that this is not the case. Some adults are better at social encoding than others. One theory about the variation in ability is proposed by the British sociologist Basil Bernstein. He believes that different social settings can generate different modes of communication—in other words, different styles of linguistic encoding. The two codes Bernstein discusses, the restricted and the elaborated code, are based on his analysis of speech patterns in the United Kingdom.

A **restricted code** is *created by a community-based culture;* it emphasizes the community rather than the individual ("we" rather than "I," Bernstein explains). It is largely concerned with shared or context-bound meanings rather than abstractions. The message sender assumes that the receiver knows what he or she is talking about. Therefore the message tends to be simple and relatively brief, the syntax simple and rigid, and the vocabulary undifferentiated. A restricted code creates social solidarity by minimizing the verbal elaboration of individual experience. According to Bernstein, this is the linguistic code of the working classes.

An **elaborated code,** on the other hand, is *person-oriented, emphasizing individual rather than group experience* ("I" rather than "we"). The sender's view of the receiver is different here. The sender does not know the receiver's intent; nor does the sender take it for granted—he or she assumes very little. Therefore the sender elaborates meanings to make them more comprehensible to the receiver. This linguistic code requires a more differentiated vocabulary, one suitable for making subtle distinctions. It also demands a style of speech that is analytic and abstract rather than concrete. This is the linguistic code available to the middle and upper classes, who, unlike the working classes, have the advantage of being able to use both codes.

Bernstein's theory has one very practical application. In many countries of the world, including our own, children of low socioeconomic status tend to get lower scores on intelligence tests, especially on the verbal tests, than do children of higher status. It has often been argued that children from lower-status families do poorly because they are less intelligent. Bernstein accounts for poor performance in another way. Intelligence tests are cast in the language of the elaborated code. Although middle- and upper-class children are fluent in both the restricted and elaborated codes, lower-class children know only the restricted code. Once lower-class children enter school they are caught between two radically different communication systems. Bernstein comments:

> Thus the relative backwardness of many working-class children who live in areas of high population density or in rural areas, may well be a culturally induced backwardness transmitted by the linguistic process. Such children's low performance on verbal IQ tests, their difficulty with abstract concepts, their failures within the language area, their general inability to profit from the school, all may result from the limitations of a restricted code. (Bernstein, in Williams, 1970, p. 37)

We have seen that the message sender's expectations about the receiver can have a crucial effect on how he or she prepares the message and on how that message is decoded by the receiver. Bernstein's theory suggests that message encoding is a form of social learning, a part of the socialization process itself. It further suggests that to some degree each of us may be able to improve our social encoding abilities.

Bernstein's views on the superiority of middle-class language over working-class language are much more controversial, particularly since they have been used by some educators and psychologists to support a **theory of verbal deprivation** among ghetto children. *According to this view, children brought up in urban ghettos receive very little verbal stimulation.* They grow up in a culture that is not verbal, a culture in which people rarely speak in well-formed sentences. Such children *cannot express themselves verbally* and often lack the vocabulary with which to conceptualize their thoughts. Their poor performance in a school setting is explained as a result of this handicap.

Foremost among the critics of this theory is William Labov. Labov's linguistic research has led him to challenge what he calls the "myth of verbal deprivation" among ghetto children and "the corresponding myth that middle-class language is in itself better suited for dealing with abstract, logically complex, or hypothetical questions" (1972, p. 220). Indeed, Labov argues,

> black children in the urban ghettos receive a great deal of verbal stimulation, hear more well-formed sentences than middle-class children, and participate more fully in a highly verbal culture. They have the same basic vocabulary, possess the same capacity for conceptual learning, and use the same logic as anyone else who learns to speak and understand English. (Labov, 1972, p. 201)

And judging from the variety of words that describe different kinds of verbal behavior among black Americans *(rapping, gripping, jiving, sounding, shucking, running it down, signifying, copping a plea,* and so on), the black community does seem to have an extremely verbal culture (Kochman, in Smith, 1972, pp. 58–59).

What then accounts for the poor academic performance of ghetto children—their difficulty, for example, in learning to read and in mastering the grammatical principles of standard English? Labov and other linguists believe that the school problems of ghetto children often have their basis in communication difficulties. For example, among black children verbal forms of expression that seem to many teachers to be failures to master standard English ("She don't know nobody," "I have live here five years," "He crazy," "Her my friend") are acceptable forms of a separate, complex linguistic system. Though closely related to English, it has its own grammatical principles and subtleties. Labov calls this system **black English vernacular,** or BEV. His studies of black English vernacular are based on the speech patterns of black youth in the majority of inner-city zones across the country. There is a strong possibility that future linguistic studies will confirm the existence of other non-standard forms of English, each with its own idioms and principles. But whether we side with Bernstein's advocates or with Labov's, it seems clear that when the sender and the receiver have overlapping linguistic codes and assume that they are always using language in the same way, possibilities for misunderstandings multiply rapidly.

LANGUAGE AND THOUGHT

Language and thought are often said to be interrelated, but the nature of their relationship is far from clear. Is language a precondition of human thought? Is thinking simply inner speech? Does language shape our ideas, or is it merely an instrument of thought? There seem to be no easy answers.

Students of communication have been particularly concerned with the last question. One version of the view that our thought is shaped by the language we speak was proposed by the linguist Benjamin Lee Whorf (1956), and is often referred to as the **Whorfian hypothesis.** Whorf believes that *the world is perceived differently by members of different linguistic communities* and that *this perception is transmitted and sustained by language,* which he regards as the primary vehicle of culture. In short, the language we speak determines our experience of the world.

Whorf supports his theory with findings from his studies of American Indian languages. In English, he points out, we tend to classify words as nouns or verbs; in Hopi the words tend to be classified by duration. For example, in Hopi "lightning," "flame," "wave," and "spark" are verbs, not nouns; they are classified as events of brief duration. In Nootka, which is spoken by the inhabitants of Vancouver Island, categories such as things and events do not exist; thus it is said that "A house occurs" or "It houses."

Is it the case that differences in language reflect differences in perception? An Amazon tribe called the Bororo have several different single words for types of parrots. The Hanunóo of the Philippines have single words for ninety-two different kinds of rice. The Eskimos distinguish at least three kinds of snow in this way. We have only one word for parrot, one for rice, and one for snow. Does this mean that we are incapable of perceiving several types of each? Probably not. Social psychologist Roger Brown suggests that the perceptual categories we use more frequently are merely more "available" to us:

> It is proposed, really, that categories with shorter names (higher codability) are nearer the top of the cognitive deck—more likely to be used in ordinary perception, more available for expectancies and inventions. . . . [Other things being equal,] the presence in someone's vocabulary of a one-word name for a category instead of a phrase name should indicate a superior cognitive availability of the classifying principle involved. . . . The man who readily identifies a set of faces as *Jews* should be more prone to form expectancies about Jews than the man who names the same array *a lot of people, most of them are rather dark, quite a few are wearing button-down shirt collars.* (Brown, 1958, pp. 236–237)

Linguistic distinctions tell us something about priorities within a given culture. Eskimos have several words for snow because they need to make finer verbal distinctions than we do when communicating about it. By and large, we are unaffected by different kinds of snow and therefore expend little effort on making such distinctions. This does not mean that we are incapable of seeing or making them. In fact, members of certain subgroups within our own linguistic community make more verbal distinctions than the rest of us—weather forecasters, bobsled owners, ski resort managers, and so on. We can qualify the Whorfian hypothesis by saying that as a person learns the language of a given culture or subculture, his or her attention is directed toward aspects of reality or relationships that are important in that context, and this focus affects the category system in the memory. Similarly, if someone tells you about several ways to view a certain painting, you will in some sense see more when you look at it—but not because the image on the retina is different.

Language may not determine thought completely, but it seems to do two important things. First, language serves as an aid to memory. It makes memory more efficient by allowing us to code events as verbal categories. Researchers have shown, for example, that we find it easier to recognize colors of low codability again if we named them for ourselves the first time we saw them (Brown and Lenneberg, 1954). It is now believed that an adult's memory is primarily verbal. Language also enables us to abstract indefinitely from our experience, which is especially important in communicating about abstract relationships (something animals are unable to do).

Ideally, language is a valuable instrument of thought; yet we know that language can sometimes interfere with our ability to think critically. Although Whorf was best known for his writings on linguistics, he was trained as an engineer. When he became an accident investigator he began to realize that a certain percentage of accidents occurred as a result of what might be called "careless thinking." For example, people would be very careful around barrels labeled "GASOLINE" but would smoke unconcernedly around barrels labeled "EMPTY GASOLINE BARREL," though the fumes in the empty barrels were more likely to ignite than the actual gasoline (Whorf, 1956, p. 135). There are many ways in which an imprecise use of language interferes with our thought processes. In the balance of this chapter, we shall examine four that have a direct influence on our communication.

Inferences

Every day you make dozens of inferences. When you sit down, you infer that the chair will support your weight. When you go through a green light, you infer that the traffic moving at right angles to you will stop at the red light. When you drive down a one-way street, you infer that all the traffic will be going in one direction. You may have good reason to expect these inferences to be correct, but there is also some uncalculated probability that events will not go as you expect. Drivers who have been involved in traffic accidents frequently say that the accident occurred because they inferred that the other party would act in a certain way when in fact he or she did not. Every year we read of people who were accidentally shot with guns they inferred were not loaded.

As students of communication we are concerned with the inferences implicit in verbal messages. If you say, "It is sunny outside today," your statement can be easily verified. It is a factual statement based on an observed and verifiable event. If you say, "It is sunny outside; therefore, it is sunny fifty miles from here," you draw a conclusion based on more than what you have observed. You have made a statement based in part on an inference.

Like "unloaded" guns, inferential statements also involve a certain amount of risk. Imagine yourself as the witness in this courtroom scene:

Prosecuting attorney:	Would you tell us in your own words what you saw on the night of December 5, 1972?
Witness:	First I heard yelling and then I saw a girl coming out of the defendant's apartment. She was crying, and her dress was torn. She also had a bruise on her cheek.
Prosecuting attorney:	Would you say that it looked as if the girl and the defendant had been brawling?
Defense attorney:	Objection! The question calls for a conclusion from the witness.
Judge:	Sustained. Would counsel please restate the question?

You, the witness, describe what you have seen. You have made a factual statement. The prosecutor asks whether "it looked as if the girl and the defendant had been brawling." The prosecutor wants to lead you into an inferential statement, one that goes beyond what you have observed. In such a situation an incorrect inference on your part can have serious consequences for the defendant. Suppose, for example, that the girl in question had fallen, and that was why she appeared to have been beaten.

We make inferences in every imaginable context, and it is neither possible nor desirable to avoid them entirely. Nevertheless, to use language more precisely and to be more discerning when we hear others speak, we should learn to distinguish between factual and inferential statements. "You spend a great deal of time with my roommate" is a statement of fact. It involves a low level of uncertainty, it is made as a result of direct observation, and it can be verified. Add to it "I'm sure he won't mind if you borrow his coat," and you have an inferential statement that may well jeopardize a friendship. In becoming more conscious of inference making, we can at least learn to calculate the risks involved.

Dichotomies

Some semanticists classify English as a two-valued rather than a multi-valued language. By this they mean that English has an excess of polar words and a relative scarcity of words to describe the wide middle

Success	__	X	__	__	__	__	Failure
Brilliant	__	__	X	__	__	__	Stupid
Handsome	__	X	__	__	__	__	Ugly
Winner	__	__	X	__	__	__	Loser
Honest	__	__	X	__	__	__	Dishonest
Black	X	__	__	__	__	__	White

ground between these opposites. Obviously, every person, entity, or event can be described in terms of a whole array of adjectives ranging from very favorable to very unfavorable. Yet we tend to say that a student is a "success" or a "failure," that a child is "good" or "bad," that a woman is "attractive" or "unattractive." Try, for example, to think of some words to describe the spots marked on the continua in the scale of dichotomies. As you search for words, you begin to see that there are a lot of distinctions for which we lack single words. The continua also illustrate how our language suggests that certain categories of experience are mutually exclusive, when in truth they are not.

Consider the first set of terms, "success" and "failure." Every human being undoubtedly meets with some success and some failure during the course of a lifetime. An insurance broker who has been unemployed for many months and is unable to find work may also be a supportive and much-loved father and husband. Yet our language suggests that he be classified as either a success or a failure. Similar difficulties crop up if we are asked to apply such adjectives as "brilliant" and "stupid" or "winner" and "loser" to other people. Is the math major with a straight A average brilliant or stupid if she can't learn to drive a car or ride a bike? If the author of a recent best-seller is divorced for the third time, is he a winner or a loser?

Even the distinction between life and death now involves more than just two mutually exclusive categories. With the perfection of heart transplants, for example, has come the problem of how to decide when a heart donor is beyond all hope so that his or her heart may be taken for another human being. We know today that there is usually a time lag between the loss of some capacities (brain functioning, for example) and others (heartbeat and respiration) and that in the interval the person is not "dead." Compare this with the days when the absence of breathing and pulse alone meant that life was gone.

When polar terms are used in a misleading way, they suggest false dichotomies, reducing experience in a way that it need not be reduced. Differences are emphasized and similarities are overlooked, and in the process a great deal of information is lost. This is certainly true in our country at election time. During a political campaign each candidate presents his or her finest qualities and avoids mention of any shortcomings. At the same time the candidate calls as much attention as possible to his or her opponent's shortcomings while ignoring the person's good qualities. Each candidate tries to create the impression of great contrast between his or her position and the opponent's, even when it does not exist. The voter is encouraged to vote a straight ticket. But must one be either a Democrat or a Republican, a Liberal or a Conservative? Don't we sometimes split our votes? Don't we vote differently in different elections?

One way to avoid making false dichotomies, as Haney (1973, p. 374) has pointed out, is to make use of the questions "How much?" and "To what extent?":

How much of a success am I?
How much of a change is this from his former stand on gun control?
To what extent is he honest?
To what extent is her plan practical?

With the aid of such questions, perhaps we can keep in mind that we have many options, that we need not cast our messages in black-and-white terms, and that we need not accept these either-or distinctions when they are made by others.

Word Power

> I said that English was my goddamn enemy. Now why do I use "goddamn" to illustrate this aspect of the English language? Because I want to illustrate the sheer gut power of words. Words like "nigger," "sheeny," "Dago," "black power"—words like this. . . .
>
> These words have a power over us; a power that we cannot resist. For a moment you and I have had our deepest physical reactions controlled, not by our wills, but by words in the English language. (Davis, in Smith, 1972, pp. 50–51)

Ossie Davis, in a speech titled "The English Language is My Enemy," was talking about one very specific power of language: the power to foster racism. Consider the words "white" and "black," keeping in mind that we live in a predominantly "white" society. "White" denotes the reflection of nearly all the rays of the sun. It also has many other associations: purity, chastity, freedom from stain, innocence. When we speak of "white magic," we refer to harmless magic. We even have the expression "That's very white of you" (honest or decent). The word "black," on the other hand, denotes the absorption of light, without reflection of any of the rays composing it. Like "white" this word has several other associations, but most of them are negative: gloomy, soiled, disgraceful, evil, wicked, and so on. These are not merely lists of connotations drawn from a dictionary. Duncan (1970) corroborated the differences in feeling evoked by "white" and "black" by asking his students to describe the associations these two words brought to mind.

Another writer takes this distinction a step further by arguing that our language reflects a kind of white racism and that such connotations influence our thinking:

> We *blacken* a man's reputation, *whitewash* a political mistake. A den is a *black sink of iniquity,* war is a *black crime against humanity,* Englishmen were stuffed into the *Black Hole of Calcutta.* The loss of a football game is a *black day* for the Navy; to anticipate such a loss is to *look on the black side of things.* To fail to mow one's lawn is to receive a *black mark* in the community. We are *black-balled* at the club, *blackmailed* by our onetime friends, and *blacklisted* by our enemies. (Haller, 1969, p. 203)

If you study our language from this angle, you may begin to see the rationale behind such expressions as "Black is beautiful."

Of course, the users of the English language have no premium on racism. In Nazi Germany a conscious effort was made to prepare the German people for the extermination of the Jews by redefining them constantly in terms of violent, threatening adjectives. In this way, "the Nazis were able to substitute the words for the objects in the minds of the German audiences" (Rich, 1974, p. 132). On many occasions, the use of racist language does more than simply express racist attitudes: "it helps to develop such attitudes in those learning the symbolic system" (Rich, 1974, p. 131).

Words reflect and influence our thinking in other, more insidious ways. In ancient times words were believed to have magical powers. For example, in ancient Egypt a man received two names: his true name, which he concealed, and his good name, by which he was known publicly. Even today there are many primitive societies in which words are regarded as magical. Members of some cultures go to great lengths to conceal their personal names. They avoid saying the names of their gods. The names of their dead are never uttered. Presumably, we moderns are far more sophisticated. Yet we have our own verbal taboos. Thus we often hear not that someone "died" but "passed away" or that he or she has "CA," not "cancer." When the airline industry switched over from propeller aircraft to jets, flight crew members whose services were no longer needed were "furloughed," not "fired."

Some empirical studies of word power examine the ways in which a speaker's use of profane words can affect our judgments of his or her credibility (Rossiter and Bostrom, 1968; Basehart and Rossiter, 1973; Mabry, 1975). In these experiments three classes of profanity were used: religious, excretory, and sexual. The experimenters hypothesized that religious profanity would be the least offensive kind of profanity and referred to it as "mild usage"; sexual profanity was referred to as "extreme usage." Subjects were asked to rate speakers who included various degrees of profanity in their messages. Under some conditions the speaker seemed to be provoked by the circumstances surrounding the speech; at other times the profanity seemed unjustified. Although religious profanity was less offensive when circumstances appeared to justify it, sexual profanity—whether provoked or unprovoked—always seemed to bring the speakers significantly lower credibility ratings. These results are surprisingly consistent: they are the same for males and females, older and younger women, and freshmen and graduate students.

In addition to affecting our feelings, words may have a direct effect on the way we behave. Novelist Herbert Gold was advised by one publisher that any book with the word "virgin" in the title would automatically receive an advance of $25,000—presumably because the book's sale was guaranteed. In other words, sometimes our decisions are based in part on how a thing is labeled.

Some words clearly have greater prestige than others. The same desk commands different prices when it is called "used," "second-hand," or "antique." "Doctor" is another powerful word. For years the basic law degree was called a "bachelor of laws," or "LL.B." Early in the 1960s, some law schools began to call the same degree by a more prestigious title: *"juris doctor"* ("doctor of law"), or "J.D." By 1969 more than 100 of the nation's 150 law schools had switched over and were granting J.D.s instead of LL.B.s. In the meantime J.D.s were getting better job offers than LL.B.s.

Diplomats and politicians are particularly sensitive to how they use words, but sometimes they slip up. While campaigning for the Democratic presidential nomination in 1976, Jimmy Carter used the phrase "ethnic purity" in a pledge to maintain the distinctive ethnic character of individual neighborhoods. Many of Carter's critics pointed to the racist connotations of the phrase. Even one of his foremost supporters in the black community described Carter's remark as "a disaster for the campaign." Carter promptly apologized for his choice of words, and the retraction did seem to mitigate whatever damage had been done. In 1975 the word "bailout" became a major source of contention between Governor Carey of New York and Gerald Ford. Carey appealed to Ford for federal assistance that would prevent default by the City of New York. Ford replied that he was "prepared to veto any bill that has as its purpose a Federal bailout of New York." Offended by the word "bailout," Carey proposed that Ford "do just that. Because we don't want a bailout, and I would welcome that kind of a veto." Carey's objection to the term "bailout" stemmed from the fact that the city was not asking that the federal government assume New York's debt by giving the city cash. Instead, the city was asking for government backing of securities.

Sometimes special-interest groups attempt to use words for their own purposes. Maddocks describes this well when he writes about "the monstrous insensitivity that allows generals to call war 'pacification,' union leaders to describe strikes or slow-downs as 'job-actions,' and politicians to applaud even moderately progressive programs as 'revolutions'" (1971, p. 36). Advertisers want to know which brand names are appealing because market research has shown that the same product often sells differently under different names.

When the receiver is swayed by the sender's choice of language rather than by message content, the receiver reacts to words as if they did have magical powers. Perhaps it is reasonable to expect this reaction occasionally, but when the receiver fails to distinguish between symbols and referents, he or she forfeits the ability to think clearly. On the other hand, in using language a communicator has many options. With increasing sensitivity to the responses of others, he or she comes to understand that there are certain choices that will facilitate communication and others that will undermine it.

Single Meanings

We spoke in outlining our model of communication about semantic interference, the interference that takes place when the receiver does not attribute the same meaning to the signal that the sender does. A common cause of such interference is the assumption that a word, a phrase, or even a sentence has only one meaning. There seem to be two sources of confusion about words or phrases. First, two people may assume that because they are using the same word, they agree, when in fact each of them interprets the word differently. In a comical incident a woman asks a pharmacist for a refill of her prescription for "the pill." "Please hurry," she adds, "I've got someone waiting in the car." Much humor is based on such double meanings. In daily communication this type of confusion may not be so funny. For example, one of the authors and spouse—and we're not saying which one—were drawn into a needless argument:

Husband: You know, the travel literature on Switzerland that I borrowed is still in the house. Since we're not going I'd better return it to that fellow in my office. Could you get it together for me so I can take it in tomorrow?
Wife: I don't know where it is.
Husband: What kind of an answer is that? If it's too much trouble, forget it.
Wife: What do you mean, "What kind of an answer is that?" How can I do anything with it if I can't find it?
Husband: There's nothing to *do*. All I asked you to do was find it. You don't have to give me a smart answer.
Wife: But you said "get it together." I thought you meant put it in some sort of order.
Husband: I meant "find it." Don't you know what "get it together" means?
Wife: Well, I didn't know it meant *that*.
Husband: If you didn't know, why didn't you ask me?
Wife: Because I thought I knew. I speak English, too, you know.

For a time this misunderstanding created a lot of ill feeling. Both husband and wife were insulted—the husband because he felt his wife had refused to do something relatively simple for him, and the wife because she felt her husband had insulted her intelligence.

A second type of misunderstanding about the meaning of a given word occurs when two people assume that they disagree because they are using different words when actually they may agree on the concept or entity represented by those words. That is, they use different terms that have the same referent. This heated discussion between two college professors was due to just such a semantic breakdown:

Professor Williams: Are we having a meeting at lunch?
Professor Ross: Well, it isn't exactly a meeting. It's a seminar.
Professor Williams: (*a little angry*) Then we are having a meeting.
Professor Ross: No, it's a seminar.
Professor Williams: (*walking away*) Thanks, *I* call that a meeting.
Professor Ross: (*yelling after him angrily*) Good for you. I call it a seminar.

As it turned out, to Professor Williams "meeting" meant getting together with other faculty members; to Professor Ross "meeting" meant solving problems as opposed to presenting research papers. Yet neither was flexible enough to ask the other what he intended by his term or to grant that any symbol can be interpreted ambiguously. When two people cannot agree to use the same words for the same referents, each thinks that the other should switch to the word he or she prefers. Neither is likely to give in unless one requests that they stop and redefine their terms.

Although in this chapter our attention has been given to words or phrases, most messages take the form of sentences. "It's a rainy day," remarks Jack to Jill. What could be clearer than the meaning of that sentence? Yet Laing (1969, pp. 139–140) suggests five ways in which Jack might intend his statement. Perhaps he wishes to register the fact that it is a rainy day. If yesterday Jack and Jill agreed to go for a walk instead of going to a movie, he might be saying that because of the rain he will probably get to see the movie. He might be implying that because of the weather Jill should stay at home. If yesterday the two argued about what the weather would be like, he might mean that Jill is right again or that he is the one who always predicts the weather correctly. If the window is open, he might be saying that he would like Jill to close it. No doubt each of us could come up with several other interpretations. The point is that any message derives a great part of its meaning from the context in which it is transmitted. Our knowledge of the speaker and the speaker's use of language, our own associations with the words he or she chooses, our previous relationship, and the messages we have already exchanged should all play a part in how we interpret what is said.

Although all our behaviors have possible meaning for a receiver, language is by far our most explicit form of communication. In using it our desire is to facilitate thought, not to obscure it. Language is potentially the most precise vehicle we have for human communication. Even if we grant the infinite richness of language and the precision it is capable of expressing, however, a look at intercultural communication makes clear that often people are divided not because of a failure to understand grammar or vocabulary but to understand rhetoric or point of view. "Grammar," one communication expert has observed, "is an instrument used to promote clarity and understanding, but often the problems between Blacks and whites do not suffer as much for clarity as for the ability to look beyond the words to the source of the other person's ideas and to his frame of reference" (Smith, in Samovar and Porter, 1972, p. 296). It is especially difficult to look beyond the words—to listen empathically, if you will—when one or both communicators are feeling defensive.

We have already seen in Chapter 2 that culture is a major determinant of set. Many people believe that culture is so pervasive that it shapes our way of thinking. For example, Kenneth Kaunda, the presi-

INTERPERSONAL COMMUNICATION

Sharing meanings can create a bond.

dent of Zambia, insists that Westerners and Africans have very different ways of seeing things, solving problems, and thinking in general. He characterizes the Westerner as having a "problem-solving mind." Once a Westerner perceives a problem, he or she feels compelled to solve it. Unable to live with contradictory ideas, the Westerner excludes all solutions that have no logical basis. Supernatural and nonrational phenomena are regarded as superstition. The African, on the other hand, allows himself or herself to experience all phenomena, nonrational as well as rational. The African has a "situation-experiencing mind." Kaunda believes that "the African can hold contradictory ideas in fruitful tension within his mind without any sense of incongruity, and he will act on the basis of the one which seems most appropriate to the particular situation" (Legum, 1976, pp. 63–64).

The Arab, too, communicates from a very different rhetorical frame of reference than our own. In daily communication Arabs will emphasize their points by exaggeration and overassertion. For them this is not a deceitful pattern; it is a necessity. Arabs have a long history of exaggeration not only in their linguistic communication but in their prose and poetry. Their linguistic tradition requires that they speak in this way if they are to be taken seriously by other Arabs. Conversely, they do not believe non-Arabs if their speech is simple and unassertive (Suleiman, in Prosser, 1973, p. 293). What Westerners might characterize as "coming on strong" would be a natural communication style to most Arabs.

Oliver makes the point forcefully when he writes:

> If we would communicate across cultural barriers, we must learn what to say and how to say it in terms of the expectations and predispositions of those we want to listen.
>
> The great over-riding fact which we need to accept is that there is no such thing as *a rhetoric* which is common at all; instead there are *many rhetorics*. Peoples in separate cultures and separate nations are concerned with *different* problems; and they have *different* systems of thinking about them. (Oliver, 1962, pp. 154–155)

Summary

Our analysis of verbal communication began and ended with a consideration of the concept of meaning. In discussing the symbolic nature of language, we saw that symbols and referents are associated with each other only by convention and that it is human beings who assign meanings to words. We reviewed the traditional distinction between denotation and connotation and went on to suggest that it might be more useful to distinguish between private and shared meanings.

Our second subject was message encoding, which we approached through a comparison of the encoding abilities of children and adults. Piaget's research on socialized and egocentric speech made it clear that the message sender's perceptions and expectations about the receiver affect his or her ability to communicate accurately. The distinction between elaborated and restricted codes, the theory of verbal deprivation, and the objections to that theory were all discussed in terms of their relevance to communication difficulties (particularly as they relate to the school setting).

Our last concern was the relationship between thought and language, and here we examined several ways in which language can either facilitate or interfere with our thought processes. In our discussion of inferences, dichotomies, word power, and single meanings, we stressed the direct influence that language can have on our communication (Tubbs, 1967). We went on to observe, however, that when people of different cultures communicate, they may be separated not so much by grammar or by vocabulary as by frame of reference.

Review Questions

1. What is intended by the statement "The word is not the thing"?
2. What is the difference between denotation and connotation?
3. Explain the difference between private and shared meanings.

4. What is the concept of overlapping codes? What is its relevance to intercultural communication?
5. What is the distinction between egocentric and socialized speech?
6. Explain the differences between a restricted code and an elaborated code.
7. Sum up the theory of verbal deprivation and the criticism it has received.
8. What is black English vernacular (BEV)?
9. What is the Whorfian hypothesis?
10. What are two ways in which language affects thought?
11. Describe four imprecise uses of language. Give an example of how each affects communication.
12. Identify two sources of confusion about words or phrases. Give an example of each.
13. What is the influence of viewpoint or frame of reference (as distinguished from grammar and vocabulary) on communication between people of different cultures?

Exercises

1. a. Construct a Semantic Differential consisting of ten bipolar adjectives. Assess the potential marketability of a fictitious product name by asking several classmates to react to two or more names using the Semantic Differential. The sample scale below shows two names for a Christmas wrapping paper:

Holly Filigree

good	X					bad
sharp		X				dull
active			X			passive
pretty		X				ugly

Green Lace

good				X		bad
sharp					X	dull
active			X			passive
pretty			X			ugly

   b. How do the responses on the Semantic Differential reflect the difference between denotation and connotation; private and shared meaning?

2. Construct a two-column list with proper names in one column and stereotypical occupations associated with those names in the second. Randomize the order of names and occupations in each column. Present the lists to several people and ask them to match the names and occupations. A sample list appears below:

Bubbles   Policeman
Killer   Stripper
Nick   Librarian

O'Malley	Mobster
Miss Penwinkle	Boxer
Lance	Actor

   a. To what extent do people agree in their responses? How do the results relate to the statement "The word is not the thing"?
   b. How do the results relate to the three factors that affect stereotype perceptions (see Chapter 4)?
   c. What implications do these results suggest about the relationship between language, stereotyping, and communication effectiveness?
3. Interview two people who are ostensibly very different—a local politician and an artist, for example. Ask each of them to make a list of adjectives describing (a) himself or herself and (b) a member of the other group. Compare the lists to see how differently each group member perceives himself or herself from the way he or she is perceived by the other person. Notice how the perceptual differences are manifested in the words chosen for the descriptions.
4. Prepare an oral persuasive message in two forms. Use the most tactful language possible in one and the most inflammatory terms you can think of in the other. Give the messages to two groups, and try to assess their reactions on an attitude scale. Which message is more effective? If the audiences are similar and your messages alike except for word choice (and assuming the nonverbal cues are similar), any difference in your results should be due to the difference in the language you use.
5. In a chance conversation deliberately assume that individual words have only one meaning, and try to interpret them in a way that the other person does not intend. What are the results?

Suggested Readings

Haney, William V. *Communication and Organizational Behavior.* 3rd ed. Homewood, Ill.: Irwin, 1973. This classic book represents an excellent overview of the field of study referred to as general semantics. Although the book's slant is on the business environment, its principles apply to most everyday situations. The cases that are included make excellent class discussion starters.

Mercer, Jane R. "The Lethal Label." *Psychology Today* (September 1972), 6:44–46, 96, 97. This article is part of an issue investigating "I.Q. Abuse." The series emphasizes the importance of language in intelligence tests and of labeling children on the basis of test scores. The written IQ test is largely oriented toward the white middle class, which causes many minority children to be classed as "retarded" and placed in special-education classes. Mercer's studies, using a cross-section of children and adults in Riverside, California, result in a way to test subjects not only for academic ability but for behavioral ability—how well they get along in everyday situations.

Premack, David. "The Education of S*A*R*A*H." *Psychology Today* (September 1970), 4:54–58. After a brief discussion of the function of language, highlighting its symbolic nature, the article outlines the methods for teaching Sarah, a chimpanzee, to "talk" using different-shaped plastic pieces as "words." Gradually, she learns a vocabulary of about 120 words, and ends up understanding enough to ask questions and give short word tests to her trainers.

Rich, Andrea L. "Language and Interracial Communication," in *Interracial Communication*. New York: Harper & Row, 1974, Chapter 6. Part of a broad survey of the dynamics of interracial communication, this chapter is concerned with racist language as well as with the language codes developed by various countercultures. The author points out that many kinds of countercultures develop such codes, including those of teen-agers, criminals, homosexuals, and members of labor movements. Her examples are timely and vivid.

Smith, Arthur. *Language, Communication, and Rhetoric in Black America*. New York: Harper & Row, 1972. In this collection of articles there are both scholarly and popular discussions. Part I, "Black Language," discusses the communication problems faced by teachers and children that result from overlapping codes.

Chapter 8 The Nonverbal Message

OBJECTIVES

After reading this chapter the student should be able to:
1. Distinguish between sign language, action language, and object language.
2. Identify four kinds of interpersonal distance and give an example of each.
3. Discuss the concept of personal space.
4. Explain the concept of chronemics and give an example of how timing might interfere with intercultural communication.
5. Define the term "kinesics."
6. Specify four unstated rules in our culture about eye contact.
7. Identify three categories of nonverbal courtship behavior and give an example of each.
8. State the relationship between head and body movements in communicating emotion.
9. Describe how a person's choice of physical objects, including clothing, communicates messages to others.
10. Define "paralinguistics" and give examples of paralinguistic cues.
11. Identify four categories of emotion consistently identified by paralinguistic cues.
12. Specify three ways in which nonverbal messages relate to verbal messages.
13. Explain the double bind and describe how it relates to nonverbal and verbal communication.
14. Discuss how verbal and nonverbal messages can be mutually qualifying.

8

In silent films wordless communication reached the perfection of an art form. Take this scene from one of Harry Langdon's movies: "watching a brazen showgirl change her clothes, he sat motionless, back to the camera, and registered the whole lexicon of lost innocence, shock, disapproval and disgust with the back of his neck" (Agee, 1967, p. 1).

Each of the silent comedians had a style all his own. Buster Keaton played every role with an absolutely blank face. Harold Lloyd portrayed a meek soul with glasses; sometimes he looked rather like a schoolboy. Charlie Chaplin was the beloved tramp: everything about him seemed comic and endearing—his shy smile, ill-fitting suit, cane, and funny gait. Without words these actors were able to communicate not only isolated ideas but complete sequences of behavior. We are not speaking here only of comic experience. The Russian film maker Sergei Eisenstein was masterful in his treatment of social and political themes, and even the silent comedians could bring their audiences to tears.

Actors and directors have to be keen observers of nonverbal communication, and mimes, of course, have been students of human expression for hundreds of years. But what about the rest of us? We are not actors. Yet unwittingly we are fairly skilled observers—and performers. Even though we may be unaware of much of it, nonverbal communication is going on all the time.

Jurgen Ruesch, a psychiatrist, and Weldon Kees, a film producer, were two of the first people to devote themselves to a serious study of nonverbal communication in daily experience. They suggest that we express nonverbal messages in one of three languages: sign language, action language, or object language (Ruesch and Kees, 1956).

We are using **sign language** when we deliberately *use gestures to replace words, numbers, or punctuation marks*. Such gestures are among the intentional nonverbal communicative stimuli we spoke of in Chapter 2. The gesture might be as simple as the peace sign or the hitchhiker's signal or as complex as the system of signals baseball players use during a game.

Ruesch and Kees classify as **action language** *all the movements that we do not use exclusively as signals*—walking, running, eating, and so on. In terms of our communication model in Chapter 2, many if not most of these actions would be considered unintentional nonverbal stimuli. For example, if your head droops and your shoulders sag while you walk, your posture expresses your mood. If you slam your fist on a table during a stalemated argument, your action conveys anger and frustration very directly. Action language is the principal means of expressing emotion.

Object language is *the intentional or unintentional display of material things*—art objects, machines, clothing, jewelry, and so on. A social worker who appears in a ghetto neighborhood driving a big car and wearing expensive clothes is obviously using the wrong language if he or she hopes to establish rapport with the residents.

Again and again we find nonverbal communication described in terms of language. Thus we hear that someone "talks" with his hands or that his gesture made a powerful "statement." One writer reminds us that

> We communicate every minute of the day with others and the outside world through "speaking" gestures, peculiarities in gait and dress, a sense of touch while shaking hands, the mannerisms of another person's glance or looks, the condition and texture of his skin, the color of his eyes, his lips, his body build and a multitude of similar bodily characteristics. (Barbara, 1963, p. 167)

Haiman refers to the sit-ins, mass marches, silent vigils, black arm bands, hair styles, and clothing of the 1960s as a form of "body rhetoric" (1969, p. 159). One popularist has written a book called *Body Language*. Anthropologist Edward T. Hall refers to "the silent language of space and time" (1959, p. 15).

There are so many special studies of this sort that we can think of nonverbal communication as made up of many different languages. Regardless of how we classify them, however, these languages have at least one thing in common. They all provide us with cues for interpreting human behavior. In this chapter we are going to speak about nonverbal cues rather than languages, and we shall begin with a closer look at how the word "cue" is used.

One of the broadest dictionary definitions of **cue** is *anything that excites to action; stimulus*. In the theater a cue is "anything said or done, on or behind the stage, that is followed by a specific line or action." If you fail to respond to a cue or you miss the point someone is making, you are said to "miss a cue." You "cue someone in" by giving him news, instructions, or information. A cue is also defined as *a hint or intimation,* and this definition is important to our discussion.

Psychologists often use the word "cue" (or "sign") in place of "signal."

> We ask what "cues" a rat follows in finding his way through a maze, and we seek an answer by depriving him of visual cues, olfactory cues, etc.

This convenient word has spread from the animal to the human laboratory so that we speak of visual cues of distance and of auditory cues of direction, when perhaps the word "clue" would be more in accordance with general usage. (Woodworth and Schlosberg, 1954, pp. 267–268)

This suggestion that "clue" may be a more appropriate word brings us back to the dictionary definition of cue as "a hint or intimation." Through their nonverbal messages people give us many clues, or hints, about their emotions, their intentions, their personalities, and even their social status. In this chapter, we shall speak about several kinds of cues—spatial, temporal, visual, and vocal—and then about the broader issue of how we interpret these cues and what their relationship is to verbal messages. In terms of our model, then, we are speaking about all nonverbal communicative stimuli—both intentional and unintentional.

SPATIAL AND TEMPORAL CUES

Only when we interact with people of other cultures or subcultures do we begin to realize that some of our most cherished ideas about what is appropriate conduct are **norms**, or *rules about behavior;* that is, they are relative, not absolute, values. Indirectly, our culture teaches us to communicate in many ways—through our voices, our gestures, and even our style of dressing. Yet each of us interprets and expresses these conventions somewhat differently. Culture has an even more subtle and pervasive influence on nonverbal communication, however. Each culture continually provides its members with input about how the world is structured. (We saw this with respect to visual perception when we discussed the Müller-Lyer illusion in Chapter 2.) Slowly we develop preconceptions about the world. It is the cues derived from these preconceptions that we take most for granted and that imperceptibly set the limits for our style of communication. Our cues about space and time are among those most significantly influenced by culture. It is not surprising, therefore, that they should also be the source of a great many difficulties in intercultural communication.

Space

If you were to enter a restaurant with only one customer in it, chances are that you would not sit down right next to him or her. Edward Hall explains that though this behavior seems natural to an American, an Arab might have a very different notion of appropriate distance between strangers. Students of nonverbal communication are indebted to Hall for his cross-cultural studies of space. Because of his work we probably know more about this dimension of cultural experience than we do about time, color, and many other factors.

Hall has given the special name of **proxemics** to *the study of space*. Social scientists make use of the Scale of Social Distance, an instrument that uses the term "distance" figuratively, to indicate degree of liking or preference. Hall goes a step further and speaks of measurable distances between people—1½ inches, 1 foot, 3 feet, and so on. In fact, he offers a four-part classification of distances between people. There is **nothing** arbitrary about this classification, as he explains:

> it is in the nature of animals, including man, to exhibit behavior which we call territoriality. In so doing, they use the senses to distinguish between one space or distance and another. The specific distance chosen depends on the transaction; the relationship of the interacting individuals, how they feel, and what they are doing. (Hall, 1969, p. 128)

Human relationships are described in terms of four kinds of distance: intimate, personal, social, and public. Each of the four distance zones is further differentiated by a close phase and a far phase within which different behaviors occur. Let us take a look at these four distances and Hall's findings about what they mean to most North Americans.

Intimate distance.

At **intimate distance,** which is *eighteen inches or less,* the presence of another person "is unmistakable and may at times be overwhelming because of the greatly stepped-up sensory inputs" (Hall, 1969, p. 116). In its close phase (six inches or less) intimate distance lends itself primarily to nonverbal communication. Any subject discussed is usually top secret. The far phase (six to eighteen inches) is often used for discussing confidential matters, with the voice usually kept to a whisper. Such close proximity is considered improper for public places, though dormitories at closing hours seem to be exceptions to the rule. In general, Americans try hard to avoid close contact with one another on buses and other public vehicles.

Hall compares **personal distance,** which is from *1½ to 4 feet,* to "a small protective sphere or bubble that an organism maintains between itself and others" (1969, p. 119). Topics discussed would still be personal. The close phase (1½ to 2½ feet) is still a distance reserved for very close relationships; the far phase (2½ to 4 feet) is a comfortable distance for conversing with friends.

Social distance, ranging from *four to twelve feet,* is described as a psychological distance, "one at which the animal apparently begins to feel anxious when he exceeds its limits. We can think of it as a hidden band that *contains* the group." The close phase (four to seven feet) is suitable for business discussions and conversations at social gatherings. The far phase (seven to twelve feet) is appropriate for meetings in a

Personal distance.

INTERPERSONAL COMMUNICATION

Social distance.

business office. People who are in the room but outside the seven-foot boundary can be ignored without being offended. Those who violate the seven-foot boundary tend to be surprised if we do not acknowledge their presence, unless we are very busy. Humans have extended social distance by means of the walkie-talkie, telephone, radio, and television.

The largest of the zones, **public distance,** denotes *twelve feet or more* of space, and it exists only in human relationships. In fact, the public relationships and manners of Americans and Europeans are considerably different from those of other cultures. At the close phase (twelve to twenty-five feet) a more formal style of language and a louder voice are required. At the far phase (twenty-five feet or more) further accommodations to distance are usually made; experienced public speakers exaggerate body movements, gestures, enunciation, and volume while reducing their rate of speech. Figure 8.1 is a brief summary of how message content and vocal shift vary with distance between communicators.

Within a country as diverse as the United States, various subcultures develop their own proxemic norms. One study (Baxter, 1970) shows sizable differences in the way Anglo-, black, and Mexican-

Public distance.

Americans regulate distance when communicating. Mexicans stand closest to one another, Anglos are intermediate, and blacks are most distant. Age and sex also make differences. Children interact at the closest range and adults at the farthest, with spacing between adolescents intermediate. The range in male-female groups is closest and **in male-male groups farthest, with female-female groups intermediate.**

Hall and Baxter are not saying that we calculate these differences while communicating. On the contrary, our sense of what distance is natural for a given interaction is so deeply ingrained in us by our culture that we automatically make spatial adjustments and interpret spatial cues. Frenchmen, Latin Americans, and Arabs, for example, stand so close to each other that if they exercise their own distance norms while conversing with an American, they arouse hostile or sexual feelings. If you want to test this concept in proxemics, the next time you converse with someone, keep inching toward him or her. See how close you can get before he or she starts backing away.

A somewhat different approach to space has been developed by Robert Sommer. His concern is with **personal space,** *"an area with invisible boundaries surrounding a person's body into which intruders may not come"* (1969, p. 26; italics added). In effect, he says that the

INTERPERSONAL COMMUNICATION

Figure 8.1

Distance	Description of Distance	Vocal Characteristics	Message Content
0–6 inches	Intimate (Close Phase)	Soft Whisper	Top Secret
6–18 inches	Intimate (Far Phase)	Audible Whisper	Very Confidential
1½–2½ feet	Personal (Close Phase)	Soft Voice	Personal Subject Matter
2½–4 feet	Personal (Far Phase)	Slightly Lowered Voice	Personal Subject Matter
4–7 feet	Social (Close Phase)	Full Voice	Non-Personal Information
7–12 feet	Social (Far Phase)	Full Voice with Slight Over Loudness	Public Information for Others to Hear
12–25 feet	Public (Close Phase)	Loud Voice Talking to a Group	Public Information for Others to Hear
25 feet or more	Public (Far Phase)	Loudest Voice	Hailing, Departures

Adapted from Hall, 1959 and Hall, 1966.

concept of personal space can be thought of as a person's portable territory, which each person carries along wherever he or she may go. Sommer is careful to distinguish his use of personal space from Hall's use of the term "territory":

> The most important difference is that personal space is carried around while territory is relatively stationary. The animal or man will usually mark the boundaries of his territory so that they are visible to others, but the boundaries of his personal space are invisible. Personal space has the body at its center, while territory does not. (Sommer, 1969, p. 248)

At least one investigator (Rosenfeld, 1965) has suggested that personality variables influence the size of one's personal space. He found that people who were rated high in their need for affiliation (see Chapter 3) sat an average of fifty-seven inches away from a target person, whereas those who were low in their need for affiliation sat approximately ninety-four inches away. In his study of prison inmates who had committed violent crimes, Kinzel (1969) observed that these men had a personal space, or "body buffer zone," twice as large as that of nonviolent prisoners. Members of the violent group felt threatened when a person came close to them, as if the person were an intruder who was "looming up" or "rushing in" at them.

Other research on personal space focuses on the relationship between spatial arrangements (architectural elements, interior design, seating, and so on) and human feelings and interaction. The college campus furnishes numerous examples. For instance, it is estimated that college students begin to identify a particular seat in the classroom as "their chair" by as early as the second class period. Although you probably would not ask another student to give up what you considered to be your chair if you arrived a little later and he or she was sitting in it, you might feel some annoyance at having to move to another one. This feeling is somewhat reminiscent of the belief that there is a home court advantage for basketball teams, so that a team traditionally plays better on its home court than it does at games elsewhere.

Sommer and his associates have been particularly interested in the study halls of college libraries, where students have a tendency to protect their privacy by sitting as far away from each other as possible. One way of communicating this need is by occupying a corner position. Or a student can sprawl out, resting his legs on the chair next to him. If he gets up from the table, he may "reserve" his place by spreading out his books and papers or leaving a jacket draped over the chair he was sitting in (Sommer, 1969, pp. 46–47). How far one goes in defending one's personal space will depend, of course, on both personality and communication style. If you sit too close to me in the library, I may get up and move. But if our roles were reversed, it's possible that you might glare at me and even spread out your notebooks and papers so that they take up a good part of the table.

Time

When we study *how human beings communicate through their use of time* we are concerned with **chronemics**. For example, have you ever written a letter to a friend only to wait what seemed to be an endless time for a reply? What inferences did you make about the strength of the friendship? Or have you ever received a phone call at three in the morning? You probably thought that it was a very important call, a wrong number, or a prank. How far in advance can a first date be arranged? Must it be several days ahead, or can one call thirty minutes before? In each of these cases, timing leads to certain expectations on the part of the people involved, and these expectations influence the face-to-face communication that subsequently occurs. A late entrance that violates standards of courtesy can have a disastrous effect, not just a dramatic one. Much of the verbal communication that ensues may have to be spent explaining away the nonverbal message that has already been conveyed.

Conceptions of what is "late" or "early" vary from culture to culture. Americans are "busy" people. We use our watches throughout the day. We like schedules and agendas. We value doing things "on time." To us five years might be a long period. To Asians a long time is more like a thousand years. (Think what differences in point of view toward the length of war must be!) It is sometimes disarming to see ourselves as other see us. Here is a Brazilian reaction to "Anglo-American" time:

> The rigid Anglo-Saxon attitude—"Time is money"—with an almost mystical cult of minutes and seconds on account of their practical, commercial value, is in sharp contrast to the Latin American attitude, a sort of "more-or-less" (*"mais ou menos"*) attitude. It is easy to understand why a Nordic was so shocked in Spain to know that a Spanish or Latin American guest in a hotel asked the desk to call him next morning not exactly at ten or ten-fifteen, as an Anglo-Saxon or an Anglo-American would have asked, but at ten or eleven. (Freyre, 1963, p. 264)

Hall relates an amusing anecdote about a friend of Spanish extraction whose business affairs were managed "Latino" style:

> This meant that up to fifteen people were in his office at one time. Business which might have been finished in a quarter of an hour sometimes took a whole day. He realized, of course, that the Anglo-Americans were disturbed by this and used to make some allowance for them, a dispensation which meant that they spent only an hour or so in his office when they planned on a few minutes. . . . If my friend had adhered to the American system he would have destroyed a vital part of his prosperity. People who came to do business with him also came to find out things and to visit each other. (Hall, 1959, pp. 19–20)

It's been pointed out that for the American businessman discussion is simply "a means to an end: the deal" (Hall and Whyte, in Smith, 1966, p. 568). Moreover, it's a sign of good faith to agree on major issues, assuming that details will be worked out later on. But like the Latin American, the Greek businessperson engages in what seems to us prolonged discussion and is excessively preoccupied with details. For the Greek these concerns signify good will (Hall and Whyte, in Smith, 1966, p. 568).

Our assumptions about appropriate timing vary so much from culture to culture that they can make for all sorts of misunderstandings. The story is told of an Indian man who invited an American and his family to come to his home. "Come anytime," the Indian urged. After waiting several weeks, the Indian extended the invitation once more. But despite the American's assurance that he would like to come, he never did. He was certain that if the Indian really expected him to visit, he would state a time. The Indian, on the other hand, assumed that the American did not wish to pay him a visit. By the standards of his own culture, the Indian had indeed extended the invitation—for in India the polite host allows the guest to determine the time of the visit (Hall and Whyte, in Smith, 1966).

One French sociologist (Gurvitch, 1964, p. 14) believes that each country has its own time or tempo, and his argument seems well taken. If we could just remember that "Time in France is not identical with time in Norway nor with time in Brazil" (Gurvitch, 1964, p. 14), our political, economic, and social relationships with other countries would improve rapidly. Even for personal effectiveness with people of our own culture, we have to be more aware of time as an aspect of communication.

VISUAL CUES

At the end of the nineteenth century, a German horse named Hans was discovered that ostensibly knew how to add. If you asked him to add two and six, for example, he pawed the ground eight times. The curious thing was that Hans could do sums only in the presence of human beings. His mysterious talent was later explained rather simply: when he unwittingly reached the answer, he saw his audience relax, and he stopped pawing.

The people who came to see Hans perform would have been shocked to learn that they were, by their body movements, transmitting the correct answers visually. Yet they were probably leaning forward eagerly to take in every aspect of the spectacle before them, for we all know how much we gain by seeing a performer, a lecturer, or any person we are speaking to. In fact, one study (Steinzor, 1950) found that members of discussion groups interacted more frequently when seated facing each other rather than side by side. In other words, the greater the visibility, the greater the potential for communicating. And as we saw in Chapter 2, the greater the number of channels the sender uses, the more information is received.

Visual cues add to the information transmitted through other channels, and at times stand alone. Specific motions of the head, for example, give the equivalents of certain brief verbal messages such as "Yes" and "No," and these movements may vary from culture to culture. Even head orientation, the direction in which we turn our heads, communicates something. Defining head orientation as the percentage of time two people direct their faces toward each other, Mehrabian (1967) found that a person who gives more head orientation to the person he or she speaks with conveys to the second person a more positive feeling. Reece and Whitman support this conclusion in their study of how "warmth" and "coldness" are conveyed during an interview: "Leaning toward the subject, smiling, and looking directly at him enabled the subject to judge the experimenter as warm. Conversely, looking away from the subject, leaning away from him, not smiling, and intermittently drumming the fingers on the table impressed the subject as coldness" (1962, p. 250).

Notice that the nonverbal cues described include facial expression, eye contact, and body movements. We shall be discussing each of these sources of information. We ask you to bear in mind, however, that when you look at another person, you get a total impression. We separate various cues here only to examine the kind of information that each conveys.

A pioneering figure in research on nonverbal communication, Ray Birdwhistell believes that the entire communication context must be observed in all its complexity and that it is only productive to isolate individual variables if they can be integrated into "the general communicative stream, including verbal behavior" (Weitz, 1974, p. 129). It was Birdwhistell (1952) who introduced the term **"kinesics"** to refer to *the study of body movements in communication*. "Body movements" is used in a broad sense and refers also to movements of the head and face. Birdwhistell has estimated that there are over 700,000 possible physical signs that can be transmitted via body movement.

Facial Expression

One of the things that made Buster Keaton's silent films so hilarious was his facial expression—or rather his lack of expression. He was the original deadpan. Film critic James Agee describes his style this way:

> He used this great, sad, motionless face to suggest various related things: a one-track mind near the track's end of pure insanity; mulish imperturbability under the wildest of circumstances; how dead a human being can get and still be alive. . . . Everything that he was and did bore out this rigid face and played laughs against it. When he moved his eyes, it was like seeing them move in a statue. (Agee, 1967, p. 13)

Keaton must have had superb control over his facial muscles. Most of us couldn't manage a poker face for very long. In fact, the human face is so mobile that it can effortlessly register boredom, surprise, affection, and disapproval one after another in a few seconds. This brief scene from *War and Peace,* for example, probably takes place in less than one minute:

> On the way to his sister's room, in the gallery that united one house to the other, Prince Andrey encountered Mademoiselle Bourienne smiling sweetly. It was the third time that day that with an innocent and enthusiastic smile she had thrown herself in his way in secluded passages.
> "Ah, I thought you were in your room," she said, for some reason blushing and casting down her eyes. Prince Andrey looked sternly at her. A sudden look of wrathful exasperation came into his face. He said

nothing to her, but stared at her forehead and her hair, without looking at her eyes, with such contempt that the Frenchwoman crimsoned and went away without a word. (Tolstoy, n.d., p. 93)

With the exception of one sentence, almost all the communication that takes place is conveyed by means of facial cues. Yet the episode seems realistic because even in less dramatic encounters, we constantly read expressions from people's faces. In fact, facial cues are the single most important source of nonverbal communication. Comments such as "If looks could kill" and "It was all over her face" bear witness to the significance we give to facial expression.

It has been learned that we tend to describe faces in terms of a general evaluative dimension (good or bad, beautiful or ugly, kind or cruel, and so on) and a dynamism dimension (active or passive, inert or mobile, interesting or boring) (Williams and Tolch, 1965). And apparently some people are much more adept than others at interpreting facial cues.

So we like a face or we don't; we think it is animated or relatively inert. These are general impressions. But what do we see that makes us judge someone to be sad or happy or frightened or angry? Isolating which facial cues specify particular emotions is more difficult than simply judging a face. In one attempt (Harrison, in Campbell and Hepler, 1965) to decipher a facial code, subjects were shown simple illustrations (pictomorphs) such as those in Figure 8.2. A statistical analysis of the results led to the conclusions that half-raised eyebrows indicate worry; a single raised eyebrow, skepticism; half-closed eyes, boredom; closed eyes, sleep; an upcurved mouth, happiness; and a downcurved mouth, unhappiness. We are reminded of the smile button, which became so popular not long ago; its brief suggestion of a face—pinpoints for eyes and a single upcurved line for the mouth—was enough to suggest to most people a happy face.

The study of facial cues as expressions of specific emotions has a long history. One of the most eminent scientists to examine this subject was Charles Darwin. Darwin set himself an even larger task: he tried to find out whether the facial behaviors associated with particular emotions are universal. One method he used was to ask subjects to identify specific emotions from still photographs of people's faces. In *The Expression of the Emotions in Man and Animals,* published in 1872, Darwin presented some of his conclusions and speculations about

Figure 8.2

expressive behavior. He felt that most of man's expressive actions, like those of other animals, are instinctive, not learned behaviors:

> So little has learning or imitation to do with several of them that they are from the earliest days and throughout life quite beyond our control; for instance, the relaxation of the arteries of the skin in blushing, and the increased action of the heart in anger. We may see children, only two or three years old, and even those born blind, blushing from shame. (Darwin, in Loewenberg 1959, p. 398)

Darwin's argument about the facial expressions of blind children is given further support by several studies done more than half a century after his book was published. The facial behaviors of blind and sighted children seem to have many similarities. More recently Ekman and Friesen (1971) asked members of a preliterate New Guinea culture to judge emotions from the facial expressions of Westerners. The subjects had had virtually no exposure to Western culture either through direct experience or through literature. Yet they made the same identifications that Westerners made, with one exception: they were not able to differentiate between fear and surprise. Ekman and Friesen conclude that, at least in some respects, expressive facial behavior is constant across cultures. They acknowledge that cultural differences exist, but they argue that the differences are reflected "in the circumstances which elicit an emotion, in the action consequences of an emotion and in the display rules which govern the management of facial behavior in particular social settings" (Ekman and Friesen, 1971, p. 129).

Other experts on nonverbal communication, including Ray Birdwhistell and Weston La Barre, argue against the possibility of universal facial cues. The issue is far from settled. Experimental evidence is scarce and somewhat contradictory. Several researchers report negative results with techniques such as still photographs and illustrations that reveal only the face. Generally, accuracy in identifying emotion seems to increase with the number of cues one sees.

Eye Contact

Proper street behavior among Americans permits passers-by to look at each other until they are about eight feet apart. At this point both parties cast their eyes downward so that they will not appear to be staring. Goffman refers to this phenomenon as a "dimming of our lights" (1963, p. 84). The many other rules implicit in our culture about looking at others are a tacit admission that eye contact is perhaps the single most important facial cue we use in communicating. The *study of the role of eye contact in communication* is called **oculesics**.

Although the face has been called "the major nonverbal liar"

(Ekman and Friesen, 1969), cues given in eye contact seem to reveal a good deal about personality. Apparently, we have greater control of the muscles in the lower part of our face than we do of the muscles around our eyes. (There are exceptions, of course. High Machs are able to sustain good eye contact even when telling lies.) It has even been suggested that "the lower face may follow culturally transmitted display rules while the eyes may reveal the spontaneous or naked response" (Libby and Yaklevich, 1973, p. 203).

One researcher estimates that in group communication we spend 30 to 60 percent of the time in eye contact with others (10 to 30 percent of the looks last only about a second). He sums up several of the unstated rules about eye contact:

> a. A looker may invite interaction by staring at another person who is on the other side of a room. The target's studied return of the gaze is generally interpreted as acceptance of the invitation, while averting the eyes is a rejection of the looker's request.
> b. There is more mutual eye contact between friends than others, and a looker's frank gaze is widely interpreted as positive regard.
> c. Persons who seek eye contact while speaking are regarded not only as exceptionally well-disposed by their target, but also as more believable and earnest.
> d. If the usual short, intermittent gazes during conversation are replaced by gazes of longer duration, the target interprets this as meaning that the task is less important than the personal relation between the two persons. (Argyle, 1967, pp. 105–116).

Argyle's second point is corroborated by other researchers: frequent eye contact does seem to be a sign of affection or interest. And personality will affect the degree of eye contact. For example, people who are high in their need for nurturance (the desire to give help and comfort) maintain eye contact to a much greater degree than do people who are rated low on this need (Libby and Yaklevich, 1973). Even in the public communication context, the frequency of eye contact will affect the message sender. When an audience gives negative feedback (including poor eye contact), the speaker tends to lose fluency and to do poorly in presenting his or her message (Blubaugh, 1969). It has also been discovered that audiences prefer speakers who give good eye contact (Cobin, 1962).

Why is eye contact so rewarding to others? Perhaps it is because the eyes are considered such a valuable source of information. Hess (1965) found that Chinese jade dealers watch the eyes of their prospective customers for interest in a particular stone because the pupils enlarge with increased interest; similarly, magicians are able to tell what card a person is thinking about by studying his or her eyes. Hess' studies confirm that pupil size is indeed a sensitive index of interest.

There are other popular beliefs about what can be learned from watching someone's eyes. For example, two people who exchange knowing glances at a party seem able to communicate without words. Being able to look another person in the eye traditionally implies that you are being truthful and that your intentions are not to be questioned. Conversely, it is said that the person who averts his or her eyes is hiding something. But this is not always the case. According to a study of patterns of nonverbal communication among black Americans, many black people avoid eye contact (especially with people who are in authority) because they have been taught since childhood that it is disrespectful to look other people straight in the eyes. Thus, while a person from another culture may interpret this avoidance of eye contact as a sign of unreliability or even dishonesty, the black person may be communicating a feeling that his is a subordinate role (Johnson, in Samovar and Porter, 1972, p. 184).

A very different feeling is communicated by black Americans through what is called "rolling the eyes," which is a nonverbal way of demonstrating hostility and impudence to a person in a role of authority:

> The main message is hostility. . . . First, the eyes are moved from one side of the eye-socket to the other, in a low arc (usually . . . preceded by a stare at the other person, but not an eye-to-eye stare). The lids of the eyes are slightly lowered when the eye balls are moved in the low arc. The eye balls always move *away* from the other person. The movement is very quick, and it is often unnoticed by the other person, particularly if the other person is not Black. (Johnson, in Samovar and Porter, 1972, p. 183)

Apparently, this is a nonverbal message for which black children tend to be punished by black teachers, but it is a message that often goes unnoticed if the teacher is white.

Body Movements

If during a party you were asked to record and classify all the body movements of two people in conversation during a five-minute period, you would probably think this an impossible task. Nothing short of a film could capture the rapid, often subtle changes of the body even during so brief a time. Much of what we know about kinesics has come to us indirectly, from such disciplines as anthropology, psychiatry, and psychotherapy.

The work of Scheflen (1965) is a case in point. He noticed that patterns of nonverbal flirting, or "quasi-courtship," emerged during psychotherapy. After studying films of a great many therapy sessions, he was able to classify some of the typical behaviors he observed. Signs of **courtship readiness** included preening hair, pulling at stockings, adjusting the tie, and so on. **Positioning** was another source of cues about interpersonal attraction. For example, two people might face each other and lean forward eagerly. Sometimes they sat with the upper half of their torsos turned in an open position so that a third person might enter the conversation but with their legs forming a circle and thus excluding the intruder. A third category, **actions of appeal,** included flirtatious glances and head cocking. Women signaled sexual invitation by crossing the legs, exposing the thigh, exhibiting the palm of the hand, and protruding the breast. Here is an example of these behaviors in context:

> At the beginning of the sequence . . . the therapist . . . turns to watch an attractive research technician walk across the room. The patient [female] begins to preen. . . . The therapist turns back to the patient and also preens, but he then disclaims courtship by an ostentatious look of boredom and a yawn. . . . Immediately afterward, the patient tells him she is interested in an attractive male aide. (Scheflen, 1965, p. 252)

It seems clear that "courtship" and "flirting" occur between males and females primarily. As we point out on p. 204, however, homosexuals act in similar ways.

Courtship behaviors occur in many other settings, such as business conferences, neighborhood parties, and other social gatherings. If we omit people's identities in the sequence just described, the scene could easily have taken place during a university seminar, an interview, or a committee meeting. Scheflen's observation that courtship behaviors tend to occur most often when a person feels he or she is not receiving enough attention can probably be extended to many interpersonal relationships.

An interesting question raised by Ekman (1965) is whether the cues given by body movements are different from those given by head and facial movements. His findings suggest that cues from the head and face suggest what emotion is being experienced whereas the body gives off cues about how intense that emotion is. The hands, however, can give us the same information we receive from the head and face.

Hand Gestures

Anthropologists distinguish humankind from other animals by their use of language and also by their superior manual dexterity. Flexible hands have enabled human beings to use tools and to draw on a wide range of gestures in communicating. It is not surprising, therefore, that as a mode of nonverbal communication, hand gestures rank second in importance only to facial cues.

Although it is said that some people "talk" with their hands, it is not only broad, expansive gestures that communicate mood. Less animated people often communicate inadvertently by means of their hands. The rather reserved husband of a psychotherapist we know repeatedly drums his fingers on a table or chair whenever his wife speaks about her practice. This behavior is the only sign of his impatience with her deep involvement in her profession.

INTERPERSONAL COMMUNICATION

GRIN AND BEAR IT by Lichty & Wagner

"Remember, one finger is the signal for a fast ball, two fingers for a curve, and three fingers means I think you're cute."

In his analysis of foot, head, and hand movements of mental patients under treatment in hospitals, Ekman (1965) was able to distinguish more than 100 different hand acts. Coding them along with the other body movements, he discovered that from the time of the patient's admission to his or her discharge, hand movements corresponded with various stages of treatment.

Hand gestures sometimes substitute for verbal communication. For example, solely by means of hands, one person can give another instruction on how to park a car. Deaf-mutes use a system of hand signals so comprehensive that it literally replaces spoken language. The signals themselves are arbitrary. It seems, for example, that many of our hand movements are culturally determined. Thus the same gesture can convey different things to members of different cultures. La Barre offers some interesting examples:

> Placing to the tip of the nose the projecting knuckle of the right forefinger bent at the second joint was among the Maori of New Zealand a

sign of friendship and often of protection; but in eighteenth-century England the placing of the same forefinger to the right side of the nose expressed dubiousness about the intelligence and sanity of a speaker—much as does the twentieth-century clockwise motion of the forefinger above the right hemisphere of the head. (La Barre, in Bennis et al., 1968, p. 204)

In *Bitter Lemons,* a book about the years he spent living in Cyprus, Lawrence Durrell gives us a more contemporary example. Durrell, an Englishman, is trying to persuade Mr. Sabri, a Turkish real estate agent with a reputation for cunning, to find him a cheap village house. Durrell announces that he has come to Sabri because of Sabri's reputation for being a rogue. In this part of the world, says Durrell, being a rogue can mean only one thing: being more clever than other people:

> I accompanied this with the appropriate gesture—for cleverness in the hand-language is indicated by placing the forefinger of the right hand slowly and portentously upon the temple: tapping slightly, as one might tap a breakfast egg. (Incidentally, one has to be careful, as if one turns the finger in the manner of turning a bolt in a thread, the significance is quite different: it means to be 'soft in the head' or to 'have a screw loose'.) I tapped my skull softly. (Durrell, 1957, p. 49)

Such differences in meaning are a potential source of communication difficulty. To an American, for example, making a circle with one's thumb and forefinger and extending the other fingers means "okay," but to a Brazilian it is an obscene sign of contempt. Apparently, American visitors and even statesmen unwittingly offend their Brazilian hosts with this gesture.

In addition to what can be learned from observing hand gestures, the cues we receive from physical contact are especially revealing. The term **haptics** refers to *the study of how we use touch to communicate.* In our culture we often shake hands upon meeting, and a handshake can set the tone for the exchange that follows. A limp handshake evokes negative feelings in most Americans; we interpret it as a lack of interest or vitality. A moist hand is often considered a sign of anxiety, especially if the handshake precedes a potentially stressful situation such as an interview. Hands, it seems, suggest a great deal more than many of us would care to reveal.

At times, however, our interpretation of how other people communicate with their hands interferes with our ability to perceive accurately. For example, hand holding between men is quite rare in the United States, but this is not the case in parts of Africa, in some Arab states, and in Southeast Asia. Hand holding in these areas is strictly a sign of friendship. Apparently, these differences created some problems during the Vietnam War. American G.I.s did not feel confident about their allies after seeing them holding hands off the battlefield (McCroskey, 1972, p. 117).

INTERPERSONAL COMMUNICATION

Physical Appearance and the Use of Objects

Clothes may not make the person, but dress, grooming, and general physical appearance are often the basis of first and relatively long-lasting impressions. As we saw in Chapter 4, even glasses affect the way the wearer is perceived by others. When Ruesch and Kees speak about object language, they include "the human body and whatever clothes or covers it" (1956, p. 189).

Uniforms tell us a great deal about rank and status; many people believe that dress and grooming do too. For example, Lefkowitz, Blake, and Mouton (1955) found that people dressed in high-status clothes were more influential in getting others to jaywalk than those who wore low-status clothes. Freedman's study of beards led him to the conclusion that beards make men more appealing to women and give them "more status in the eyes of other men"; he also observed that beards "may increase the social distance between two men" (1969, p. 38).

Sometimes people deliberately attempt to increase social distance. In colonial Brazil people of rank used a parasol to indicate their social

Dress is the basis for first and long-lasting impressions.

status as well as to protect themselves from the sun; their long nails were another sign of superior social standing. Even today we sometimes dress to impress others, to be more like them, or—when we dress counter to prevailing norms—to express rejection of their values.

In our country great emphasis is placed on democratic values. As we saw in Chapter 5, people tend to dislike those who differ from themselves, and elegant, expensive-looking clothes can be a barrier to communication. Politicians, as a rule, are aware of this phenomenon, for on campaign tours they often adopt signs of local dress (ten-gallon hats in Texas, for example) in an effort to be more appealing to voters. Even when worn casually, smart clothes are noticed by others. Novelist F. Scott Fitzgerald once took a supervisory position at the Northern Pacific car barn. Told to wear old clothes on the job, he turned up wearing a blue cap, a polo shirt, a sweatshirt, and—perhaps most inappropriate—dirty white flannels. The men who worked for him must have been put off by the way he dressed, because Fitzgerald complained about not being able to converse with them. Conditions improved when he came to work in overalls (Mizener, 1949, p. 94).

The study of how we select and make use of physical objects in our nonverbal communication is referred to as **objectics.** Objectics is concerned with every kind of physical object from the clothing we wear to the bumper stickers we choose for our cars. For example, what is implied about drivers A, B, and C by the bumper stickers seen on their trucks?

Driver A | I FOOL AROUND |

Driver B | AMERICA. LOVE IT OR LEAVE IT. |

Driver C | CHRIST IS THE ANSWER. |

In this case, of course, the physical object has a verbal message. But objectics is especially concerned with the exclusively nonverbal message. We communicate about ourselves by our choice of car, home, furniture, magazines, and many other things. Even the way in which we hold and light a cigarette, cigar, or pipe transmits cues about us. The woman who smokes little cigars or the man who carries a shoulder bag are seen by some as violating their role expectations. Goldhaber (1974) found that nonverbal communication plays a major role in the "gay" world. His description of the interaction between male homosexuals illustrates the complex mix of nonverbal cues involved.

> Most street interactions take place between two people on foot. . . . One of the more important nonverbal cues is the street or neighborhood you are in. Coupled with the time of day, this is a major indicator of your

INTERPERSONAL COMMUNICATION

204

interest. Eye behavior (lengthy stare, return glances, looking at other men, looking at the crotch area, etc.) along with the clothing you are wearing are other key street behaviors. Particular clothing depends upon the neighborhood and your own personal desires, but common street cruising garb in many cities includes tight-fitting blue jeans, boots or sandals, denim or leather jackets or clothing articles. After initial decisions are made about attraction and suitability of mate, a ritual usually follows involving a gambit of slow-downs, lingers, stops, glances into store windows, crossing streets, reversing directions, etc., until physical space is diminished sufficient to allow for ritualistic verbal interactions focusing on cigarettes, matches, residences, or the old stand-by, the weather. (Goldhaber, 1974, p. 17)

In plush athletic clubs, the shower room is an active place for meeting:

The towel, the only item of clothing worn in the baths, can be cleverly used to display parts of the body or emphasize others, or in some cases, be totally removed and draped around the shoulders. Many people watch closely for the message in the towel. (Goldhaber, 1974, p. 19)

Homosexuals also communicate their interest in each other by displaying keys on a ring outside of their pants. This practice sometimes creates difficulties for the uninitiated, as we see in this letter to the editor of *Time* magazine:

My husband has to carry a number of keys because of his work. Because of worn-out pockets, sore legs from keys digging into them and unsightly bulges, he decided to carry his keys on a hook on his belt. Now we find out this is a homosexual signal. Needless to say, he will go back to worn-out pockets, sore legs and unsightly bulges.

Mrs. Gordon Burke
San Jose, Calif. (*Time*, 1976)

Whether we intend to communicate or not, the way we choose and display physical objects is taken by others as a source of information about us. It should go without saying that such information is not always accurate.

VOCAL CUES

"I hate you." Imagine these words being said to show anger or in a much different way to sound seductive. The simple sentence "I'm glad to meet you" can sound cold and insincere despite its verbal message. We make the distinction here between the verbal and the vocal message, between what is said and how it is said. Mehrabian puts it well when he explains vocal information as "what is lost when speech is written down" (1968, p. 53).

To give the study of vocal phenomena a special name, anthropologist George L. Trager has coined the term "paralinguistics." *"Para"* is Greek for beside, near, or beyond; hence **paralinguistics,** or **paralanguage,** refers to *something beyond or in addition to language itself.* According to Trager (1958) paralanguage has two principal components: *voice qualities,* such as pitch, range, resonance, lip control, and articulation control; and *vocalizations,* or noises without linguistic structure, such as crying, laughing, and grunting. Our primary concern will be with voice qualities, but we shall touch on vocalizations in our discussion of fluency later in this section.

Vocal cues, as we shall see, differentiate emotions and also influence our judgments about personality and social standing. Yet though we are self-conscious about the visual impressions we make on others, we pay little attention to our vocal impressions. There is a good reason for this. If someone is staring at your face, you can look into a mirror and find out what he or she is staring at. And you probably look into a mirror at least once a day. On the other hand, you never hear your voice as others hear it. The first time you listen to a tape recording of yourself, you are likely to be shocked or disappointed; you may not even recognize your own voice.

Unlike most of us, actors, singers, public speakers, and others who have had voice training are keenly aware of how they sound. For example, Katharine Hepburn sued the makers of Vita Herring products for $4 million because a character named Harriet allegedly imitated her voice in a series of their radio commercials. Miss Hepburn charged that Harriet's voice sounded like her own, which she described as "distinctive with a unique, characteristic quality of sound, style, delivery, pitch, inflection and accent" (*The New York Times,* 1971, p. 39).

In truth, every human voice is distinctive because it is a unique combination of qualities. After discussing some of the information provided by vocal cues, we shall look briefly at four significant voice qualities and their effects on communication. Keep in mind, however, that when you speak, all these voice qualities as well as several others are interacting simultaneously.

The Information in Vocal Cues

Intuitively we feel that we can make some judgments from a person's voice about what he or she is communicating. Perhaps you have been in an argument during which someone said, "Don't answer me in that tone of voice!" At a point like this, tempers really begin to escalate, for an objection to someone's tone of voice is based on inferences about his or her feelings. Vocal cues are the sources of several kinds of inference, and those that we know most about have to do with emotion.

In contrast to the conflicting evidence about facial cues and specific emotions, studies all seem to support the notion that several distinct emotions can be accurately identified solely on the basis of vocal cues. Several different emotions can be distinguished just from hearing people recite the letters of the alphabet (Davitz and Davitz, 1959a). One study (Davitz and Davitz, 1959b) using the alphabet-recital technique shows, however, that the more similar the emotions are to each other (admiration and affection, for example), the greater the difficulty in identifying them.

Much of the research on vocal characteristics and emotions parallels the studies of facial expressions; instead of photographs or illustrations, tape recordings are used. A popular instrument for isolating vocal cues from verbal messages is an electronic filter. The filter eliminates the higher frequencies of recorded speech so that words are unintelligible but most vocal qualities can still be heard. Using this method Mehrabian (1968) found that people are easily able to judge the degree of liking communicated vocally. One team of researchers (Soskin and Kauffman, 1961) used a comparable filtering process for several male voice samples. They then played a tape recording of the samples for forty-nine inexperienced judges and asked them what emotions they thought each voice conveyed. Four categories of emotion were consistently and reliably identified: positive feeling, dislike, sadness, and apprehension or fear. The results of this research confirm "the generally held view that voice sounds alone independent of semantic components of vocal messages carry important clues to the emotional state of a speaker" (Soskin and Kauffman, 1961, p. 78).

Other emotions can also be determined solely from vocal cues. Starkweather (1956) found, for example, that people could reliably detect aggressiveness from a tape recording of a speaker, though not from a written transcript of the speaker's message. In a later study Starkweather (1961) showed that we can also judge intensity of emotion from vocal characteristics.

Vocal cues are sometimes the basis for inferences about personality traits. For example, it has been found that speakers who increase the loudness, pitch, timbre, and rate of their speech are thought to be more active and dynamic (Davitz and Davitz, 1961). And those who use more intonation, higher speech rates, more volume, and greater fluency in their speech than others have been judged more persuasive (Mehrabian and Williams, 1969).

Despite wide agreement about certain relationships between voice qualities and personality traits, no conclusive evidence supports such inferences. These judgments seem to derive from vocal stereotypes.

Even if our beliefs have no basis in fact, however, they have striking effects on our response to others, for we act on what we believe to be true. Thus when the talkies appeared several stars of the silent films were ruined because the public expected their voices to sound consistent with their screen personalities. The great lover with the high-pitched voice was too great a disappointment.

In discussing how the voice can be used to convey social status, Goffman quotes from a nineteenth-century book of etiquette. The subject—how to speak to one's servants:

> Issue your commands with gravity and gentleness, and in a reserved manner. Let your voice be composed, but avoid a tone of familiarity or sympathy with them. It is better in addressing them to use a higher key of voice, and not to suffer it to fall at the end of a sentence. The best-bred man whom we ever had the pleasure of meeting always employed, in addressing servants, such forms of speech as these—"I'll thank you for so and so,"—"Such a thing if you please."—with a gentle tone, but very elevated key. The perfection of manner, in this particular, is to indicate by your language, that the performance is a favour, and by your tone that it is a matter of course. (Anonymous, cited in Goffman, 1967, p. 62)

Quaint perhaps, but accurate in its appraisal of the impact of vocal characteristics—and not totally outdated.

A study by Harms (1961) suggests that status cues in speech are probably based on a combination of "word choice, pronunciation, grammatical structure, voice quality, articulation, and several other observable features." An interesting sidelight of Harms' research is that most subjects apparently made judgments about status (and credibility) after listening to the recorded samples for only ten to fifteen seconds, even though the samples were from forty to sixty seconds long. Apparently, we make such inferences with a high degree of accuracy.

Volume

One precondition of effective verbal communication is adequate volume. The person who speaks so low that he or she can barely be heard is a burden to others; they rapidly become too tired or too embarrassed to ask this person to repeat his or her last remark. In such a case, it is the message sender who becomes a source of interference for the receiver. Of course, adequate volume varies from situation to situation.

Aside from circumstantial differences in speech volume, appropriate sound level varies considerably from culture to culture. In describing voice level at social distance, Hall observes that "in overall loudness, the American voice . . . is below that of the Arab, the Spaniard, the South Asian Indian, and the Russian, and somewhat above that of the English upper class, the Southeast Asian, and the Japanese" (1969, p. 121).

Human sensitivity to unpleasant levels of sound is reflected in the present concern with noise pollution. But the noises of jet aircraft are not the only disturbing sounds. The person who speaks too loudly often offends others. In fact, most people link volume to certain personality traits; thus it is commonly thought that an aggressive person speaks in a louder voice than one who is reserved and shy. Volume, however, is not necessarily a function of personality. A person's models as a child can influence his or her volume level somewhat apart from his or her personality.

The best check on volume is the feedback from the receiver. If you are not getting through or if you are coming on too strong, then you should adjust your voice accordingly.

Rate and Fluency

Your rate of speech is *the number of words you utter within a specified time.* The unit most often used is one minute, and the average speaking rate is about 125 to 150 words per minute.

Although research on rates of speech has been limited, we do know that rates are highly stable for individuals. For this reason a faster rate (as well as shorter comments and more frequent pauses) seems to be linked to fear or anger and a slower rate to grief or depression (Barnlund, 1968, p. 529). Some people are able to control their rate of speaking despite their emotions, but the strain of maintaining this control is often expressed in other vocal or facial cues.

There is no optimum speaking rate. One speed may be appropriate for a comedian addressing an audience; another is needed for talking to a foreign student, a translator, or a secretary taking dictation. Speaking quickly when explaining technical material to those unfamiliar with the subject can completely undermine a verbal message. Think of the instructor who lectures so rapidly that the students become paralyzed. They do not have time to follow what is being explained or to take notes so that they can study after class. No matter how high the caliber of the teaching, students may think of this instructor in very negative terms. If the same lecture were given to a group of graduate students, they might have no objection to the rapid speaking rate.

There are, of course, rates of speech that are too fast or slow for the majority of listeners. Take the machine-gun delivery of certain people. These individuals tend to speak so rapidly that they run the risk of being unintelligible; at the very least, they may make others feel tense. At the opposite extreme are people who speak so slowly that their listeners become bored or impatient. When you hear people like this drone on and on, you almost want to finish their sentences for them.

Thus rate of speech can have a definite effect on people's responses to a communicator. And like many other vocal qualities, rate of speech is most effective when it is adapted to the verbal content of the message and to the specific receiver.

The **fluency,** or *continuity,* of our speech is closely related to rate, and pauses, of course, affect fluency. Pauses are usually described in terms of three dimensions: length (from milliseconds to minutes), filled (vocalized) or unfilled (silent) time, and location (at the end of a thought or within the context of an idea, for example). A person who pauses continually, whose speech is full of vocalizations such as "um," "er," and "ah," may destroy his or her effectiveness as a communicator. Let us take an extreme case. If during a press conference the president pauses frequently in responding to a controversial question, we are not inclined to give credence to his answer. Instead we think he is stalling for time or he is lying or he doesn't know.

Pauses that are frequent, long, and vocalized and that come in the middle of an idea are usually distressing and serve to undermine the sender's purpose. When used selectively for emphasis and variation, pauses often enhance the verbal message—particularly if they are infrequent, short, and unfilled and are used at the end of an idea.

Pitch

When, in *My Fair Lady,* Professor Higgins speaks with distaste about someone's "large Wagnerian mother with a voice that shatters a glass" (Lerner and Loewe, 1956), he is referring to **pitch**—*the frequency level (high or low) of the voice.* Each person has a pitch range determined by the size and shape of the vocal bands within his or her larynx, or voice box. Optimum pitch, the level most comfortable for you, is usually one-third above the lowest pitch you are capable of producing (Eisenson and Ogilvie, 1963, p. 283). Most untrained speakers use a pitch somewhat higher than their optimum pitch, but it has been found that lower pitches are most pleasant to listen to.

Pitch is an important element in people's judgments about a speaker. A voice with unvaried pitch is monotonous and is usually disliked; in fact, a monotone seems to be as unpopular as a poker face. People expect a voice to be varied in pitch and sometimes derive information about emotions from changes in pitch. In a summary of recent research, Weick writes:

> The potential significance of pitch measures lies in the fact that they may be accurate indices of emotional states. . . . Mahl suggested that the general pitch level at which one speaks is unimportant in the English language, people receive little explicit training in it, therefore, it may be

more sensitive to drive states. (Weick, in Lindzey and Aronson, 1968, p. 392)

Apparently, pitch level does not affect the amount of information a receiver comprehends (Diehl, White, and Satz, 1961), but it does influence his or her attitude toward the communicator and the content of the message. One study (Eakins, 1969) showed that exaggerated pitch changes are even more unpopular than the monotone. A naturally expressive voice has a variety of pitch levels, which are spontaneous and unforced changes.

Quality

The primary difference between a portable record player and a console hi-fi unit is the quality of the sound reproduction. In fact, "hi-fi" stands for "high fidelity," or small loss of quality in the reproduction of sounds. Differences in the **quality,** or *timbre,* of the human voice become easier to explain if we use another musical analogy. Think of a violin, a viola, and a cello. Each is a stringed instrument, but each has a different size and shape. The same note played on each of these instruments will therefore have a different *resonance*—a distinctive quality of sound. Similarly, each of us has a distinctive voice quality because the *resonance* of our voice—which to a great extent determines its quality—is a function of the size and shape of our body as well as of our vocal cords.

There seems to be wide agreement in responses to vocal qualities. One study (Bowler, 1964) shows that judges could reliably distinguish voices described as shrill or harsh from those considered pleasant, or "resonant." Although it is common practice to refer to a pleasant voice as one that is "resonant," Anderson reminds us that a voice with "a disagreeable quality or lacking in general effectiveness is not necessarily lacking in resonance—it may have too much of the wrong kind. Mere resonance alone does not make a superior voice" (Anderson, 1961, p. 435).

There are several particularly unpleasant voice qualities, and we shall mention five of them here. See if you recognize a familiar voice or two among them.

Hypernasality is talking through the nose; think of someone imitating a whining child. *Denasality* sounds as though the person has a constant head cold. *Hoarseness* will sound like perpetual laryngitis. *Harshness,* or *stridency,* results in a piercing voice. One writer comments, "Strident voices seem to be able to make themselves heard more easily than normal voices even though the effect is often unpleasant." *Breathiness* is caused by air wastage, and like *huskiness* it occurs most often in women; sometimes these have organic origins, but frequently they are due to faults in phonation (voice production), which can be relearned and improved (Van Riper, 1963, pp. 172, 174).

Through practice and training almost all of us can make improvements in our vocal quality. One of the best media available for studying communication style in general is the videotape recorder, though even videotape loses some of the nuances of vocal inflection, eye contact, postural cues, and the like. The audiotape recorder is another valuable aid and one that is perhaps more accessible to students.

INTERPRETING NONVERBAL MESSAGES

Nonverbal communication—indeed the entire communication process—must be viewed as a whole that is greater than the sum of its parts. Outside the laboratory we do not depend on isolated cues. As one writer has explained:

> The still photo of a face alone is a radically reduced situation; in life there are more cues and so more accuracy. Reading an emotion from a still photograph of a face is rather like trying to identify animals from the tracks they leave in the snow. (Brown, 1965, p. 624)

In face-to-face communication, all the cues we have been discussing are available to us. Therefore it is not surprising to find some scholars estimating that at least 65 percent of all social meaning in face-to-face communication is conveyed through nonverbal stimuli (Harrison, 1965, p. 161). Our knowledge of the setting in which the message occurs is another advantage. As we saw from Laing's example at the end of Chapter 7, meaning is, to a great degree, determined by context. Barnlund also reminds us that changes "in the speed or direction of a particular movement may carry as much meaning as does its form" (Barnlund, 1958, p. 525).

We learn most about the meaning of nonverbal messages by studying them in relationship to verbal messages. Essentially, a nonverbal message functions in one of three ways: it replaces, reinforces, or contradicts a verbal message.

A nonverbal message that substitutes for a verbal one is often easy to interpret. Our culture provides us with gestures and expressions that are the equivalents of certain brief verbal messages: "Yes," "No," "Hello," "Goodbye," "I don't know," and so on. Likes and dislikes can also be expressed without words. It will be a long time before anyone forgets Khrushchev pounding a United Nations table with his shoe.

When a nonverbal message reinforces a verbal message, meaning is conveyed quickly and easily, and with increased comprehension. Sometimes a single cue such as a hand movement or a long pause gives special emphasis to one part of a message so that we are able to discern what the speaker feels is most important.

As receivers most of our problems in interpreting meaning arise when we receive a nonverbal message that contradicts a verbal message. Let us explore this subject briefly.

You are familiar with the word "bind" as used to describe a situation one cannot get out of. In 1956 the anthropologist Gregory Bateson and a group of his associates presented a theory of the **double bind** that revolutionized the study of schizophrenia. They proposed that schizophrenic communication—particularly within families—was characterized by the constant exchange of contradictory messages between two or more people, one of whom was designated the "victim."

The recurrent theme in the double bind is a sequence of three injunctions or commands. The first says, "Do not do so and so, or I will punish you," or "If you do not do so and so, I will punish you." The second command contradicts the first and is often communicated nonverbally: "Posture, gesture, tone of voice, meaningful action, and the implications concealed in verbal comment may all be used to convey this more abstract message" (Bateson et al., 1956, p. 254). (Note the multiple channels through which these commands may be communicated.) The third negative command makes the victim's position completely untenable by forbidding him or her to leave this paradoxical situation. Laing has given us this summary of a chilling example taken from Bateson's work:

> A mother visits her son, who has just been recovering from a mental breakdown. As he goes towards her
> a. she opens her arms for him to embrace her, and/or
> b. to embrace him.
> c. As he gets nearer she freezes and stiffens.
> d. He stops irresolutely.
> e. She says, "Don't you want to kiss your mummy?"—and as he still stands irresolutely
> f. she says, "But, dear, you mustn't be afraid of your feelings."

Laing notes that the description does not include the patient's double-binding behavior toward his mother. "For instance, between steps (b) and (c) above, the patient in moving towards his mother may have succeeded by minute nuances in his expression and walk, in putting into his mother *his* fear of closeness with her, so that she stiffened" (Laing, 1969, p. 127).

Bateson's double-bind thesis explains a great deal about contradictory messages and the breakdown of interpersonal relationships that may result from them. Although the theory applies specifically to schizophrenic communication, it is relevant to more general studies such as ours because normal and so-called abnormal, or deviant, behavior exist along a continuum. Suppose, for example, that a supervisor always cautions her employees not to postpone discussing problem areas in their work. "Don't wait till it's too late to remedy the situation. I want you to come and tell me when you run into problems," she repeats. Yet as one of the asssistant managers enters her office, she looks up annoyed. "Yes. What is it *now?* I'm busy." Then, as the employee starts to back out of her office, the supervisor comments, "Well, don't stand there looking so frightened. Tell me what's on your mind."

Within the normal range of experience, Birdwhistell uses the term **kinesic slips** for *contradictory verbal and nonverbal messages.* Imagine this conversation between a married couple who have just had a bitter quarrel. The wife asks the husband, "Honey, are you still angry?" "No," he replies, "it's all right." "But you *sound* as though you're still angry," she says, "I'm telling you I'M NOT ANGRY!" he answers. The husband's words give one message, his voice another. He may not even be aware of the second. Which message is his wife likely to believe?

Recall for a moment the estimate we spoke of earlier: if nonverbal stimuli account for at least 65 percent of all social meaning in face-to-face communication, verbal stimuli can account for no more than 35 percent. Nonverbal cues predominate by sheer number. In general, if as receivers we are caught between two discrepant messages, we are more inclined to believe the nonverbal message.

One reason for this is that nonverbal cues give information about our intentions and emotional responses. A seasoned editor once commented that he always preferred to discuss any major problems with an author in person rather than over the phone or by mail, because "then you can see the author's face and tell how far you can go with him" (Corry, 1975, p. 42).

Another reason that the nonverbal message seems to have greater impact is the popular belief that body movements, facial expressions, vocal qualities, and so on cannot be simulated with authenticity by the average person. Even children are quick to sense gestures or expressions that are not spontaneous. Caroline, an exuberant first-grader, was fond of imitating what she called her teacher's "phony smile" for her mother. One day Caroline followed up with the observation that when the teacher, Mrs. McDonald, was angry, she smiled sweetly, then said, "Caroline, *come here,*" and the smile vanished.

For purposes of analysis we have spoken of verbal and nonverbal messages as distinct. In actual communication, however, multiple channels, contexts, and messages are involved. These, as Weakland points out, "are never absolutely separable, but interact, so that, for example, messages and contexts, verbal message and vocal or facial expression, or related verbal messages are mutually qualifying in ways crucial to interpretation and response—and therefore to effective analysis of communication" (Weakland, in Prosser, 1973.)

A lighthearted illustration of this point appears in a recent account by an American woman of a trip abroad. On her last day in Greece the woman tries to buy several dozen olive oil pitchers for a friend in America. The day, she observes, was fated to begin with an *"Ochi"* (the Greek word for "No"), and she goes on to make the distinction between two different methods of refusal in Greece. When she tries to cash her friend's check, for example, the reply of the bank manager is an *"Ochi"* of the following order:

> a slight lift of the chin, a slight lift of the fingers of one hand, meaning "I'm sorry, but you are asking the impossible." (Yerxa, 1976, p. 1)

As the day progresses, her frantic efforts to purchase the oil pitchers and have them properly crated for shipping are finally successful. But when she tries to find a taxi and later to get the parcels accepted by post office employees, the prevailing response seems to be this kind of *"Ochi"*:

> eyes chinward, chin heavenward, and an upward flip of both hands means, "You are not only insane but probably dishonest and almost certainly of dubious parentage to even ask such a thing. Besides, I can't, I don't want to, there isn't any and you can't get there from here." (Yerxa, 1976, p. 1)

In these latter instances a verbal response ("No") is qualified not only by eye movements but by hand gestures and head movements. The same verbal response accompanied by different nonverbal responses (chin and fingers up) takes on different shades of meaning and a different emphasis. These examples are extreme. There are many, more subtle ways in which verbal and nonverbal communicative stimuli are mutually qualifying. Yet even in a situation as clear-cut as that in which the American tourist found herself, it is difficult to weight the individual importance of the verbal and the nonverbal stimuli.

If at times in the last two chapters we have spoken of verbal and nonverbal messages as if they could be separated, this has not been our intention. Face-to-face communication is a total experience. No matter what a person is saying, you see his or her face, body movements, clothing, and so on, and you are responding, whether you are aware of it or not, to all this input.

Summary

Nonverbal communication is going on all the time. In this chapter we have looked at three kinds of nonverbal cues. We discussed space and time, two cues that have a subtle but pervasive influence on our style of communication and are, to a significant degree, determined by culture. We saw that assumptions about space and timing can sometimes be a source of difficulty in intercultural communication. Visual cues from facial expressions, eye contact, body movements (particularly hand gestures), and physical appearance and the use of objects were analyzed. We found that these cues give us information about human emotions and intentions; they are also the basis for some of our judgments about personality and social status. Vocal cues are another source of information. We spoke in some detail about volume, rate and fluency, pitch, and quality. Although all these cues were discussed separately for the purpose of analysis, it is misleading to speak about individual cues without considering the entire communication event.

We concluded with a look at how we interpret nonverbal messages, particularly in relation to verbal messages. The source of most communication difficulties, double or contradictory messages, was considered in terms of double-bind situations and the kinesic slips common in daily experience. We also suggested that verbal and nonverbal responses qualify each other in so many ways that they are not totally separable.

Review Questions

1. Describe the difference between sign language, action language, and object language.
2. Discuss four kinds of interpersonal distance. Give an example of each kind.
3. What is personal space?
4. What is chronemics? Give an example of one way in which timing could be a source of interference in intercultural communication.
5. What is kinesics?
6. What are four unstated rules in our culture concerning eye contact?
7. Describe three categories of nonverbal courtship behavior. Give an example of each type.
8. What is the relationship between head and body movements in the communication of emotion?
9. Describe how the physical objects we choose for ourselves can communicate messages.
10. What is paralinguistics? Give some examples of paralinguistic cues.
11. What four categories of emotion are consistently identified by paralinguistic cues?
12. What are three ways in which nonverbal and verbal messages may be related?

13. What is a double bind? How does it relate to both verbal and nonverbal communication?
14. Explain how verbal and nonverbal messages can be mutually qualifying.

Exercises

1. Form several two-person teams consisting of one male and one female. Have each team select a place where several people are likely to pass by. Have both members take turns asking strangers the time of day, or some other standard question. While speaking, slowly violate the stranger's proxemic norms until you are very close to him or her. The other member of the team should observe and record the stranger's reactions. When all the teams have collected data, discuss these questions in light of the data collected:
   a. In what ways did the strangers demonstrate sign language, action language, and object language and under what conditions?
   b. How did the strangers respond to the questioner as he or she began to violate proxemic norms?
   c. Did male and female strangers respond differently to proxemic norm violation depending on whether a male or female did the violating?
2. Repeat the exercise just described, but this time have one questioner dress very neatly, and the other in a sloppy, unkempt manner. Discuss the differences in the strangers' reactions to the questioner.
3. Make a list of the various paralinguistic and vocal cues discussed in this chapter. Tape-record a series of short messages presented by a male and female that illustrate the various types of paralinguistic and vocal cues. Construct a Semantic Differential similar to the one suggested in exercise 1a in Chapter 7; then ask a number of people to listen to the taped messages and rate the speakers using the Semantic Differential. How did the various paralinguistic and vocal cues affect the listeners' perceptions of the speaker? Relate the results to the concepts discussed in Chapter 4 on person perception.
4. The next time you get angry with someone, try to observe your own nonverbal behavior. Who do you sound like? Who do you remind yourself of? Most people look and sound like their parents or other members of their family. Facial expressions, posture, gestures, and vocal cues are often similar among family members. Do you notice similarities? What differences can you detect? Can you account for these similarities and differences?
5. Try playing charades. Notice how much more aware of nonverbal communication everyone is during the game. Do all players communicate equally well? What differences can you identify between the good players and those who are less skilled?

Suggested Readings

Fast, Julius. *Body Language*. New York: Evans, 1970. This lively, popularized introduction to nonverbal communication is an entertaining treatment of the subject, including such topics as "To touch or not to touch," "Winking, Blinking and Nods," and "Putting it all together." The reader should be aware that this treatment is not considered to be wholly accurate.

Knapp, Mark L. *Nonverbal Communication in Human Interaction*. New York: Holt, Rinehart and Winston, 1972. This book is an excellent resource for the student of nonverbal communication. Professor Knapp writes in a readable and lively style, and he has a significant message to convey. One interesting feature is the illustrative material that is included (pictures, diagrams, charts).

Mehrabian, Albert. *Silent Messages*. Belmont, Calif.: Wadsworth, 1971. Mehrabian has contributed still another of his absolutely first-rate publications to the literature. This little book synthesizes a lot of experimental and theoretical material on nonverbal communication.

Rich, Andrea L. "Interracial Implications of Nonverbal Behavior," in *Interracial Communication*. New York: Harper & Row, 1974, Chapter 7. The author discusses the importance of nonverbal communication in interracial contexts, where a mutual lack of trust results in a search for nonverbal rather than verbal cues as "indicators of real meaning."

Weitz, Shirley (Ed.). *Nonverbal Communication: Readings With Commentary*. New York: Oxford University Press, 1974. The many readings in this collection are organized around five themes: facial expression and visual interaction, paralanguage, body movement and gestures, spatial behavior, and multichannel communication. In her commentary preceding each of these five sections, the editor provides an excellent overview of the topic.

Chapter 9 Two-Person Communication

OBJECTIVES

After reading this chapter the student should be able to:
1. Describe the relationship between disruptive power and norms in dyadic communication.
2. Distinguish between expected roles and enacted roles.
3. Define intrarole and interrole conflicts and give an example of each.
4. Describe two ways in which involvement on the part of communicators is related to dyadic communication.
5. State the relationship between one's level of arousal and the ability to perform effectively.
6. Describe the relationship between need for dominance, need for achievement, and self-concept.
7. State the relationship between need for affiliation and need for dominance.
8. Describe at least two ways in which status affects dyadic communication.
9. Describe the MUM effect.
10. Illustrate a complementary transaction.
11. Distinguish between a complementary and a crossed transaction.
12. Illustrate an angular and a duplex transaction, and give examples of both.
13. Identify ten different types of interview objectives.
14. Distinguish between standardized interviews and unstandardized interviews.
15. Distinguish between five types of interview questions and give an example of each type.
16. Identify five types of inadequate responses to interview questions and describe a strategy that may be used to handle each type.
17. Describe three responsibilities of the interviewer at the beginning of an interview.
18. Describe the funnel sequence as it is used in the body of an interview.
19. Describe three steps in terminating an interview.

9

In preceding chapters we have developed several elements of the model illustrated in Figure 2.1: the social behavior and motivation of individual communicators, their perceptions of other human beings, some of the bases of their attraction to others, the relationship aspects of their communication, and the components of their verbal and nonverbal messages. In this chapter we finally bring the two communicators in our model together, and we raise two basic questions concerning their encounters: What if anything do we know about two-person communication? What predictions can we make about how two people will interact?

You will recall that our model focuses on **dyadic,** or *two-person communication*. The dyad is the smallest unit of interaction, and in many ways it is a microcosm of all larger groups. Wilmot (1975) characterizes dyadic communication in the following manner:

> Two people involved in a face-to-face transaction. Any direct communicative transaction between *two people,* whether it be fleeting or recurring, is dyadic. Friendship pairs, marital couples, business partners, a parent-child relationship, or two persons having coffee for the first and last time, all constitute dyads. (p. 4)

THE SOCIAL SETTING

When we consider the two communicators in our model, we find that we have set our actors on a rather bare stage. We have already discussed some of the variables that make them unique and others that influence their responses to one another. Now we must place them within a social setting.

Norms

Attraction, we have seen, is in part based on perceived similarity of relevant or salient characteristics. We tend to like others whom we view as resembling ourselves. We find it comfortable to believe that they share our attitudes, beliefs, or values. In effect, these similarities confirm us: they suggest that we must be right because others think the way we do.

When we speak of attitudes, beliefs, or values that are shared by several people, we approach the subject of social norms. **Norms,** as we saw in Chapter 8, are *rules about behavior,* rules from which we develop certain expectations about how people should act. We have norms for sex, eating, grading exams, tipping, and child rearing—in fact, for every aspect of human life. Even in casual encounters there are norms for how to communicate: "There are rules for taking and terminating a turn at talking; there are norms synchronizing the process of eyeing the speaker and being eyed by him: there is an etiquette for initiating an encounter and bringing it to an end" (Goffman, 1971, pp. 3–4).

The word "norm" refers to a standard or average, and it often implies that the standard or average is acceptable. Behaviors that violate a given norm are called "deviant," the implication being that deviant behaviors are in some way unacceptable or even abnormal. Of course, extremely deviant behavior is more likely to elicit strong negative responses than behavior that deviates only slightly from any given norm. A man who eats with his hands in an elegant restaurant will get more disapproving glances than one who uses the wrong knife.

Norms develop at a number of social levels. Some norms are shared by almost all members of a given culture. Some are specific to countries, regions of a country, communities, smaller social groups, or families. Certain norms are transferred from one relationship to another. Thus when two people meet, each already has a great many expectations about how the other will behave. Both will be strongly influenced by the norms they have already adopted. As they interact, however, they may also establish some norms of their own—rules, whether implicit or explicit, by which they agree to behave. During courtship, for example, a couple decides on a number of acceptable and unacceptable behaviors concerning love making, use of profanity, topics of conversation, places to go on dates, and so on.

An interesting question that has been raised is whether certain dyads establish more norms than others. Suppose that Will and Barbara are friends. When *Will can keep Barbara from doing something she wants to do,* Will may be said to have **disruptive power** over her. In some dyadic relationships one person has more disruptive power than the other. In others both members may have relatively high or low disruptive power. One team of researchers reports that the frequency with which norms are established in dyads is linked to the disruptive power each person has over the other. When both members have high disruptive power, they tend to establish more normative agreements—perhaps, it has been suggested, because both are conscious that "the overuse of their power can be self-defeating" (Murdoch and Rosen, 1970, p. 273). When disagreements between two people are a common occurrence, normative agreements will often reduce the level and frequency of conflict. If Will always prefers films and Barbara always favors hockey games, they can decide to alternate these activities. If Barbara has greater disruptive power than Will, they may end up always going to hockey games. Either arrangement would be considered a normative agreement.

Norms then are guidelines that limit and direct behavior. We accept them because they allow us to establish standard operating procedures—ground rules, if you will—that make the behavior of others more predictable and decrease the need for communicating about that behavior. If a married couple reaches an agreement about where to spend Christmas and Easter holidays each year or about who handles the finances, there is no need to renegotiate these decisions repeatedly. Thibaut and Kelley put it well when they write that effective norms "can reduce the costs of interaction and eliminate the less rewarding activities from a relationship. They can act to improve the outcome attained by members of a dyad and to increase their interdependence" (1959, p. 147). They also point out that a conformity agreement tends to become rewarding in and of itself.

Not all normative agreements are rewarding. Some are inappropriate for a given relationship. Some restrict communication in an unhealthy way. Others are too rigid. For example, if a normative agreement exists between father and son that the son will never question the father's judgments or decisions, the son may forfeit his own good judgment simply because it conflicts with his father's opinion. Ellis (1962) believes that a great deal of psychological damage can be attributed to attempts to live by norms that we are virtually unaware we have assumed, standards inappropriate for our own wellbeing. He bases his rational-emotive school of psychotherapy on the premise that norms can best serve us if we know that they exist and can periodically evaluate their appropriateness.

Roles

In public places adults are expected to use cutlery when eating certain foods. People who borrow library books are expected to return them. In any given culture some norms apply to all members and others apply only to some members. A **role** is a *set of norms that applies to a specific subclass within the society*. The term itself is unsettling. Actors play roles. What have they to do with us? If a college student is expected at various times to play the role of son, student, friend, lover, employee, grandson, Catholic, and tennis player, how seriously can he assume these roles without becoming an automaton or sacrificing his individuality?

"Mr. Edwards, this is your secretary, Melissa. When you have a moment, would you run down and get me a regular coffee and a pineapple Danish?"

Drawing by Whitney Darrow, Jr.; © 1976 *The New Yorker Magazine*, Inc.

To answer this question a distinction must be made between **expected roles** and **enacted roles**. For example, in parent-child relationships the parent is expected to minister to the needs of the child, to provide for him or her financially, and so on. The enacted role of parent may in fact be quite different. A father who is an alcoholic or an invalid may be tended to and even supported by his child. Even if such an obvious reversal of roles does not take place, different men will interpret the role of father differently—one as a stern disciplinarian, one as a completely permissive companion, one as a firm but loving teacher. Granted, we "enact" roles. We shall not say, however, that we are "actors" in a completely theatrical sense, but rather that some roles are more central to us than others. Thus the intensity with which a person takes on various roles differs; some will be enacted casually, with little or no involvement, and others with great commitment.

We are, of course, more comfortable in some roles than in others. The roles we do not enjoy playing are those that create conflict. There are two types of role conflict, and both tend to lead to communication difficulties.

A person is likely to experience **interrole conflict** when occupying *two (or more) roles that represent contradictory expectations about a* *given behavior.* Suppose that a student who is proctoring an exam sees her friend cheating during the test. As a proctor she feels obliged to report the cheating. As a friend she may feel that out of loyalty she should overlook what she has just seen. The options in interrole conflicts seem clear. The demands of role 1 and role 2 are known. They conflict. One must be chosen over the other.

What about **intrarole conflict**—*conflicting expectations concerning a single role?* Let us consider an example that concerns us all: the conflict in sex roles.

Much has been written about redefining the traditional female role, especially as it relates to marriage. Must a woman assume the roles of wife and mother to be totally feminine? And what after all are her obligations as wife and mother? Are housework and child rearing exclusively female responsibilities? No, say many women—and some men.

For the moment the women's movement has focused attention on the female sex role. But male and female roles are complementary; a redefinition of the female role will, of necessity, require changes in the male role. Some men are already aware of this possibility. One group

Parental roles are becoming more and more flexible.

of husbands whose wives had committed themselves to instituting some change in their marriages discussed some of the problems entailed by redefinition of roles and the confusion that often results. For example, Dick, one of the participants, commented that he had "a hard time calling a waiter or a cab" and that his wife's ability to do these things well made him even less effective (Gould, 1972).

Trivial as it may seem, Dick's concern over not being able to get the attention of a waiter or a cab driver illustrates some of the problems of intrarole conflict. Is success in getting a cab or calling a waiter essential to fulfilling a masculine role? Do others expect a man to do this? Does he expect it of himself? Dick is not sure. The issue is complicated by the fact that as a result of her consciousness-raising sessions, Dick's wife wants him to change some of his expectations about her behavior. Yet the roles of male and female are complementary. Would she be flexible enough to change some of her expectations about his behavior? How would she react when he said, "If you want the waiter, call him yourself"?

Role conflicts and the misunderstandings to which they give rise illustrate the interdependence of role, self-concept, and communication. When we enact a role with any measure of intensity, we communicate from within that role—that is, we take a certain stance. We also internalize certain expectations about how we should respond and how other people should respond to us. Most communication takes place within the boundaries of these expectations.

UNSTRUCTURED TWO-PERSON COMMUNICATION

Much of the day-to-day interaction between members of dyads is casual and spontaneous. We can describe their encounters as relatively unstructured if we contrast them with more structured two-person exchanges such as interviews. We emphasize the word "relatively." Daily interactions do have some structure; conversely, some more formal encounters have only the barest minimum of structure. With this qualification in mind, we turn to some elements of unstructured two-person communication.

Involvement and Arousal

Researchers have known for some time that as the number of people interacting increases, the individual satisfaction of each member of the group decreases. Thus the dyad is potentially the most satisfying social context within which communication can occur, partly because there is likely to be more opportunity to participate than there is in larger groups. Also there is convincing evidence, as we saw in Chapter 3, that the opportunity to talk is in itself satisfying. Consequently, members of dyads are more deeply involved than are members of larger groups. **Involvement** has another side, however. Although experiences in a dyad tend to be satisfying, they may also be intensely unsatisfying. Because of the depth of involvement, members of a dyad are likely to have more intense negative feelings about an unpleasant experience in the relationship than are members of a larger group. For example, everyone acknowledges the importance of listening in communication. Yet when tempers begin to flare, less listening occurs. Sereno and Mortensen (1969) found that dyads consisting of slightly involved members were able to reach effective compromises more often and with a more favorable private attitude change than were highly ego-involved members of dyads. (They point out, however, that a number of variables are probably relevant to the communication process that may in time help us negotiate conflict with maximum effectiveness.) It is known that in open-ended or unstructured situations, high Machs, who have greater emotional detachment than low Machs, seem to "direct the tone and content of interaction—and usually also the outcome" (Christie and Geis, 1970, p. 313). Low Machs, who are more open to emotional involvements, are less effective strategists but more sensitive to the feelings of others. It is particularly interesting that the differences between high Machs and low Machs show up most in face-to-face interactions.

Another concept relevant to dyads as well as to larger groups is arousal level. It is well known that one's ability to behave efficiently may be activated by a certain level of physiological arousal. Athletes as well as entertainers are better able to perform if they can first get "psyched up" for the effort. In fact, all of us need a minimum level of arousal in order to use cues efficiently; otherwise, we fail to perceive them. But arousal level works against us beyond a certain point—overexcitation can make us unable to organize the stimuli we receive. This is what seems to happen when a person is overcome by stage fright or becomes so deeply involved in an argument that he or she is virtually unable to communicate. As Figure 9.1 illustrates, the relationship between the ability to perform effectively and one's level of arousal seems to follow an inverted U curve. We need a minimum arousal level to function and in fact a moderate level of arousal facilitates communication, but we reach a point of diminishing returns, beyond which high arousal level results in poor performance.

Some Dimensions of Interpersonal Relations

The dyad, like all social units, presupposes certain norms and roles. This means that we need not start afresh in analyzing the behaviors of

Figure 9.1

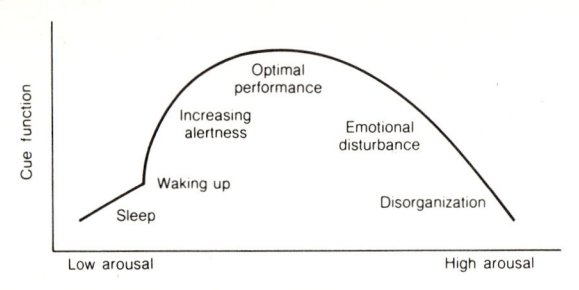

AROUSAL LEVEL AND PERFORMANCE

SOURCE: Donald Hebb, *A Textbook of Psychology*, 3rd ed. (Philadelphia: Saunders, 1972), p. 235.

the two communicators; we have at least some basis for prediction. Another variable that will qualify any predictions we make will be motivation.

Certain dimensions of motivation have more relevance for communication than others. One important predictor of how two people will interact is the strength of their affiliative needs, discussed in Chapter 3. For present purposes the **need for affiliation** may be seen as a continuum from highly affiliative to antisocial behavior. The high affiliater prefers being with others to being alone. He or she enjoys and seeks out companionship. Such a person may be described as friendly, gregarious, and generally sociable. The person who is low in the need for affiliation probably prefers being alone. He or she has much less desire for companionship and is not very reinforcing to other people. In fact, the low affiliater is usually described as unfriendly or unsociable.

Given a knowledge of two people's affiliative tendencies, we can make some predictions about how they will respond in a face-to-face encounter. But suppose that we add to this knowledge some information about a second important dimension of interpersonal relations: the **need for dominance**. Like the need for affiliation, the need for dominance can be imagined as a continuum: at one end we have the person who wants control over others, and at the other the person with a relatively submissive style of communication. Need for dominance seems to have some correlation with need for achievement—those who rate high in the first also tend to rate high in the second.

A correlation also seems to exist between dominance and self-concept. A person with an unfavorable self-concept, chiefly measured by level of self-esteem, tends to be low in the need for dominance, and he or she is likely to defer to the other dyad member. For example, in one of your authors' classes, students were assigned two-person projects. Student A on one team complained to the instructor that his partner, B, was bossing him around and preventing him from taking part in planning. Yet each time the instructor observed the two at work, he noticed that A made no attempts to get B to let him participate in the planning. This submissive behavior seems typical of the person with low self-esteem: he or she is unable to influence others but is not satisfied with the role he or she must play when others become more dominant. Furthermore, such hesitancy tends to bring out the dominating tendencies of others.

When we combine what we know about behaviors associated with the needs for affiliation and dominance, as in Figure 9.2, we see some communication patterns possible in a dyad as well as in a larger group. Allowing for the individuality of each member of the dyad, we can still make some predictions about how the two will interact if we know something about the strengths of their needs for affiliation and dominance. If Will has a high need for dominance but a low need for affiliation, we expect him to be analytic, to make many judgments, to be resistant, and so on; if Barbara has a low need for dominance but a high need for affiliation, we expect her to acquiesce much of the time, to cooperate with Will, and so on. But if, like Will, Barbara has a high need for dominance, it is likely that a power struggle will ensue, or, as we suggested in discussing norms, the two will work out some satisfactory normative agreements that regulate their behavior—at least for a time.

No discussion of power or dominance would be complete without

Figure 9.2

Some Behaviors Associated with Needs for Dominance and Affiliation

	High dominance	**Low dominance**
High affiliation	Advises Coordinates Directs Initiates Leads	Acquiesces Agrees Assists Cooperates Obliges
Low affiliation	Analyzes Criticizes Disapproves Judges Resists	Concedes Evades Relinquishes Retreats Withdraws

SOURCE: Adapted from David W. Johnson, *Reaching Out: Interpersonal Effectiveness and Self-actualization* (Englewood Cliffs, N.J.: Prentice-Hall, 1972), p. 35. By permission of Prentice-Hall, Inc.

some mention of **status.** Potter (1952) has written at length about a familiar strategy for achieving higher status in human relationships; he calls it "one-upmanship." No doubt the popularity of his tongue-in-cheek descriptions of how to gain the upper hand stems from their authenticity. In one guise or another, the one-upper is known to you all. He or she is always busier than you are, goes to more expensive places, knows more important people, and—most telling of all—is a chronic name dropper. A remark such as "When I was talking to Skinner at the A.P.A. meetings last week," may leave a colleague or graduate student duly impressed. An undergraduate who doesn't know that A.P.A. stands for the American Psychological Association but who has seen B. F. Skinner's name in a psychology text may be even more impressed.

Potter comes through with one-upmanship techniques for all of us: doctor and patient, businessman, artist, sportsman, wine lover. And he has not forgotten the college student. If you want to be one up before exams have started or after they are over, you might give either of two impressions: that you spend all your time studying or that you never open a book. For example, "to Harvard," the second strategy, is "to seem, even when the examination is only two days off, to be totally indifferent to the impending crisis, and be seen walking calmly and naturally about, out of doors, enjoying the scenery and taking deep breaths of air" (Potter, 1952, p. 22). Efforts to outdo another person or group clearly take place on both verbal and nonverbal levels.

Status has marked effects on the form of all communication, no matter how unstructured. It makes a great difference, for example, whether the status of both members of a dyad is the same. If two people are unequal in status, there is a good chance that the one with higher status will control the topics of conversation as well as the length of the discussion. Higher status may even enable that person to avoid the discussion entirely if he or she so chooses. If the president of a bank and one of his tellers are engaged in conversation, for example, and the teller asks a question that seems too personal, it is likely that the bank president will respond in such a way that the teller will feel uncomfortable pursuing the subject.

Perceptions of status are immediately reflected in greetings as well as in forms of address. Thus "Hi" may be permissible for some encounters but "Hello" or "Good morning" may be more appropriate for others. The higher-status person is often addressed by title and last name ("Good morning, Dr. Jones"), and the lower-status person by first name or even a briefer version of that name ("Hi, Mike"). One sociologist (Goffman, 1971, pp. 3-4) observes that greetings may also affirm a subordinate's willingness to maintain his or her lower status. American military practice, for instance, requires that the subordinate salute first and hold the salute until it is returned by the person of higher rank. Observe people of different status greeting one another and see whether these behavior patterns are borne out by your own experience.

Status differences between members of a dyad affect not only communicative style but the actual content of the communication. For years we have known that in larger social systems those interested in achieving higher status tend to distort what they say to their superiors in order to create the most favorable impression possible. In other words, they create a filter through which only the more pleasant information passes. This phenomenon has been called the **MUM effect** —from *Mum about Undesirable Messages* (Rosen and Tesser, 1970).

No doubt the status filter operates at a number of levels within the federal government. One Vietnam veteran observed that the South Vietnam military efforts appeared to be more successful than they were because combat officers were eager to report considerable progress to their superiors each month. We also expect this filtering process to exist in all sorts of institutions and businesses—hospitals, schools, legal firms, department stores. And some of us can personally attest to the presence of the MUM effect within our own families.

It is not surprising, therefore, that the MUM effect is also present in dyads—even when two people are relatively similar in status. Each tries to communicate so that he or she either maintains his or her existing status level or achieves a higher one. And though each enters the relationship with a certain status, it may change as a result of interaction with the other.

The MUM effect can be thought of as a form of interference. In a dyadic relationship the temptation to distort messages and thus put oneself in a favorable light is especially great for the person who occupies the lower-status position. On the other hand, the higher-status person in a dyad may be aware that he or she sometimes receives distorted messages.

Sound communication depends upon accurate information, and this is true not only of informal communication but communication in groups of all sizes, including large organizations. Beckhard (1969) identifies ten characteristics of a healthy organization: at least three of them depend on minimal distortion of information not only between superiors and their subordinates but between peers. And clearly, there is less message distortion when people communicate within an atmosphere that encourages feedback.

We have discussed other aspects of interpersonal relations in earlier chapters. For example, in Chapter 5 we spoke about attitude influence with special emphasis on dyadic communication. In Chapter 6 we went on to discuss confirmation, self-disclosure, and trust. In concluding this part of our discussion, we shift our attention to a theory that proposes to analyze the structure of individual transactions in the dyad.

Transactional Analysis

Chapter 1 referred to most of the informal communication activities we engage in as "transactions." **Transactional analysis,** or TA, was first developed by the late Eric Berne and is today a popular approach to *the analysis of communication behaviors—particularly in two-person contexts.* Many laymen have become familiar with this method through such best-sellers as *Games People Play* (Berne, 1964), *I'm OK—You're OK* (Harris, 1967), and *Born to Win* (James and Jungeward, 1971).

The basic premise of transactional analysis is that each human being has three coexisting ego states: parent, adult, and child.

> The *Parent ego state* contains the attitudes and behavior incorporated from external sources, primarily parents. Outwardly, it often is expressed toward others in prejudicial, critical, and nurturing behavior. Inwardly, it is experienced as old Parental messages which continue to influence the inner Child.
>
> The *Adult ego state* is not related to a person's age. It is oriented to current reality and the objective gathering of information. It is organized, adaptable, intelligent, and functions by testing reality, estimating probabilities, and computing dispassionately.
>
> The *Child ego state* contains all the impulses that come naturally to an infant. It also contains the recordings of his early experiences, how he responded to them, and the "positions" he took about himself and others. It is expressed as "old" (archaic) behavior from childhood. (James and Jungeward, 1971, p. 18)

What sort of responses represent parent, adult, and child? Suppose you were trying to give up smoking and a friend offered you a cigarette. Your parent response might be, "I should have one. I'm too tense, and a cigarette would relax me." Your adult response might be, "I think I'll pass and just have a Coke." On the other hand, if you respond on the level of the child you might answer, "I could smoke the whole pack."

Making use of this parent-adult-child-ego classification, transactional analysis describes all transactions between two (or more) people as complementary, crossed, or ulterior.

In a *complementary transaction* only two ego states are involved. It is not the particular ego states involved that make a given transaction complementary. It is complementary because it satisfies two conditions: "the response comes from the same ego state as that to which the stimulus is directed, and the response . . . is directed to the same ego state from which the stimulus is initiated" (Woollams, Brown, and

"I find you guilty, young man. And don't
let me hear of you running off appealing this decision
to a higher court, like some spoiled child."

Drawing by Handelsman; © 1972 *The New Yorker Magazine*, Inc.

Huige, 1974, p. 17). Here the lines of communication, which are represented by the stimulus (the first message) and response (the second message), are parallel, and the communication can go on indefinitely. In Figure 9.3 we see two examples of complementary transactions.

In a *crossed transaction* communication lines are not parallel. Notice in Figure 9.4 that in both situations the first message, or stimulus, is disregarded, and there is a momentary failure in communication. The first message is ignored because the response, often defensive, involves other ego states. Harris (1967, pp. 80–81) recalls Berne's classic example of a crossed transaction. "Dear, where are my cuff links?" a husband says to his wife. "Where you left them!" shouts the wife, responding to an adult stimulus with a parent rather than an adult response. (Her adult response might have been, "I really don't know, but I'll help you look" or "I think they're in the first drawer of the bureau.") Crossed transactions often occur when one person is very defensive and interprets a statement as personal criticism, even when that was not the other person's intention.

An *ulterior transaction* involves the communication of multiple messages. The most complex of the three types, such a transaction is described as either angular or duplex. As we see in Figure 9.5, an *angular transaction* involves three ego states. For example, the apparent message of the salesman ("The price on the new merchandise will

Figure 9.3

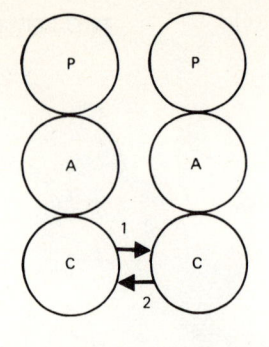

BETWEEN LOVERS

1. I love you.
2. I love you, too.

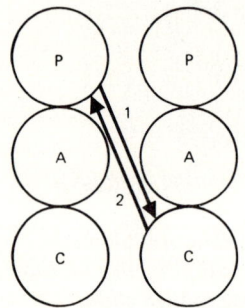

BETWEEN ROOMMATES

1. I told you to keep your side of the room clean.
2. Why don't you kiss off.

COMPLEMENTARY TRANSACTIONS

Figure 9.4

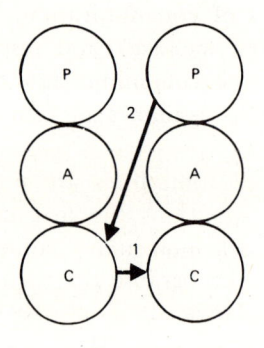

BETWEEN SPOUSES

1. What do you say we get drunk and fool around a little?
2. All you ever think of is sex. I wish you'd put some of that energy to good use.

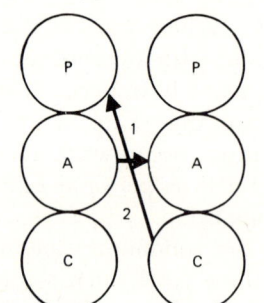

BETWEEN FELLOW EMPLOYEES

1. Ron, will you help me on the T15 project this afternoon?
2. I can't do that. Who'll do my work for me?

CROSSED TRANSACTIONS

Figure 9.5

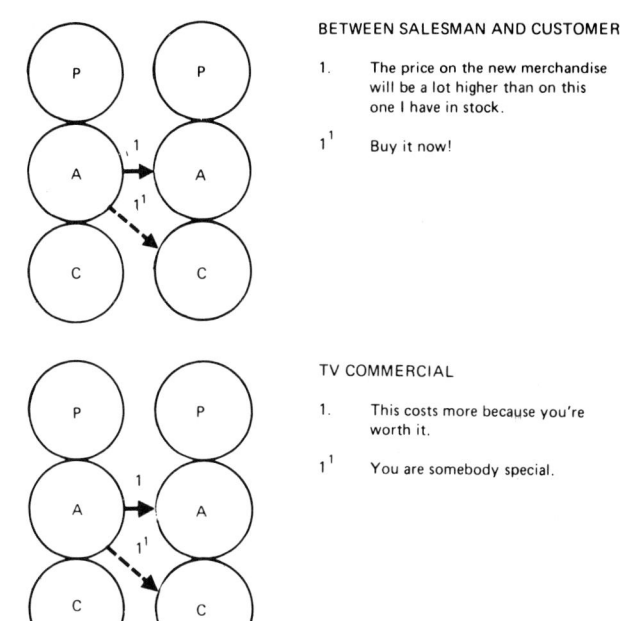

TWO-PERSON COMMUNICATION
BETWEEN SALESMAN AND CUSTOMER

1. The price on the new merchandise will be a lot higher than on this one I have in stock.
1^1 Buy it now!

TV COMMERCIAL

1. This costs more because you're worth it.
1^1 You are somebody special.

ANGULAR TRANSACTIONS

be a lot higher than for this one I have in stock") is an adult stimulus, but his second message ("Buy it now!") is directed to the child ego state of his customer. A *duplex transaction* involves four rather than three ego states. Like the angular transaction, this exchange appears to be taking place on one level, but another message is being transmitted on a second level (see Figure 9.6). In many ulterior transactions a person does not realize that he or she is transmitting more than one message. Such encounters bring to mind the contradictory verbal and nonverbal messages discussed at the end of Chapter 8.

We also spoke in Chapter 6 about the content and relationship aspects of communication. It is the relationship aspects of communication with which transactional analysis is particularly concerned. According to Harris and others, both crossed and ulterior transactions tend to reduce the effectiveness of communication and often undermine the relationship between the parties involved. Advocates of transactional analysis believe that many communication problems arise because a person is more or less "locked into" a particular ego state so that he or she responds from this frame of reference regardless of what the other person is communicating. One person we know is so locked into her critical parent state that the following incident occurred:

INTERPERSONAL COMMUNICATION

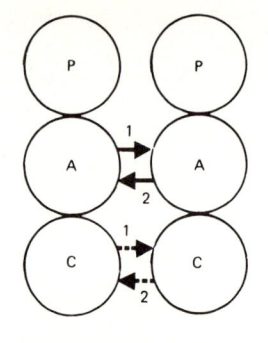

Figure 9.6

BETWEEN MAN AND WOMAN

1. How would you like to see my art collection?
2. Fine, I appreciate good art.
1. Let's make love.
2. I'm available.

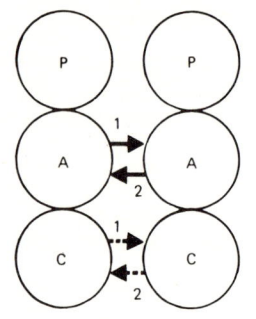

BETWEEN SALESMAN AND CUSTOMER

1. This high performance engine is a real safety feature for passing other cars.
2. Yes, that is important for safety.
1. Wouldn't you love to buy this mean machine?
2. Man, that speed would be fun.

DUPLEX TRANSACTIONS

Jean: (smiling as she walks by) Hi, how are you today?
Thelma: Fine, thank you.
Thelma: (behind Jean's back) Can you believe how short her skirt is? And she's a grandmother! She has no business dressing that way.

Thelma overlooked Jean's warm and sincere effort to be friendly. Instead, she got caught up in her own critical appraisal of Jean's dress. In Thelma's case, this reaction is chronic and almost pathological in its severity.

The aim of transactional analysis is to enable us to get in touch with all three ego states so that we can respond to other people appropriately. According to this school of thought, identifying our crossed or ulterior transactions would be a first step in limiting and ultimately eliminating them. Whether or not we accept the classification of parent, adult, and child ego states as valid (and there are some who question it), transactional analysis offers an interesting way of looking at the dynamics of two-person communication.

As we turn to the interview, a more structured form of two-person communication, keep in mind that the variables we have been discussing will still be present.

STRUCTURED TWO-PERSON COMMUNICATION: THE INTERVIEW

If you associate interviews only with job hunting, your definition of "interview" is too narrow. The interview encompasses many of the elements of all two-person communication. When you consult a doctor, canvass door to door for a political candidate, or ask a stranger for detailed instructions on how to get to a particular place, you are in some sense involved in an interview, or a "conversation with a purpose," as it was once defined (Bingham and Moore, 1924, p. 3). The interview has also become a popular form of entertainment: witness the television talk shows as well as the more formal interviews on press-panel programs.

Interviews serve a number of functions, as can be seen from the table of interview objectives. The interviewer may gather or convey information; he or she may influence people's attitudes; at times he or she may affect their behavior. An appraisal interview, for example,

Ten Interview Objectives

Objective	*Description*	*Example*
Getting information	Interviewer gathers facts, opinions, or attitudes from respondent	Census taker collects data
Giving information	Interviewer presents facts, opinions, or attitudes to respondent, often as a form of instruction	Doctor explains to his patient how to maintain a balanced diet
Persuading	Interviewer attempts to influence respondent's attitude and ultimately his or her behavior	Student tries to convince his or her instructor to give a make-up exam
Problem solving	Interviewer and respondent attempt to identify causes of a problem and together seek a possible solution	Parent and teacher discuss child's reading difficulties
Counseling	Respondent seeks advice from interviewer on a matter of personal concern (closely related to problem-solving interview)	Client requests legal advice from his or her attorney
Job seeking or hiring	Interviewer and respondent exchange information on which to base an employment decision	Campus recruiter meets with senior students

Receiving complaints	Interviewer tries to minimize the respondent's dissatisfaction	Store manager speaks with customer about defective merchandise
Reviewing performance	Interviewer offers feedback on respondent's performance and helps him or her establish specific goals to be met by next appraisal interview	Editor-in-chief of newspaper gives periodic evaluation of each of the editors
Correcting or reprimanding	Interviewer and respondent, usually in the roles of superior and subordinate, meet to discuss respondent's need to improve his or her performance (ordinarily most effective when handled informally and with a helpful rather than critical tone)	Maintenance supervisor of airline discusses with mechanic areas in which technical competence must be improved
Measuring stress	Interviewer determines how respondent acts under pressure	Personnel director of large corporation selects a top executive
	Interviewer gathers information from a respondent who does not wish to divulge it	Army officer questions a military prisoner

often exercises a major influence on an employee's morale. The interview is also a valuable research tool. It allows the interviewer to gather more complete information than could be obtained in a questionnaire or a telephone conversation and to make full use of nonverbal as well as verbal cues. It also enables the interviewer to interpret or explain questions more easily, thus increasing the likelihood of getting answers from the respondent.

Standardized and Unstandardized Interviews

Whatever his or her objectives, the interviewer may use one of two approaches: standardized or unstandardized. The **standardized interview** consists of *a set of prepared questions from which the interviewer is not allowed to deviate.* The interviewer poses the questions precisely as they are worded on the form. He or she does not even have the option of changing their order. The standardized interview has one distinct advantage: uniform responses over a large number of interviewers and respondents. An inexperienced interviewer may still be able to conduct a fairly successful interview. As a rule more skill is required as the interview becomes less structured.

The **unstandardized interview** *allows the interviewer as well as the respondent considerable latitude.* The interviewer may deviate from any of the prepared questions. He or she may follow up a prepared question with one of his or her own to obtain a more complete or appropriate answer. He or she may drop a question that seems unsuitable or one that might put the respondent on the defensive. If he or she suddenly discovers an interesting subject that had not been anticipated, the interviewer has the freedom to pursue this line of questioning as far as is desired. In short, the unstandardized interview gives the interviewer considerable flexibility and potential for discovery.

As we have described them, the standardized and unstandardized interviews are extremes. In fact, some standardized interviews allow some departure from the prepared questions; some unstandardized interviews to not permit the interviewer unlimited freedom. No matter how the interview is structured, however, some feedback must flow between interviewer and respondent. In the discussion that follows, let us assume that the interviewer is conducting an unstandardized interview in which he or she can make maximum use of feedback from the respondent by departing where necessary from the list of questions.

Questions and Answers

Interviewing is essentially dialogue, dialogue in which one party, the interviewer, guides the direction of the conversation by means of a series of questions. A skillful interviewer knows a great deal about the art of questioning. He or she responds to the answers received by modulating subsequent responses—particularly the kinds of questions that are being asked. We can illustrate by first looking at several categories of questions.

The **open question** resembles an essay question on a test; it *places no restrictions on the length of the respondent's answer.* It also allows the respondent more latitude in interpreting the subject to be discussed. Examples of open questions would be, "Would you please summarize your work experience?" and "What are your feelings about your marriage?" The interviewer may want to use open questions early in the interview to get the respondent to relax and reveal more personal information.

The **closed question** is more specific and *usually requires a shorter, more direct answer.* Contrast the following with the two open questions just given: "How many years of work experience have you had in this field?" and "What aspect of your marriage seems to trouble you most?" Closed questions may restrict the respondent still further by requiring a simple yes-or-no answer. "Would you like to work for a small corporation?" or "Do you feel you have a happy marriage?"

Another alternative is the **probing question,** which *encourages the* *respondent to elaborate on what he or she has been saying.* Such remarks as "I see. Can you tell me more?" or "Why don't you go on?" tend to bring about further comment on a previous statement. Short pauses may elicit the same reaction, allowing the respondent to express thoughts more completely.

A more volatile and often annoying type of question is the **loaded question,** which *stacks the deck by implying the desired answer.* This is a form of the closed question that may be used to back the respondent into a corner. In effect, the interviewer poses and answers his or her own questions: to a left-wing militant, "Isn't it true that violence can only make matters worse?"; to the secretary of defense at a press conference, "Hasn't your new policy been tried in the past with no success?" Such questions are emotionally charged, and they immediately put the respondent on his or her guard. Undeniably, loaded questions are sometimes used to advantage, especially in the news media. Thus a reporter can ask a politician questions that are on the lips of many voters, forcing him or her to meet the issues head on. Nonetheless, if we are interested in getting information, the loaded question is a doubtful technique. A better way, for example, to question the secretary of defense might be, "Would you explain the advantages and disadvantages of your new policy?"

Another type of question to steer clear of is the **obvious answer question,** which by its phrasing *implies the expected response.* For example, if during an employment interview a college professor is asked, "You wouldn't be opposed to teaching freshmen, would you?" he or she knows that the expected answer is something on the order of "I don't mind at all" or "No, I enjoy teaching freshmen." The professor who wants the job is likely to give the "right" answer, regardless of actual preference.

Regardless of the kinds of questions chosen, the interviewer is never completely sure of obtaining the number and quality of answers he or she would like to have. Interviewing is a dynamic process, not a programed event. It cannot move forward without the participation of the respondent. Thus another aspect of interviewing skill involves handling inadequate responses. Let us look at five that the interviewer can anticipate and try to avoid.

First, suppose that the respondent gives **no answer**—that is, either refuses to answer (the familiar "No comment" or "I'd rather not say") or says nothing at all. A sufficient number of such responses will bring the interview to a dead end. The interviewer might follow up such a response with a second, related question. If necessary, the line of inquiry might be dropped altogether.

Imagine instead that the respondent gives a **partial answer.** The interviewer might then restate the part of the question that has not been answered. If the respondent gives a good many partial answers, the interviewer should review the questions asked. Perhaps some could be subdivided and posed individually. In general, it is best to avoid asking more than one question at a time.

Reacting appropriately to an **irrelevant answer** is more complex because there are two reasons the respondent may have gone off on a tangent: he or she may not have understood the question completely, or he or she may be making a conscious effort to avoid answering it. Politicians, it seems, frequently evade questions by offering irrelevant answers.

Often a respondent who does not wish to disclose information will offer an **inaccurate answer,** especially if revealing the truth will be embarrassing. Unfortunately, an inaccurate answer is often difficult for the interviewer to detect, especially in an initial interview. Of course, the accuracy of the information the interviewer receives is determined in part by the respondent's motivation. A person who feels threatened by an interview is more inclined to provide data within what he or she perceives to be the interviewer's expectations. And as we saw in discussing the MUM effect, people sometimes respond inaccurately in an attempt to maintain their status level or achieve a higher one. It has been found, for example, that people (particularly those with high incomes) overestimate the number of plane trips they have made but play down any automobile loans they have taken out (Lansing and Blood, 1964).

Whether they are intentional or not, inaccurate responses are damaging not only to the interviewer but to the respondent. If he or she will be seeing the interviewer again—as is probable after an employment, appraisal, or counseling interview—it is likely that some of these distortions will be revealed at a later date. If the interviewer finds that over a series of meetings the respondent has been giving inaccurate answers, he should consider possible reasons for this behavior. The interviewer has much to gain from establishing greater rapport with the respondent, putting him or her at ease so that he or she feels it will not be personally damaging to tell the truth.

The respondent who gives an **ververbalized answer** tells the interviewer much more than he or she wants to know. Sometimes lengthy answers contain a great deal of irrelevant information. A high percentage of ororverbalized responses will severely limit the number of topics that an interviewer can cover in the time allotted. He or she should try as tactfully as possible to guide the respondent back to the heart of the question, and to do this the interviewer may wish to increase the number of closed questions.

As if these difficulties were not enough to contend with, it now seems that there are people who have a response set to agree (yea-sayers) or to disagree (naysayers). Couch and Keniston (1960), two psychologists who have analyzed response tendencies as a personality variable, describe yeasayers as impulsive people who respond easily to stimuli. Naysayers, on the other hand, inhibit and suppress their impulses and tend to reject emotional stimuli. The language in which statements are cast also affects response bias. Yeasayers are particularly attracted to statements that are enthusiastic and colloquial in tone. On the rare occasions when naysayers do agree, they are inclined to go along with statements that seem guarded, qualified, or cautious. Further research findings will be needed, however, before the interviewer can attempt to offset response bias by the way he or she constructs questions.

Interview Structure

In addition to developing skill in the art of questioning, the interviewer is sometimes responsible for giving the meeting structure. Much of what we have said thus far can be applied to relatively unstructured communication as well as to interviews. But in most cases an interview should have an apparent structure—an opening, body, and closing—and the interviewer will have specific responsibilities during each part.

In beginning an interview, an interviewer has three basic responsi-

The interview is a valuable research tool.

bilities. The first is to introduce the objectives of the interview to the respondent. Although these usually seem obvious to the interviewer, a brief statement of purpose is reassuring to the other party: an employee who is called in for a routine appraisal, for example, may perceive it as a reprimand interview unless the purpose is made clear. A second task for the interviewer is to establish rapport with the respondent, to get him or her to feel that he or she can trust the interviewer and that the meeting does not present a threatening situation. The interviewer's third and most important responsibility is motivating the respondent to answer questions. Sometimes the respondent's interest seems assured. For example, a person applying for a job will probably do his or her utmost to answer questions. But what if you are conducting some research interviews? Typically, door-to-door canvassing is considered a nuisance, and respondents may be reluctant to talk. An interviewer should never assume that a potential respondent is just waiting to be interviewed. Instead he or she should act as though the person is busy and try to show briefly why it is important that the person take a few moments of his or her time.

The body of the interview constitutes the major portion of time spent with the respondent, and it should be carefully planned for best results. If at all possible, it should be free from interruptions, phone calls, and other distractions so that both parties remain as relaxed as possible. We have seen that a number of different types of questions can be used in an interview. Each has advantages and disadvantages; the student of interviewing should at least be familiar with them. In addition, the sequence of questions used is important.

The first step in interview planning is to determine the topics to be covered. What, for example, is the typical content of the employment interview? One analysis of twenty employment interviews lists the topics shown in the table on the following page as the most frequently discussed.

After selecting the topics, the interviewer than determines the actual sequence of questions. At this point a strategy known as the **funnel sequence** is often useful: *the interviewer begins with broad questions and gradually makes them more specific* (Kahn and Cannell, 1957). Here is a funnel sequence that was used in a discussion of population control:

1. What are your views about increasing population growth in the United States?
2. What are your feelings about controlling our population growth?
3. Do you think legalized abortion should be used to help control population in the United States?
4. Should there be restrictions on abortions?
5. What restrictions should there be?

Themes of Twenty Employment Interviews

Theme	Percentage*
Information about the company:	
General organizational orientation	100
Specific job area	90
Promotion policies	60
Information about the candidate:	
Job expectations	80
Academic background	75
Prepared for the interviews	75
Scholastic record	70
Military status	70
Work experience	60
Geographical preference	60
Interviewing for other jobs	50
Marital status	50
Information about the interviewer:	
His job	25
His background	25
Where he lives	10

* Refers to the percentage of observed interviews in which this theme occurred.

SOURCE: Adapted from Cal Downs and Wil Linkugel, "A Content Analysis of Twenty Selection Interviews" (paper delivered at the annual conference of the International Communication Association, Phoenix, Ariz., April 1971), p. 3.

Because each question in the sequence is more specific than the preceding one, the interviewer can reconstruct a more complete picture of the respondent's attitudes and at the same time evaluate specific answers in relation to the general issue. The funnel sequence may be used for any number of individual topics within the body of the interview.

The funnel sequence is just one of several ways of organizing the exchange. In their discussion of the research interview, Cannell and Kahn offer some advice about selecting the sequence of topics that might well apply to almost any type of interview:

> The sequence of topics themselves should be planned to make the total interview experience as meaningful as possible, to give it a beginning, a middle, and an end. More specifically, the early questions should serve to engage the respondent's interest without threatening or taxing him before he is really committed to the transaction, and to exemplify and teach him the kind of task the interview represents. The most demanding of questions might well be placed later in the interview, when respondent commitment can be presumed to have peaked—and fatigue has not yet set in.

Sometimes the riskiest of questions may be put very late in the interview, so that if they trigger a refusal to continue, relatively little information is lost. This procedure seems prudent, but it risks also the possibility of an unpleasant leavetaking. (Cannell and Kahn, 1968, p. 578)

The possibility of an unpleasant or at least an unsatisfying conclusion points to the importance of skillfully terminating the interview. All too often interviews end abruptly because of a lack of time, and both parties are left feeling the need for closure, or resolution. Almost any interview profits from a summary of the ground covered. It can range from a brief statement to a review of all the major points discussed. Then, if some action is to be taken as a result of the interview (hiring a person, for example), the nature of the next contact should be agreed on. If each person thinks the other will initiate the contact, both may wait too long before following up. More than one job has been lost this way. Finally, a written summary may be sent to the respondent. In appraisal interviews this procedure is especially helpful: both parties then have a written record of the agreed-upon objectives for the employee's future job responsibilities. The summary will also serve as a record of the employee's progress.

We have seen various ways in which the interviewer can introduce or reinforce interview structure, but the **nondirective interview** demands skill of a different order. In this approach, often associated with psychotherapeutic treatment, *the interviewer merely restates the respondent's answers* without making value judgments about them or guiding the conversation along any prescribed lines. The aim is to induce the respondent to elaborate on previous statements in greater depth and realize the implications of what he or she has said. In this excerpt from the M.I.T. MAD Doctor computer program we see an exchange between computer and patient that reads like a parody of the nondirective interview:

> HOW DO YOU DO. I AM THE DOCTOR. PLEASE SIT DOWN AT THE TYPEWRITER AND TELL ME YOUR PROBLEM.
> I am unhappy.
> I AM SORRY TO HEAR YOU ARE UNHAPPY.
> What shall I do about it?
> WHY DO YOU ASK?
> I don't like being unhappy.
> YOU SAY YOU DON'T LIKE BEING UNHAPPY.
> Yes, I don't like it.
> YOU SEEM QUITE POSITIVE.
> Of course I am.
> IS IT BECAUSE YOU ARE THAT YOU CAME TO ME?
> Because I am what? (Quoted in Argyle, 1969, p. 169)

To elaborate on the skills needed to conduct a nondirective interview would go beyond the limits of this chapter. We shall simply note in passing that such an interview requires great restraint and sensitivity on the part of the interviewer and that this is not a technique to be exploited by the amateur psychologist.

Summary

The dyad is in many ways a microcosm of all larger groups. In the present chapter dyadic, or two-person, communication was viewed within a social setting. We saw that members of a dyad are strongly influenced by the norms they have already adopted, and that they also establish some normative agreements of their own as they interact. In addition, the roles they enact affect how they will respond to each other; we examined some consequences of conflicts within and between roles.

Our second topic was the dynamics of unstructured two-person communication. We found that given certain norms and roles, several other variables affect interaction. For example, greater emotional involvement is possible within the dyad than in a larger group, and this involvement is usually satisfying; such involvement can have negative consequences, however. Arousal level is another correlate of performance. Need for affiliation and need for dominance—two important dimensions of motivation—were also seen to be predictors of face-to-face interaction. Transactional analysis with its distinction between complementary, crossed, and ulterior transactions was also discussed.

The final section of the chapter examined a more structured form of communication: the interview. Interview objectives, various kinds of questions and responses, and ways of structuring the interview were all discussed, largely in terms of the interviewer's role.

Review Questions

1. How are disruptive power and norms related to dyadic communication?
2. What is the difference between expected and enacted roles?
3. Explain the distinction between intrarole and interrole conflict, and give an example of each.
4. What are two ways in which involvement of communicators is related to dyadic communication?
5. How is one's level of arousal related to one's ability to perform effectively?
6. How are need for dominance, need for achievement, and self-concept related?
7. How are need for affiliation and need for dominance related?
8. Describe two ways in which status affects dyadic communication.
9. Define the MUM effect.
10. Make a diagram of a complementary transaction.

11. Explain the difference between a complementary and a crossed transaction.
12. Make a diagram and give an example of both an angular and a duplex transaction.
13. Identify ten different types of interview objectives.
14. How do standardized and unstandardized interviews differ?
15. What are five different types of interview questions? Give an example of each.
16. What are five inadequate responses to interview questions? What strategy or strategies may be used to handle each?
17. Discuss three responsibilities of the interviewer at the beginning of an interview?
18. What is the funnel sequence?
19. Name three steps that might be used in terminating an interview.

Exercises

1. Select one of the role-playing situations listed in the Appendix. Determine what norms appear to operate in the specific role-playing situation selected. How might these norms be adhered to and violated in terms of the expected and enacted roles of the interviewer and respondent?
2. Write a short paper in which you analyze some communication difficulties that might arise for a college student as a result of his or her role conflicts.
3. Create two or three different role-playing situations similar to those listed in the Appendix. Select members of the class to role-play the situations in which the players have different dominance and affiliation needs. How do differences in these needs affect the communication patterns in the interview?
4. After observing a conversation between two people, try to determine what specific messages (nonverbal as well as verbal) reveal the dominance or submissiveness of each communicator. Make the same observations with respect to affiliative or antisocial behaviors. Do the characteristic roles shift from time to time?
5. Videotape an interview conducted by your classmates. Play back the interview and have the class evaluate it in terms of the suggested procedures for conducting the beginning, body, and end of an interview.
6. Role-play the part of respondent to a classmate, providing inadequate responses to develop his or her ability to probe for better answers. Then switch roles and take the test yourself.

Suggested Readings

Bach, George, and Wyden, Peter. *The Intimate Enemy: How to Fight Fair in Love and Marriage.* New York: Morrow, 1968. This book attempts to show constructive ways to resolve conflicts between the sexes. Numerous people have found it to be a useful guide to problem-solving communication in the love relationship.

Goldhaber, Gerald M. and Goldhaber, Marylynn B. *Transactional Analysis: Principles and Applications.* Boston: Allyn and Bacon, 1976. If you are interested in reading further into transactional analysis, this is an excellent book. It not only includes articles covering basic TA concepts, but offers three chapters applying the concepts to therapeutic, organizational and educational situations.

Gorden, Raymond. *Interviewing: Strategy, Techniques, and Tactics.* Homewood, Ill.: Dorsey, 1969. This comprehensive text has depth and breadth and covers both theory and application well. If you are interested in an extensive sourcebook, this would be a good one.

Stewart, Charles, and Cash, William. *Interviewing: Principles and Practices.* Dubuque, Iowa: Brown, 1974. These authors combine a brief but sound treatment of several types of interviewing with sample interviews and role-playing cases. Coverage includes informational, persuasive, employment, appraisal, and counseling interviews.

Chapter 10

Small Group Communication

OBJECTIVES

After reading this chapter the student should be able to:
1. Distinguish between primary, casual, learning, work, and therapeutic groups and explain what constitutes a problem-solving group.
2. Describe the concept of conformity in terms of the autokinetic effect.
3. Distinguish between private acceptance and public compliance.
4. Identify four conditions under which private acceptance is likely to occur.
5. Identify four characteristics of people likely to conform to group pressure.
6. Describe two theories that have been used to explain compliance to social pressure.
7. Explain the risky shift phenomenon.
8. Describe the relationship between group cohesiveness and the effectiveness of the brainstorming technique.
9. List twelve types of group member roles and give an example of each.
10. Identify four characteristics of group cohesiveness.
11. Describe the four phases of a typical group's development.
12. Describe the relationship between group size, member satisfaction, and group performance.
13. Draw five types of communication networks and describe their relative effectiveness in relation to group performance.
14. Distinguish between the trait and function views of leadership.
15. Distinguish between task and consideration functions in leadership.
16. Identify six common difficulties that small groups encounter in developing ideas and solving problems.
17. Distinguish between the Standard Agenda, Ideal Solution, and Single Question formats for group discussion.
18. Identify four strategies that may be used to resolve group conflict effectively.
19. Describe four ways in which a group can arrive at a decision.

10

A camel, it's been said, is a horse that was built by a committee—the implication being that group solutions are far less effective than those made by individuals. Whether or not this statement is true (and we shall examine it further in this chapter), all of us spend at least some of our time as members of problem-solving groups. A student council, a parent-teacher's committee on sex education in the public schools, a commission investigating the causes of prison riots, a fund-raising committee for a political party, and a tenants' association organized to fight rent increases have much in common. Despite the diverse issues that concern them, each group consists of several human beings with different ideas, skills, and levels of interest. Each group has a problem to solve and must determine the best way to go about solving it— ideally by making use of the resources of all its members.

This chapter is about the kind of communication that takes place in small groups, particularly in **problem-solving,** or *task-oriented,* groups. We shall focus first on the ways in which such groups typically function and second on the ways individual members can improve their effectiveness in them. In doing so, we extend the communication model outlined in Chapter 2 and developed in Chapter 9. The dyad is sometimes referred to as a two-person group, and often two people will engage in problem solving. But in discussing the small group, particularly the problem-solving group, we shall follow Shaw (1976), who summarizes the views of many scholars of small-group communication. Shaw (1976) identifies six ways in which a group may be defined: (1) perceptions (Do members make an impression on other members?); (2) motivation (Is membership in the group rewarding?); (3) goals (Do group members work together for a purpose?); (4) organization (Does each member have a specialized role—moderator, note-taker, and so on?); (5) interdependency (Is each member somewhat dependent on the others?); (6) interaction (Is the group small enough to allow face-to-face communication between members?).

These criteria represent guidelines for defining a group. A small group may meet some but not necessarily all these criteria. One that does meet all six would be described as a collection of people who influence one another, derive some satisfaction from maintaining membership in the group, interact for some purpose, assume specialized roles, are dependent on one another, and communicate face to face. Using this definition of a group, **small-group communication** may be regarded as *"the process by which [three] or more members of a group exchange verbal and nonverbal messages in an attempt to influence one another"* (Tubbs, 1978, p. 5).

Small-group experience is by no means confined to problem solving. Each of us is simultaneously a member of many small groups. The first and most informal are **primary groups,** *the basic social units to which we belong.* Our first primary group is our family. Our childhood friends constitute another.

In the company of adult friends, neighbors, and others with whom we socialize—fraternity or sorority groups, classmates, teammates, even street gangs—we continue and *extend our primary-group relationships* **to casual** or **social groups.** While these relationships may be relatively short-lived, their influence on later thinking and behavior is often considerable. Newcomb (1943, 1963) found that the attitudes and values of college students were influenced significantly by the friends and acquaintances they made while at college. To a lesser degree, these changes were still present thirty years after graduation. Occasionally, members of primary or social groups solve problems together, but much of their communication is spontaneous and informal.

As members of **learning or educational groups** we *come together* in an attempt *to teach or learn something about a given subject.* Quarterback clubs meet to learn more about football. Film buffs get together to share their interpretations of movies. Seminars and courses involving group interaction also constitute learning groups. Brilhart (1974) refers to such groups as "enlightenment groups," in which members may attempt to solve problems, but have no authority to implement their decisions.

Sooner or later, most of us will belong to **work groups,** which *have specific goals to achieve,* often within the context of a job. Membership may be required by virtue of employment in an organization rather than because of individual interest in the group. Group members may have little in common other than that their jobs require them to interact. That they receive payment for their individual contributions adds a unique dimension to this type of group. And whereas a member of a social or a learning group might remain relatively inactive, the consequences of not participating in a work group can be more severe (reprimands, ostracism, or even loss of employment).

At one time or another some of us will also belong to **therapeutic groups,** whose members *come together to learn about themselves and to improve their interpersonal relationships.* Unlike learning groups, which focus on mastering a given subject, therapeutic groups are consciously concerned with process—with the small-group experience itself. Therapeutic groups usually take one of two forms: the psycho-

This chapter is about communication that takes place in small groups—particularly problem-solving groups.

therapeutic group or the encounter group. The first usually meets over a longer period of time than the second and is largely conducted in conjunction with individual therapy. The encounter group may vary in length from a minilab that lasts two to three hours to a marathon that lasts several days. Depending on its focus, the group may be a personal growth lab, a group dynamics lab, a couples lab, or an organizational development session. It may be a group with one or more leaders or it may be a leaderless, or self-analytic, group that uses taped instructions for each of its meetings.

Homans has described membership in small groups as "the first and most immediate social experience of mankind" (1950, p. 1). More specifically, he defines a group as "a number of persons who communicate with one another often over a span of time and who are few enough so that each person is able to communicate with all the others, not at secondhand, through other people, but face-to-face" (p. 1). As you read the present chapter, you might give some thought to this definition.

GROUP DYNAMICS

One of the major complaints about committees and other problem-solving small groups is that they take up too much time and seldom accomplish as much as they should. To make better use of the time spent in small groups, we have to know something about how people ordinarily behave in them.

Conformity

One night several restless upperclassmen in a small dorm at the University of Wisconsin decided to persuade a fellow student that it was time for class. It was about 1 A.M. As the girl lay sleeping, they reset her alarm clock so that it went off at 1:15 but read 8:15. A few people were stationed in the bathroom, towels and toothbrushes in hand. Others were strategically placed along the corridor, ready to go through the motions of bustling off to class.

When her alarm rang the poor victim stumbled out of bed to see her roommate in the process of getting dressed. She couldn't believe that it was morning, despite the activity. "You can still see the stars. There's something wrong with the alarm. It's pitch dark outside," she protested, only to be told that it was "a dark morning." The sight of two students on their way to have breakfast was the final touch. It was spring, and there aren't many dark mornings in the spring. Nonetheless, other people seemed to think it was morning, and despite the evidence of her own senses, the weary girl started to dress for breakfast.

This is a common prank, not only in college but in summer camps and military barracks. It works often enough to suggest the potent influence of group opinion on individual judgment. In the 1930s a psychologist named Sherif designed a series of experiments on social influence in which he made use of a phenomenon called the **autokinetic effect**. The autokinetic effect is an optical illusion that was first pointed out by ancient astronomers: *when a stationary point of light is viewed in total darkness, the light seems to move because no frame of reference exists against which the observer can localize it.*

Individual estimates of autokinetic movement vary a great deal. To one person it might seem that the light has moved two inches; to another the distance might seem to be six inches. Yet Sherif found that a person who first views this phenomenon when he or she is isolated from others and observes it several times under these conditions will develop a standard of his or her own so that all his or her subsequent estimates of distance fall within this range. On the other hand, when a person witnesses the autokinetic effect for the first time as a member of a group, the group establishes a norm; if that person is then exposed again to the autokinetic effect, he or she will make estimates in terms of the group norm. Moreover, a person who has made initial judgments in isolation and then overhears others estimate the distance will correct his or her own estimate so that it tends to converge with that of the others. The autokinetic effect is thus also a measure of the effect of prestige on conformity:

> Miss X and I (Assistant in Psychology, Columbia University) were subjects for Dr. Sherif. I was well acquainted with the experiment, but Miss X knew nothing whatsoever about it. Since she was a close friend of mine, and I carried some prestige with her, Dr. Sherif suggested that it would be interesting to see if we could predetermine her judgments. It was agreed beforehand that I was to give no judgments until she had set her own standard. After a few stimulations it was quite clear that her judgments were going to vary around five inches. At the next appropriate

stimulation, I made a judgment of twelve inches. Miss X's next judgment was eight inches. I varied my judgments around twelve inches and she did the same. Then I changed my judgment to three inches, suggesting to Dr. Sherif that he had changed it. She gradually came down to my standard, but not without some apparent resistance. When it was clear that she had accepted this new standard, Dr. Sherif suggested that I make no more judgments lest I might influence hers. He then informed her on a subsequent stimulation that she was underestimating the distance which the point had moved. Immediately her judgments were made larger and she established a new standard. However, she was a little uneasy with it all, and before the experiment had progressed much farther, whispered to me, "Get me out of here." (Sherif, 1967, p. 150)

There could be no right or wrong answers in Sherif's experiments; yet norms developed. In another work Sherif tries to explain why social influence is so strong:

when a group of individuals faces a new, unstable situation and has no previously established interest or opinions regarding the situation, the result is not chaos; a common norm arises and the situation is structured in relation to the common norm. Once the common norm is established, later the separate individuals keep on perceiving it in terms of the frame of reference which was once the norm of the group. (Sherif, 1936, p. 111)

We discussed the concept of norms in Chapter 9. Suffice it to say that in the small group, social influence is even more powerful than it is in the dyad. Moreover, as we know from our discussion of balance theory, the judgments of other people affect our attitudes, beliefs, and values as well as our perceptions.

"Well, heck! If all you smart cookies agree, who am I to dissent?"

Drawing by Handelsman; © 1972 The New Yorker Magazine, Inc.

One of the criticisms of conformity research has been that subjects rarely get to argue their point of view against the majority opinion. Yet even in studies that allow dissenting members to present their arguments, considerable conformity behavior still occurs (Grove, 1965). These studies distinguish between **private acceptance** of a judgment or opinion and **public compliance**—that is, *between whether people change their thinking as a result of hearing opinions different from their own or whether they say they agree with the group when in fact they disagree.*

Private acceptance is more likely to occur when (1) the individual greatly values membership in the group, (2) opinion is unanimously against him or her, (3) the issue in question is ambiguous to begin with, or (4) the group is under pressure to achieve an important goal (Cartwright and Zander, 1968). Public compliance usually stems from the desire to avoid the unpleasantness of conflict. After maintaining a dissenting opinion for a long time, a person may be made so uncomfortable by social pressures that as a peace-keeping gesture he or she gives the impression of going along with the rest of the group. A number of studies have shown that the person who conforms readily tends to be (1) more submissive or dependent, (2) high in the need for social approval and low in the need to be outstanding, (3) more often female than male, and (4) lacking in self-confidence (Hare, 1962).

Sometimes, of course, compliance is forced. For example, during the Korean War the so-called confessions of American prisoners to Chinese participants holding them captive often included remarks or emphases that undercut their own statements of contrition:

> the prisoners found numerous ways to obey the letter but not the spirit of the Chinese demands. For example, during public self-criticism sessions they would often emphasize the wrong words in the sentence, thus making the whole ritual ridiculous: "I am sorry I called Comrade Wong *a no-good son-of-a-bitch.*" Another favorite device was to promise never to "get caught" committing a certain crime in the future. Such devices were effective because even those Chinese who knew English were not sufficiently acquainted with idiom and slang to detect subtle ridicule. (Schein, 1956, pp. 159–160)

The prisoner of war and the compliant group member both pretend to go along with the expectations of the group in order to spare themselves certain undesirable consequences. For the prisoner of war, these consequences are often physical—solitary confinement, lack of food, torture. For the member of a group, the consequences, while perhaps more subtle, are no less real—social pressure, loss of esteem, even ostracism by the group. At issue in the much publicized trial of kidnapped heiress Patricia Hearst was whether her apparent compliance with the demands of her kidnappers, the Symbionese Liberation Army (S.L.A.), implied private acceptance of S.L.A. precepts or merely, as her defense lawyers maintained, public compliance motivated by coercion and fear.

Social Influence

We have looked at conformity behavior in terms of the individual member. Now let us examine the behavior of the group. We know that the group tends to exert most pressure to conform on newcomers, who have not yet earned the right to deviate from group norms. Fraternities and sororities often deal out harsh criticism when rushees and pledges dress or act differently from other members of the group. Yet a great many of the same deviations are tolerated when they exist in fraternity members who are upperclassmen.

Groups with a high level of cohesiveness tend to exert strong conformity pressures. It seems that the more closely knit the group, the more the members resist allowing anyone to become a member who does not share their values. Members with the greatest prestige tend to be "super representatives" of the attributes that are highly valued by the group. The typical football team captain is usually one of the best athletes on the team. Similarly, the gang leader is often one of the gang's toughest members. In each case the person who best represents the qualities esteemed by the group has the most prestige.

How does the cohesive group behave when one of its members takes a stand quite different from that of the rest? Schachter (1951) found that initially the deviant gets most of the group's attention. Each member will probably say or do something to persuade the lone dissenter to come around to the position held by the rest of the group. These efforts may go on for some time. Eventually, the deviant either gives in—there is no way of knowing, of course, whether this is simply public compliance—or is ignored or rejected.

Newcomb (1953) has tried to account for the group's behavior in terms of balance theory. He predicts that in groups of three or more people, the need for balance (or symmetry) will operate to reduce the discrepancy between the deviant's attitude and the attitudes of the other group members. Thus, in an effort to change the deviant's mind, the group will direct a greater proportion of its communicative acts toward him or her than toward any other member for a considerable length of time. There is a point of diminishing returns, however, after which the deviant receives little or no communication from other group members, who for the most part ignore him or her.

An explanation of what makes most of us yield to social pressure is offered by Festinger's **social comparison theory.** Festinger (1954) believes that *all human beings have a need to evaluate their own* *opinions and abilities and that when they cannot do so by objective nonsocial means they compare them with those of other people.* How do you tell, for example, whether you are a good driver? Clearly, by comparing your performance with that of other drivers. Similarly, you find out whether you are liberal in your political views by comparing them with those of others. In other words, in the absence of objective criteria, you rely on the opinions of others to determine the validity of your own.

In the Schachter experiment a discrepancy existed between the opinions of one group member and the rest of the group. Social comparison theory predicts that in such a situation group members will act to reduce the discrepancy and that the person with the discrepant opinion will tend to change his or her position so that it is closer to that of other group members. We saw this to be the case not only in the Schachter experiment but in some of the studies of the autokinetic effect, where individual judgments tend to converge with group norms. However these phenomena are explained, the tendency to conform seems clear. In the following section we shall examine conformity as it affects group decisions.

The Quality of Group Problem Solving

In studying group dynamics, a reasonable question to ask is how groups compare with individuals in problem solving. Will the number of people in the group affect the quality of the decision? Will people meeting together generate a greater number of novel ideas than they would working in isolation? In short, how does the presence of others influence the way we think?

Acceptance of Risk. It has been established that members of groups tend to conform. As yet, however, nothing has been said about the direction of that conformity. When we call someone a "conformist," we usually think of him or her as somewhat conservative. Conformists don't rock the boat. They don't create dissension. They go along with group norms. They probably go along with group decisions. It would seem that because they conform, they take few risks, and from this we might guess that the decisions of the group would also tend to be conservative or at least cautious.

Suppose you are on your way to a meeting in which your group will advise Mr. A, an electrical engineer, about the pros and cons of a certain career choice. Should he remain in the large electronics corporation for which he works, where he is assured a high level of security and moderate financial rewards, or should he accept an offer from a small, recently founded company that will offer him a higher starting salary and a share in the firm's ownership but whose future is highly uncertain? What odds will you give—one in ten, three in ten, and so on—that the new company turns out to be financially sound and thus that Mr. A will do better joining it than remaining where he is? Whatever the odds you choose, chances are that if a group discussion follows, it will significantly increase your estimate of Mr. A's chances for success.

The risky shift phenomenon is the name given this *tendency for people to increase their willingness to take risks as a result of group discussions.* It is by no means confined to decisions about careers. Here, for example, are summaries of a few of the experimental problems that have demonstrated a shift toward risk after group communication:

> A man with a severe heart ailment must seriously curtail his customary way of life if he does not undergo a delicate medical operation which might cure him completely or might prove fatal.
>
> A captain of a college football team, in the final seconds of a game with the college's traditional rival, may choose a play that is almost certain to produce a tie score, or a more risky play that would lead to sure victory if successful, sure defeat if not.
>
> An engaged couple must decide, in the face of recent arguments suggesting some sharp differences of opinion, whether or not to get married. Discussions with a marriage counselor indicate that a happy marriage, while possible, would not be assured. (Wallach, Kogan, and Bem, 1962, p. 77)

Several explanations of the risky shift phenomenon have been proposed; we shall consider three of them in brief fashion. The first is that within a group no member feels totally responsible for the decision. This might explain the actions of lynch mobs: a person who might never dare commit a murder alone suddenly helps carry out a lynching. The second possibility is that those who argue in favor of risky positions are more persuasive than those who are conservative and that they therefore influence others in favor of riskier decisions. The first two hypotheses have little experimental support. A third and more likely possibility is that Western culture tends to value risk taking over conservative behavior. Witness the American idea that any newborn child has some chance of one day becoming president of the United States. In this country we hold success and achievement in high esteem, and both are linked to a good extent with a willingness to take risks. In contemplating a decision each person may feel that the course of action he or she favors involves a reasonable amount of risk, but as the group begins to communicate about the problem, more arguments for both the risky and the conservative side become apparent. The result, as Wheeler puts it, is that

> Just as an individual practices his tennis game because there is a cultural value placed on being slightly better than other people, he changes his risk level in the direction valued by the culture so that he can feel he is

slightly "better" than his peers. This does not mean that the individual automatically changes his risk level but that he reinterprets elements in the situation and focuses on arguments favoring risk. (Wheeler, 1970, p. 106)

As you find yourself participating in task-oriented groups, it is important to realize that the group decision is likely to be riskier than the average of the positions taken by individual group members before their interaction.

Level of Creativity. A second issue concerning the kinds of solutions groups reach has to do with creativity. Consider this problem. The Lang Advertising Agency has five writers on its staff. It is bidding for the Hudson's Bay Scotch account and must submit a sales presentation and advertising program to the prospective client. Should all five writers work independently and submit their own programs to the advertising director, or should the five be brought together to tackle the problem? Which procedure will generate a greater number of original ideas?

In essence we are asking whether **brainstorming** is an effective problem-solving technique. This approach, first introduced in the advertising firm of Batten, Barton, Durstine & Osborn in 1939, was designed to offset tendencies of group members to be inhibited by pressures to conform. Brainstorming had several rules. There was to be no criticism of ideas. "Freewheeling" was encouraged: the more way out the idea, the better. Quantity was desired: the greater the number of ideas, the better. Taking off on other people's ideas—either by improving one or by showing how two different ideas could be combined—was also encouraged (Osborn, 1957).

Brainstorming sessions became extremely popular not only in large corporations but in the military and in various government agencies. No one seemed to challenge the belief that people worked more effectively in groups than in isolation until 1958. At that time a study at Yale University found that people who worked alone on a problem rather than as part of a group produced almost twice the number of ideas and twice the number of unique ideas (Taylor, Berry, and Block, 1958).

Yet brainstorming is still a widely practiced technique. Are we to conclude from the Yale study that groups will always solve problems less effectively and creatively than individuals? We cannot answer this question as easily as we can the issue of whether groups make more or less conservative decisions than individuals. There is evidence that when the group is a cohesive one and when members have had previous training in brainstorming techniques, the results can be highly successful (Cohen, Whitmore, and Funk, 1960). It has been suggested, therefore, that the effectiveness of brainstorming will depend on several variables, including the relationships between group members, the nature of the problem to be solved, and the type of leadership the group has (Kelley and Thibaut, 1969).

The Role of Group Member

Nine psychotherapists have formed a group to help block the passage of mental health legislation that they consider repressive. Ostensibly, the group's members are equal in status. No leader has been appointed. In this context each of the therapists has the same role—that of group member. Because of your interest in small-group communication and your friendship with one of the therapists, you are allowed to attend the meeting as an observer.

After attending a few meetings, you begin to notice that Bob knows a lot about existing mental health laws. He also makes a number of suggestions for actions the group might take: contacting legislators, raising funds for a series of broadcasts on the issue, distributing handbills about the implications of the new law. Matt, another member of the group, has few ideas of his own and tends to go along with any concrete proposals for group action. "I'm for that. Why not try it?" he often says. Frank, on the other hand, has more ideas than he knows what to do with. He proposes solutions, one after another—some sound, others extreme. Initially, he is very enthusiastic, but he never seems to carry through any of his suggestions. To the chagrin of most of the group, Kay usually punches holes in other people's arguments. "It will never work," she chides. "What do we use for money? People aren't going to contribute. They don't understand the issue."

Here are four people in the role of group member. Each interprets it somewhat differently. You think you see some individual patterns of interaction emerging, but to be accurate you need a method of describing various behaviors.

One of the more important accomplishments of small-group research has been the development of several such systems. Undoubtedly, the most widely known is Interaction Process Analysis (IPA), developed at Harvard University by Robert Bales. The twelve categories of IPA are virtually self-explanatory (see Figure 10.1), and they offer a valuable framework from which to view the functions and patterns of communication. Each interaction is assigned to one of the categories, and when the scoring has been completed, certain behavior patterns become apparent.

In the group we have been discussing, Bob's statements would tend to fall in categories 4 (gives suggestion) and 6 (gives information), Matt's in 3 (agrees), Frank's in 4 (gives suggestion), and Kay's in 10 (disagrees). The responses of other members of the group may be more diversified so that no single category or set of categories predomi-

INTERPERSONAL COMMUNICATION

Figure 10.1

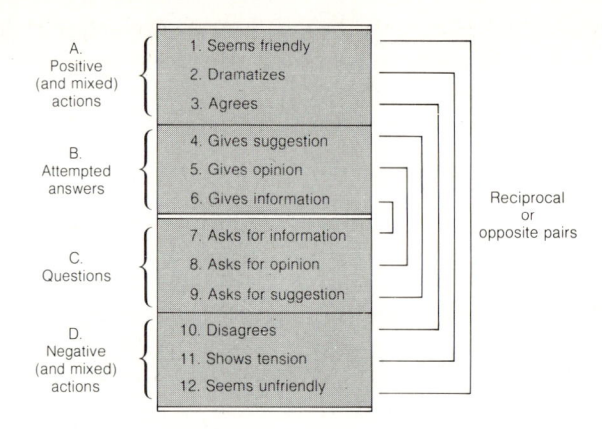

A. Positive (and mixed) actions	1. Seems friendly 2. Dramatizes 3. Agrees	
B. Attempted answers	4. Gives suggestion 5. Gives opinion 6. Gives information	Reciprocal or opposite pairs
C. Questions	7. Asks for information 8. Asks for opinion 9. Asks for suggestion	
D. Negative (and mixed) actions	10. Disagrees 11. Shows tension 12. Seems unfriendly	

CATEGORIES FOR INTERACTION PROCESS ANALYSIS

SOURCE: *Personality and Interpersonal Behavior* by Robert Freed Bales. Copyright © 1970 by Holt, Rinehart and Winston, Inc. Reprinted by permission of Holt, Rinehart and Winston, Inc.

nates, but over an extended period we could probably identify the characteristic behaviors of each member. In any case Bales' method of classifying human interaction gives us a systematic way to analyze group communication. By means of these categories, we can classify each communicative act regardless of its content.

As you look at the list in Figure 10.1, you might ask yourself which categories describe your own actions in small groups. There is a good chance that you will find yourself performing only a limited number of these behaviors. For example, one friend of ours summed up his participation in groups by saying, "I often like to play the devil's advocate and give people a bit of a hard time." If his statement is accurate, we would expect that most of his interactions (like those of Kay in the group we described) would fall in category 10 of the IPA. There are groups that need at least one critical member, someone willing to challenge others, but the last thing in the world some groups need is another devil's advocate. In general, it seems foolish to assume that any behavior or set of behaviors is appropriate in all situations; there is much to be said for developing some degree of role flexibility. Increasing one's sensitivity to the needs of the group is a first step in this direction. Cameron speaks to this point when he writes:

> To the extent that an individual, in the course of his personality development, learns to take social roles skillfully and realistically, acquires an adequate repertory of them, and becomes adroit in shifting from one role to another when he is in difficulty, he should grow into a flexible, adap-

tive social adult with minimal susceptibility to behavior disorders. (Cameron, 1947, p. 93)

Cohesiveness

Probably one of the most important by-products of group interaction is the emotional commitment that may evolve from having worked on a problem with others. In a classic study conducted during World War II, it was found that women who participated in group discussions on how best to cook unpopular cuts of meat (and thus leave favored cuts for the troops overseas) were much more likely to try out new recipes than were women who simply listened to a speech intended to persuade them to do so (Lewin, 1958, p. 202).

This kind of emotional commitment seems to increase as attraction to the group increases. **Cohesiveness** has been defined as *"the total field*

Feelings are very much involved in group behavior.

of forces acting on members to remain in the group" (Schachter, 1951, p. 191). It may also be considered in terms of the loyalty and high morale of group members. Think of groups you have either been in or observed that were closely knit. Two groups that are not necessarily problem-solving groups but that illustrate high levels of cohesion are the Carter family and the Cincinnati Reds. Cohesiveness, which connotes pride of membership, often intensifies as a group becomes more successful. We are all familiar with the popular chant of crowds at sporting events, "We're number 1, we're number 1."

In general, cohesive groups have interested and committed members who enjoy each other's company. The group is not always highly productive, but its members do tend to help each other with problems, to adapt well to crisis situations, and to ask questions openly. We referred earlier to the conformity demands made by a cohesive group on its members. It is true, however, that they may sometimes feel free to disagree more openly than members of less cohesive groups.

In discussing emotional reactions to groups, it is only fair to acknowledge that things do not always turn out so positively. Working with others can also be frustrating, boring and unsettling. The point is that the socioemotional dimension of group interaction constitutes a very real and powerful part of group behavior. Many people think that feelings have no place in a problem-solving group. On the contrary, feelings are very much involved in group behavior and should be studied as vigorously as its logical and rational aspects.

The Phases of Group Development

It has been said that like a human being, each group has a life cycle: it has a birth, childhood, and maturity, and ultimately it ceases to exist. A number of theories have been proposed about what growth typically occurs in a group, and these are based on the study of either problem-solving or therapeutic groups (especially, encounter groups).

Theorists seem to agree that growth and development in the group are the result of both the needs of the individual members and the social forces created within the group itself. Typically, these forces interact in a predictable way, with the group going through several stages or phases. Some theorists identify four phases, others three, and there are other differences in interpretation as well. For example, some theorists believe that the various phases occur even if a group meets only once (Tuckman, 1965; Fisher, 1970). Others hold that the phases occur over the life history of a group that meets repeatedly (Bennis and Shepard, 1956; Thelen and Dickerman, 1949). And still a third faction contends that all the group phases occur in each meeting and continue to recur throughout the group's life history (Schutz, 1958; Bales and Strodbeck, 1951). This third theory seems the most likely and the most valuable in providing insight into group development. Keeping these different viewpoints in mind, let us look at the four-phase model of group development as it is represented in the literature.

Phase one is a period in which *group members break the ice and begin to establish a common basis for functioning.* This stage is sometimes referred to as a period of orientation, inclusion, or group formation. Initially, people may ask questions about one another, tell where they are from, and generally make small talk. It seems that early in the life of a group, members are interested in building a working relationship that is psychologically comfortable. Even members of the most ambitious problem-solving groups usually spend some time socializing.

But **phase two** is frequently *characterized by conflict.* The social amenities are over, and sooner or later the pressure to accomplish a task reveals differences in personalities, values, and opinions. People become much more definite about their beliefs, and sometimes group members clash. This period of dissent and controversy is ripe for communication failures: the more emotionally charged the discussion, the more prone group members are to jump to conclusions, lose their tempers, or interpret the comments of others as threats or criticisms. One student description clearly tracks the movement from phase one to phase two:

> we talked about personal interests until some common ground was established, then we found we could talk about the assignment more freely. But after talking about non-subject things, it was hard to keep the line of talk on the problems at hand. Some wanted to get the assignment accomplished while two guys in the group continually swayed the conversation to things that were easier to talk about, but had nothing to do with the subject (Howard has a big thing for John Deere farm machinery). At first we were constantly trying not to hurt anyone's feelings, so we let the conversation drift. We didn't question or reject each other's ideas, and I feel we often settled for less than we should have. The longer we were in the group together, the more we got to know each other and the more times we voiced our real opinions. That's when the tempers started to flare!

In **phase three** there is a *resolution of the conflict experienced during phase two.* Group cohesion begins to emerge, and the group starts functioning more smoothly as a unit. Here is Fisher's description of phase three:

> Social conflict and dissent dissipate during the third phase. Members express fewer unfavorable opinions toward decision proposals. The coalition of individuals who had opposed those proposals which eventually achieve consensus also weakens in the third phase. (Fisher, 1974, p. 142)

The *period of consensus and maximum productivity* is **phase four**. Dissent is very much out of place at this time, so that few negative or unfavorable comments are expressed. Group spirit is high, and a great deal of mutual backpatting takes place. Group members joke and laugh and reinforce each other for having contributed to the group's success.

In an early article Thelen and Dickerman did a good job of summarizing the group phases:

> Beginning with individual needs for finding security and activity in a social environment, we proceed first to emotional involvement of the individuals with each other, and second to the development of a group as a rather limited universe of interaction among individuals and as the source of individual security. We then find that security of position in the group loses its significance except that as the group attempts to solve problems it structures its activities in such a way that each individual can play a role which may be described as successful or not in terms of whether the group successfully solved the problem it had set itself. (Thelen and Dickerman, 1949, p. 316)

Our summary of the current literature on group phases has not made specific reference to all the theories that have contributed to our thinking. These are outlined briefly in Figure 10.2.

Figure 10.2

Summary of Literature on Group Phases

	Phase 1	*Phase 2*	*Phase 3*	*Phase 4*
Thelen and Dickerman (1949)	Forming	Conflict	Harmony	Productivity
Bennis and Shepard (1956, 1961)	Dependence	Interdependence	Focused Work	Productivity
Tuckman (1965)	Forming	Storming	Norming	Performing
Fisher (1970, 1974)	Orientation	Conflict	Emergence	Reinforcement
Bales and Strodbeck (1951)	Orientation	Evaluation		Control
Schutz (1958)	Inclusion	Control		Affection

Of course, not every group will develop precisely along the lines described above. Nevertheless, an awareness of the recurring themes in group development should enable us to improve our perception and understanding of group dynamics.

GROUP STRUCTURE

The distinction between group structure and group dynamics is somewhat arbitrary, for the way a group is constituted has considerable influence on how it functions. In our discussion of structure, we shall be concerned with three communication variables: group size, networks, and leadership.

Group Size

Think back to the groups you have belonged to that ranged in size from three to fifteen members. As the group got larger, what did you notice about the quality of the communication? How did you feel about your part in the discussions? How satisfied were you with them? It has been known for a number of years that as group size increases, the satisfaction of each member decreases. In larger groups a few people account for almost all the talking; the rest do very little. If you remember larger groups as boring and slow-moving, you probably were among the more silent members. We have seen a number of student groups fail to develop into effective decision-making bodies because a great many people spent most of their time listening to a few long, complicated speeches made by a handful of members.

Group size affects performance as well as satisfaction. For example, larger groups tend to take more time to reach decisions, particularly if unanimity is required. We also know that as group size increases a number of subgroups may form, and that these factions tend to polarize and to distract members from the problems at hand.

You can get some idea of the subgroups that may develop by looking at the potential communication relationships within groups of various sizes. In a dyad, for example, Bostrom (1970, p. 257) shows that only two relationships are possible—A to B or B to A, but in a triad, or three-person group, there are nine possibilities:

1. A to B
2. A to C
3. B to A
4. B to C
5. C to B
6. C to A
7. A to B and C
8. B to A and C
9. C to A and B

To show how rapidly complexity increases as groups gain in size, Bostrom (1970, p. 258) also calculated all the communication relationships possible within groups of three to eight people:

Number in Group	Interactions Possible
2	2
3	9
4	28
5	75
6	186
7	441
8	1,056

Small wonder that to most people, belonging to a large group is less satisfying than belonging to a small one.

For our purposes the most practical qestion we can ask is: What size group seems best for problem solving? In a tongue-in-cheek discussion of government cabinets, the world's most powerful committees, Parkinson reasons that ideally a cabinet should consist of five members. Nevertheless, membership usually increases to seven or nine and then from ten toward twenty. In addition to the obvious difficulty of assembling all these people at one time, writes Parkinson,

> there is a far greater chance of members proving to be elderly, tiresome, inaudible, and deaf. Relatively few were chosen from any idea that they are or could be or have been useful. A majority perhaps were brought in merely to conciliate some outside group. The tendency is therefore to report what happens to the group they represent. All secrecy is lost and, worst of all, members begin to prepare their speeches. They address the meeting and tell their friends afterward about what they imagine they have said. . . . Internal parties form and seek to gain strength by further recruitment. (Parkinson, 1964, p. 54)

As membership expands beyond twenty, the whole quality of the committee changes so that "the five members who matter will have taken to meeting beforehand" (Parkinson, 1964, p. 55).

While not to be taken literally, Parkinson's amusing description of the life cycle of the committee has essential validity. Although it is true that a greater variety of ideas tend to be expressed in large groups, such groups have several limitations we have already mentioned. Generally, the optimum size for a problem-solving group is five to seven members. This figure seems to have the greatest number of advantages.

Communication Networks

In *Up the Organization* Robert Townsend (1970), the man who revitalized Avis Rent a Car and has headed numerous other business enterprises, has some provocative things to say about how management should be organized. One of his proposals is that all positions with "assistant to" in the title be abolished. In making his point Townsend presents three charts; these are reproduced in Figure 10.3. Unlike the regular assistant, who is given authority to make decisions, the assistant-to "moves back and forth between the boss and his people with oral or written messages on real or apparent problems—overlapping and duplicating efforts and make-working." Further on in his book, the author makes this observation about structure:

> In the best organizations people see themselves working in a circle as if around one table. One of the positions is designated chief executive officer, because somebody has to make all those tactical decisions that enable an organization to keep working. In this circular organization, leadership passes from one to another depending on the particular task being attacked—without any hang-ups. (Townsend, 1970, p. 134)

Townsend is talking about **communication networks,** *patterns of human interaction*. As you read on, try to decide for yourself whether his recommendations have merit. You might reserve your judgment, however, until after you have read the section on leadership.

Figure 10.3

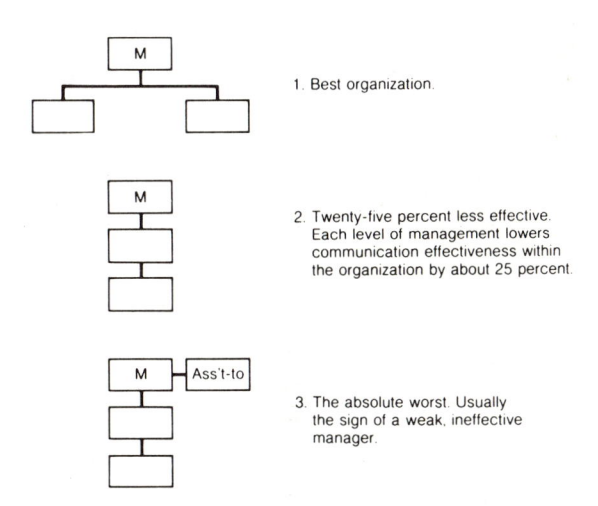

1. Best organization.

2. Twenty-five percent less effective. Each level of management lowers communication effectiveness within the organization by about 25 percent.

3. The absolute worst. Usually the sign of a weak, ineffective manager.

THREE TYPES OF MANAGEMENT ORGANIZATION

Source: Robert Townsend, *Up the Organization* (New York: Knopf, 1970), pp. 22, 23.

INTERPERSONAL COMMUNICATION

In Figure 10.4 we see several frequently used communication networks: the Wheel, Chain, Y, Circle, and All-Channel networks. Note that in this illustration each is a five-person group. In the Wheel, one person—who usually becomes the leader—is the focus of comments from each member of the group. As the central person in the network, he or she is free to communicate with the other four, but they can communicate only with him or her. In the Chain network three people can communicate with those on either side of them, but the other two with only one other member of the group. The Y network resembles the Chain: three of the five people can communicate with only one person. Unlike these systems, which are centralized and tend to have leaders, the Circle and All-Channel patterns are decentralized and sometimes leaderless. In the Circle each person may communicate with two others, those on either side of him. In the All-Channel network, sometimes called Concom, all communication lines are open; each member is able to communicate with all the other members.

In studying small-group communication, we want to know how the type of network used affects group performance in problem solving and how given patterns affect interpersonal relationships within the group. Much of the research on networks is based on an experiment by Leavitt (1951) in which five subjects were each given different information essential to the solution of a problem in symbol identification. By using various networks (the Y, Wheel, Chain, and Circle), Leavitt manipulated the freedom with which information could be transmitted from one subject to another, and he then compared the results. The Wheel, the most centralized of the four networks, produced the best-organized and fastest performance; the Circle group, the least centralized, was the most disorganized and unstable, and proved

Figure 10.4

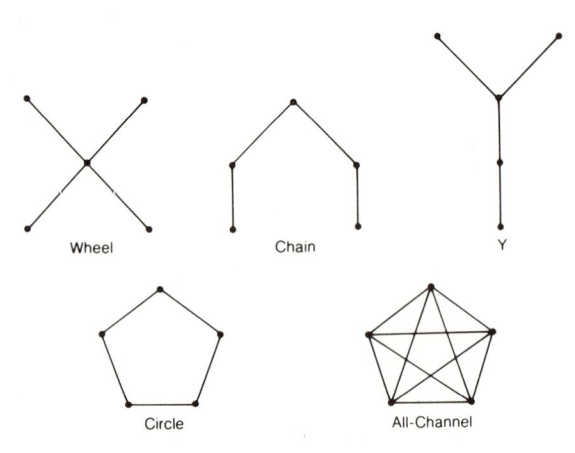

FIVE TYPES OF COMMUNICATION NETWORKS

slowest in solving the problem. The biggest drawback of the Circle network, as another researcher has observed, is that it tends to generate a large number of errors as members try to communicate information around it (Bavelas, 1950).

Numerous studies of networks have been patterned after the Leavitt experiment, but the results are not easy to summarize. It is sometimes argued, for example, that certain networks are inherently more effective because of their structure, but Guetzkow and Simon (1955) believe that there are other factors to be considered. A particular network may handicap a group not in its ability to solve a problem but in its ability to organize itself so that it can solve the problem. This is an interesting hypothesis, especially in the light of Leavitt's original finding that Y, Wheel, and Chain groups were able to organize themselves so that each eventually established one procedure it used over and over, whereas members of Circle networks did not. Guetzkow and Simon believe that once a group has established a procedure for working together, it can perform efficiently regardless of its type of network.

The nature of the problem to be solved also affects performance. Groups with centralized networks are better at identifying colors, symbols, and numbers, and solving other simple problems. Decentralized networks have the edge over centralized ones when dealing with problems that are more complex—arithmetic, word arrangement, sentence construction, and discussion problems (Shaw, 1964).

Because most of the communication we are concerned with relates not to symbol identification and the like but to more complex issues, decentralized networks will usually be most desirable. For example, the Wheel, though efficient in its use of time, tends to lower the cohesiveness of a group, reduce its inventiveness, and make it too dependent on its leader (Guetzkow and Simon, 1955). Another advantage of decentralized networks is that they tend to provide the most satisfaction for individual members. The All-Channel network seems desirable for a number of reasons. Although initially it tends to be more inefficient and time-consuming, it maximizes the opportunities for corrective feedback, which ultimately should result in greater accuracy. Furthermore, freedom to speak to anyone else in the group creates high morale. These findings are important to keep in mind in the event that group discussions you participate in are characterized by inaccuracy or low morale.

Leadership

For many years people believed that leaders were born, not made, and a search was conducted to determine the traits of the "born leader." The quest has been largely unsuccessful. We do know that usually a leader is more self-confident and more intelligent than other members of his or her group. Some studies suggest that the leader is better adjusted and more sensitive to the opinions of other group members. Nevertheless, these traits are by no means reliable predictors of leadership. No single set of traits seems important in all situations. The successful commander of an air force squadron is not necessarily effective in an administrative post at the Pentagon. The outstanding teacher is not always a worthwhile dean or department chairman.

Recent studies have led us to view leadership not as a quality but as a series of functions that groups must have performed. The leader then becomes the person who successfully performs a number of these functions, and sometimes leadership will pass from one person to another or be divided among group members. Thus far two major leadership activities have been identified: task functions and consideration functions. Neither set is in itself sufficient to satisfy all the group's needs.

Task functions are *activities that help the group achieve its goals.* In terms of the IPA categories in Figure 10.1, the activities might include giving and asking other members for suggestions, opinions, and information (categories 4–9). Other task functions might be orienting the group on how best to proceed, clarifying the remarks of others, and summarizing group progress.

Consideration functions have to do with morale. They include *any activities that improve the emotional climate or increase the satisfaction of individual members:* showing agreement, support, or encouragement; gatekeeping (that is, allowing members who might otherwise be ignored to speak); and so on.

It is often difficult for one person to perform task and consideration functions simultaneously. Suppose that an emergency meeting of a school board is called to prevent a walkout of the teachers and that two board members monopolize the discussion in an unconstructive way. Someone will have to steer the conversation back to the problem at hand, which requires immediate action, and in doing so he or she may bruise a few egos. It takes considerable skill for the person who has done the offending to also conciliate the offended. For this reason the group often develops two or more leaders: a task leader, whose primary concern is that the job be done and the group perform well, and a social leader, whose first interest is in maintaining the group's high morale. Nevertheless, the most valuable leaders are those able to perform both task and consideration functions successfully.

Support for the concept that leaders are made, not born, comes from the Leavitt (1951) study of communication networks. Whereas in decentralized networks there was found to be little agreement among members as to the identity of the group's leader, in centralized networks such as the Wheel, Chain, and Y, people who occupied central positions and were thus able to channel communication were considered leaders. (Leadership and popularity are by no means synonymous, however, as we saw in the sociograms in Chapter 5.)

Although we have stressed leadership functions rather than traits, there are specific behaviors often characteristic of leaders. If we compare those who get weeded out with those who emerge as leaders, we see some clear-cut differences. The first tend to be quiet, uninformed or unskilled, inflexible, and bossy or dictatorial; they also spend a great deal of time socializing. In contrast, emergent leaders tend to speak up, to have good ideas and state them clearly, to care about the group, and to make sacrifices and build cohesiveness (Bormann, 1976). In sum, leadership functions include a number of behaviors that can be learned.

CORRELATES OF EFFECTIVE GROUPS

Anyone who has participated in problem-solving group discussions knows that they can be time-consuming, boring, and sometimes infuriating. Furthermore, the decisions groups make may be of poor quality and may be ignored by those who must carry them out. Yet even committees that design horses which look like camels are not that easily disbanded. There are countless situations in which we cannot make decisions on our own; we must work within a group. As we have already seen, group structure—the size of a group, for example—can influence the effectiveness of problem-solving communication. In this section we shall be looking at some other correlates of small-group effectiveness.

It would be nice if we could automatically improve our communication behaviors by reading about what makes small groups successful. Unfortunately, improvement is not so easily attained. It does come, however, with participation. In summarizing several studies, McGrath and Altman comment, "The adage 'Practice makes perfect' seems to be fairly well substantiated by small group research. The more task training and experience groups and group members have, the better they perform as individuals and as groups" (1966, p. 58).

The process by which improvement takes place is probably that of social learning. Behaviors that are productive tend to be reinforced by other members of the group, and those that are unproductive tend to be extinguished because they go unrewarded. Granted that no amount of reading can replace the experience of being part of a group, there are still some lessons we can learn from reading about communication. We can learn what the behaviors are that make for successful groups and then try to practice them when we do participate. In some situations we may be able to do no more than improve our own performance within the group. In other cases we may be in a position to design as well as engage in more effective group activities.

Idea Development and Problem Solving

If you were to interview members of several different kinds of small groups about the difficulties they encounter in developing ideas and solving problems, you would find at least six recurring complaints: (1) Group objectives are not clearly stated or agreed upon; (2) Group members do not come up with enough ideas; (3) The group does not carry through discussion of each issue until it is resolved; (4) Members rarely help one another; (5) Conflict between members becomes so intense that it is counterproductive; and (6) Conclusions are not reached or agreed upon.

In an attempt to correct some of these shortcomings, many groups try to follow an agenda or schedule that will help them make better use of their time and resources. One of the most widely known group agendas is that adopted from a problem-solving sequence of questions developed several decades ago by John Dewey. This approach has often been called the Standard Agenda because, as you can see below, the questions are broad enough to be applied to just about any problem.

Standard Agenda

1. What are the limits and specific nature of the problem?
2. What are the causes and consequences of the problem?
3. What things must an acceptable solution to the problem accomplish?
4. What solutions are available to us?
5. What is the best solution?

Although groups have been aided by the Standard Agenda for years, experimental evidence shows that two other problem-solving sequences—the Ideal Solution Form and the Single Question Form—result in greater accuracy (Larson, 1969). Like the Standard Agenda both these instruments involve a series of questions intended to stimulate the thought of group members and to keep them from reaching an impasse. In the Ideal Solution Form, notice the realistic emphasis on approximating ideal goals:

Ideal Solution Form

1. Are we all agreed on the nature of the problem?
2. What would be the ideal solution from the point of view of all parties involved in the problem?

3. What conditions within the problem could be changed so that the ideal solution might be achieved?
4. Of the solutions available to us, which one best approximates the ideal solution? (Larson, 1969, p. 453)

The Single Question Form has a slightly different emphasis. By constantly referring the group back to a single objective, it attempts to concentrate the group's energies on the problem and keep members from going off on a series of tangents:

Single Question Form

1. What is the single question, the answer to which is all the group needs to know to accomplish its purpose?
2. What subquestions must be answered before we can answer the single question we have formulated?
3. Do we have sufficient information to answer confidently the subquestions? (If yes, answer them. If not, continue below.)
4. What are the most reasonable answers to the subquestions?
5. Assuming that our answers to the subquestions are correct, what is the best solution to the problem? (Larson, 1969, p. 453)

Resolution of Conflict

One value of the four-phase model of group development discussed earlier is that it enables us to see that regardless of whether a group follows an agenda or a schedule, conflict will be a legitimate part of the small-group experience. Should we avoid conflict or meet it head on? Some group members try to avoid it at all costs; others seem to thrive on it. Somewhere between these extremes is a realistic attitude toward conflict, one that will result in maximum gain for all parties concerned.

If several approaches to conflict, along with their outcomes, are plotted on a grid, our alternatives become clear. In the model of conflict resolution in Figure 10.5 (page 277), these outcomes are related to the task and consideration functions that each group must have performed. The horizontal axis, "Concern for production of results," measures task functions; the vertical axis, "Concern for people," measures consideration functions.

The 1,1 position on the grid is the laissez-faire approach. It represents complete neutrality. The person with this attitude avoids pushing for the resolution of any issue that might introduce dissension; yet he or she shows no regard for other members of the group. The 1,9 position is person oriented. Its goal is surface harmony, accomplished by subordinating task to consideration needs. The person who takes this position strives for the appearance of good feeling by suppressing conflicts wherever possible. The 5,5 position represents the desire for

Conflict will be a legitimate part of the small group experience.

compromise. Although it seems effective, this midway point leaves conflict unresolved; no one loses, but no one gains either. The hard-nosed or exclusively task-oriented approach is represented by the 9,1 position. This attitude is typified by such remarks as "Let's get the ball rolling and the job done." But the job often remains undone because of the lack of concern for group feelings.

Each of these positions has disadvantages when compared with the 9,9 approach. Here the point of view is that we must allow conflicts to be expressed openly while working vigorously at the tasks confronting the group. This means keeping the conflict directed at the problem before the group rather than at the personalities of dissenting members. Comments such as "Anyone who thinks that must be crazy" are taboo. In this view task and consideration needs are both met. Conflict is not suppressed, but it is not allowed to disrupt the progress of the group or to undercut morale.

On a grid, things look simpler than they are. Perhaps the biggest stumbling block in conflict-resolving communication in our society is the high value we place on "winning." We often cling tenaciously to our position or even move to a more extreme one just to avoid giving

Figure 10.5

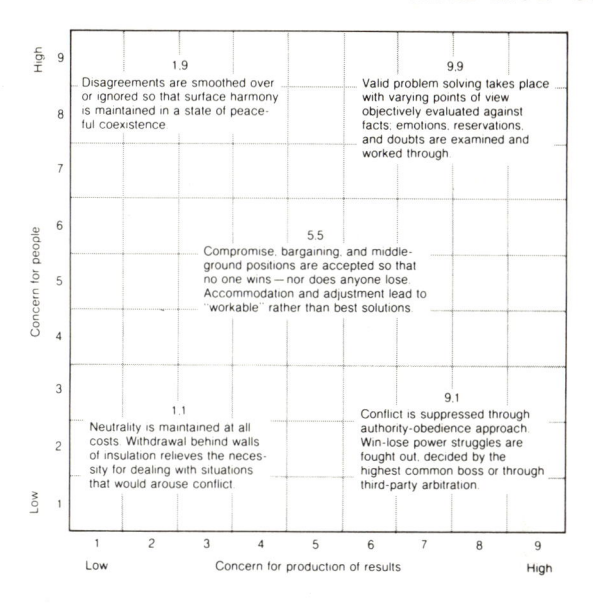

SMALL GROUP COMMUNICATION

1,9 — Disagreements are smoothed over or ignored so that surface harmony is maintained in a state of peaceful coexistence.

9,9 — Valid problem solving takes place with varying points of view objectively evaluated against facts; emotions, reservations, and doubts are examined and worked through.

5,5 — Compromise, bargaining, and middle-ground positions are accepted so that no one wins — nor does anyone lose. Accommodation and adjustment lead to "workable" rather than best solutions.

1,1 — Neutrality is maintained at all costs. Withdrawal behind walls of insulation relieves the necessity for dealing with situations that would arouse conflict.

9,1 — Conflict is suppressed through authority-obedience approach. Win-lose power struggles are fought out, decided by the highest common boss or through third-party arbitration.

(Y-axis: Concern for people, Low to High, 1–9)
(X-axis: Concern for production of results, Low to High, 1–9)

THE CONFLICT GRID

SOURCE: Robert Blake and Jane Mouton, "The Fifth Achievement," *Journal of Applied Behavioral Science*, 6 (1970), 418.

the other person the satisfaction of having "won." In a small group the win-or-lose mentality can only be destructive.

Clearly, there are more effective behaviors for resolving conflict. First, we should try to agree on a definition of what actually constitutes the problem. Sometimes people swept away in an argument do not realize that they may not even be arguing about the same point. Second, we should explore possible areas of agreement. Two parties rarely disagree completely on a given issue, and their goals may not be mutually exclusive. Next, we can determine what specific changes each faction must make to resolve the issue satisfactorily. Most conflicts are resolved by some modifications in the original preferences of both sides. And fourth, we must not resort to personal attacks but must keep the conflict directed at the issue.

Patterns of Decision Making

Decisions can be avoided, demanded, or agreed on. Assuming that decisions will actually be made, let us briefly examine four rather different ways of carrying out the process.

One writer goes quite far in stating that "Achieving consensus is the essential purpose of interpersonal communication" (Phillips, 1966, p. 39). Although this position fails to account for several other important communication goals, we heartily agree that consensus is one of the most desirable outcomes of interaction in small groups. The term can mean a majority opinion, but we use **consensus** to denote *agreement among all members of a group concerning a given decision*. Juries in criminal cases must reach consensus, and those that cannot—hung juries—are ultimately dismissed.

Few groups are as concerned as they should be about trying to reach consensus on decisions. We tend to forget that the people who help make a decision are often those who are also expected to carry it out. And given a choice, most people who disagree with a decision will resist enacting it. Therefore, problem-solving groups should try to reach consensus to ensure maximum satisfaction and commitment to the decision by all members.

The **majority vote** represents *the wishes of at least 51 percent of a group's members*. Although it is not nearly as satisfying as consensus, it does allow some group harmony in decision making. After as much deliberation on the problem as time permits, there may still be a substantial split in opinion. The majority vote allows the group to proceed despite this. The major limitation of the majority vote is that the dissenting members may be numerous and may be bitterly opposed to the decision. If so, they may be expected to resist carrying it out. When feasible the majority vote can be used to establish whether a group is near consensus. If a split still exists and time allows, deliberation should continue. If continued discussion does not prove fruitful, the majority vote may be used to reach the decision.

A still less desirable method of arriving at a decision is **handclasping**, or **pairing**. This term applies when various *minority members within a group form a coalition to help each other achieve mutually advantageous goals*. Their decision may not represent common sentiment in the group, but they overpower the majority by dint of their collective numbers. This pattern seems characteristic of political life. It is a common practice for legislators to vote for each other's bills in order to compel support for their own. In the short run, coalitions may be quite successful, but ultimately they can have disastrous effects on group morale. Furthermore, members of coalitions sometimes forget that these bargains exact obligations.

Most groups have at some time been the victims of **railroading**, which occurs when *one or a few group members force their will on the group*. This technique is used most frequently by a leader or particularly influential member, and, of course, it is the one most likely to produce resentment and resistance. All that we know about Machiavellianism leads us to expect that it is the high Machs who will be most inclined to engage in this sort of manipulating.

Since reaching consensus is the most desirable method of decision making within the small group, it is instructive to turn to a few of the research findings on the subject. Gouran (1969) compared the conversation of groups that were able to reach consensus with that of groups who were not. He found that the discussion in the first groups had a greater proportion of "orientation statements," statements explicitly directing the group toward the achievement of its goal or helping it resolve conflict. A follow-up study reported that orientation statements contained fewer self-referent words and phrases—"I," "me," "my," "I think," and so on—and that highly opinionated statements, which were characteristic of groups that had difficulty reaching consensus, contained more self-referent words (Kline, 1970).

Findings about orientation statements bear out our common-sense expectations, but we cannot always follow our hunches. We might predict, for example, that if group members expressed their ideas clearly and briefly (in one to two minutes), they would facilitate the group's progress. It has been found, however, that clarity and length of statements are not significantly related to the group's ability to reach consensus. These data need to be substantiated by further research.

Testing the Group's Effectiveness

It is to be hoped that in the near future we shall have more experimental findings pinpointing the communication behaviors that help discussion groups achieve their goals. For the time being, however, we have to agree with Mortensen (1970), who comments that "far more is known about the dynamics of groups than about the distinctive communicative properties, functions, and outcomes in groups" (p. 309), and with Gouran (1973), who states:

> Although it is relatively easy to specify a list of outcomes on which research in group communication can concentrate, the task of identifying communication behaviors potentially related to those outcomes is considerably more complex. The problem is that there are simply so many individual variables which could be associated in some meaningful way with consensus, effectiveness of decisions, satisfaction, and cohesiveness. (1973, p. 25)

For these reasons most of us learn about what goes on in groups from our firsthand experience as members. Sometimes, however, this knowledge can be increased through special exercises. One frequently used technique is called the "fishbowl discussion." Two groups form concentric circles. The inner group carries on a discussion; the outer comments on what it has observed. The two groups then switch positions and repeat the procedure. Each member is allowed to leave the discussion long enough to observe the behavior of the others in the group. He or she may be aided by a list of pointers about what behaviors to be looking for.

Summary

In this, our final chapter, we extended our model of interpersonal communication by examining the dynamics of communication within the small group. Each human being is simultaneously a member of many kinds of small groups. The present chapter has given special attention to the communication that takes place within problem-solving, or task-oriented, groups. Thus, we observed the strong influence of social pressure on individual group members, and in discussing the risky shift phenomenon, we examined the direction of conformity behavior. The larger question we raised was how the quality of problem solving is affected when people work together instead of independently. Role behavior, another aspect of group dynamics, was also surveyed. Although role flexibility is desirable, most people interpret the role of group member rather narrowly, performing only a few of the behaviors described by the IPA categories.

After touching on some characteristics of cohesive groups, and on the phases of group development, we considered three aspects of the structure of a group that affect its functioning: size, communication network, and leadership. Limiting the size of the group to five to seven members seems to assure maximum performance and satisfaction. Among communication networks the All-Channel pattern offers the greatest opportunity for corrective feedback and high morale, though the centralized systems are more efficient. Two concepts of leadership were discussed, and analysis of leadership functions rather than traits was recommended.

The last question raised was practical: How can the small group be made more effective? First, the use of an agenda makes the most of time and resources. Second, an awareness of various attitudes toward conflict allows group members to resolve conflicts in a way that respects both task and human concerns. A third correlate of small-group effectiveness is an approach to decision making that ensures commitment to the decision by all members of the group.

Review Questions

1. How do primary, casual, learning, work, and therapeutic groups differ? What distinguishes a problem-solving group from other groups?
2. How does the concept of conformity relate to the autokinetic effect?
3. What is the difference between private acceptance and public compliance?

4. Identify four conditions in which private acceptance is likely to occur.
5. What are four characteristics of people likely to conform to group pressure?
6. Discuss two theories that have been used to explain compliance to social pressure. How does each explain this phenomenon?
7. What is the risky shift phenomenon?
8. How does group cohesiveness relate to the effectiveness of the brainstorming technique?
9. Identify twelve types of group member roles. Give an example of each.
10. What are four characteristics of group cohesiveness?
11. Identify the four phases of group development and describe briefly the type of communication characteristic of each.
12. What is the relationship between group size, membership satisfaction, and group performance?
13. Draw diagrams representing five types of communication networks. Describe the relative effects of each on group performance.
14. How do trait and function views of leadership differ?
15. How do task and consideration functions in leadership differ?
16. What are six common difficulties that small groups encounter in developing ideas and solving problems?
17. How do the Standard Agenda, Ideal Solution, and Single Question formats for group discussion differ?
18. Identify four strategies that may be used to resolve group conflict effectively.
19. What are four ways of arriving at a decision in a group? What are some relative advantages and disadvantages of each?

Exercises

1. Have five people solve the "sinking ship" exercise in the Appendix independently. After individual solutions have been reached, ask these people to solve the same problem in a group. Compare the individual solutions with the group solution. In what ways is the risky shift phenomenon illustrated?
2. Ask several people to complete a sociogram as described in Chapter 5. Use the results to form a cohesive group and a noncohesive group. Ask the groups to use a brainstorming technique in discussing one of the case studies listed at the end of the book. Observe the groups' interaction using Bales' IPA categories. What differences emerge in the two groups?
3. Observe an actual problem-solving group. Listen carefully for statements that indicate the four phases of group development. Record

any statements that represent any of these phases. Notice also whether the group does *not* seem to go through these four phases. Compare your observations with others who have observed different groups. Do most of the observations correspond to the research findings?

4. Conduct an in-depth study of a group of which you are a member. Keep a journal of the group's interaction pattern and activities and write a paper in which you analyze: (1) the communication network (s) of the group, (2) the leadership functions, (3) the group's cohesiveness, (4) members' satisfaction, and (5) methods of conflict resolution.

5. Analyze the most successful group discussion that you have ever participated in. What specific factors were present that accounted for its success?

Suggested Readings

Fiedler, Fred E. "Style or Circumstance: The Leadership Enigma." *Psychology Today* (March 1969), 3:38–43. What makes a good leader? Using questionnaires and studies the author identifies three types of leaders and the group situations these leaders could handle best. Fiedler also suggests methods for improving a leader's performance. You will be able to identify types of people you know from the descriptions in this article.

Janis, Irving L. "Groupthink." *Psychology Today* (May 1971), 5:43–46, 74–76. Janis examines the infamous "Bay of Pigs" disaster of the Kennedy administration. After analyzing documented accounts of group decision making done by President Kennedy and his top advisers, Janis concludes that group conformity was largely responsible for this political disaster.

Shaw, Marvin E. *Group Dynamics: The Psychology of Small Group Behavior*. 2nd ed. New York: McGraw-Hill, 1976. This book is somewhat more challenging than most we have suggested. It synthesizes the findings of a large number of research studies in a meaningful way. It also lists several propositions that specifically capture those "rules" of small-group behavior that are confirmed by empirical research.

Rosenfeld, Lawrence B. *Now That We're All Here . . . Relations in Small Groups*. Columbus, Ohio: Charles E. Merrill, 1976. A brief, readable overview of communication in small groups, this little book has interesting chapters on nonverbal behavior, self-concept and role behavior, conflict in groups, and power and leadership.

REFERENCES

Chapter One—The Process of Interpersonal Communication

Barnlund, Dean C. "Toward a Meaning-Centered Philosophy of Communication," *Journal of Communication,* 11 (1962), 198–202.

Dance, Frank E. X. "The Concept of Communication," *Journal of Communication,* 20 (1970), 201–210.

Gardner, R. A., and B. T. Gardner. "Teaching Sign Languages to a Chimpanzee," *Science,* 165 (1969), 664–672.

Goldhaber, Gerald M. *Organizational Communication* (Dubuque, Iowa: Wm. C. Brown, 1974).

Goyer, Robert S. "Communication, Communicative Process, Meaning: Toward a Unified Theory," *Journal of Communication,* 20 (1970), 4–16.

Harris, Thomas A. *I'M OK—YOU'RE OK* (New York: Harper & Row, 1967).

Hart, Roderick P., Gustav W. Friedrich, and William D. Brooks. *Public Communication* (New York: Harper & Row, 1975).

Katz, Elihu, and Paul F. Lazarsfeld. *Personal Influence* (New York: The Free Press, 1955).

Luft, Joseph. *Of Human Interaction.* (Palo Alto, Calif.: National Press, 1969).

Premack, D. "The Education of S*A*R*A*H," *Psychology Today,* 4 (1970), 55–58.

Redfield, Charles E. *Communication in Management,* Rev. ed. (Chicago: University of Chicago Press, 1958).

Rogers, E., and F. Shoemaker. *Communication of Innovations* (New York: The Free Press, 1971).

REFERENCES

Samovar, Larry A., and Richard E. Porter. *Intercultural Communication: A Reader* (Belmont, Calif.: Wadsworth, 1972).

Samovar, Larry A., Robert D. Brooks, and Richard E. Porter. "A Survey of Adult Communication Activities," *Journal of Communication,* 19 (1969), 301–307.

Tubbs, Stewart L., and Sylvia Moss. *Human Communication,* 2nd ed. (New York: Random House, 1977).

Chapter Two—A Model of Interpersonal Communication

Barker, Larry L. *Listening Behavior* (Englewood Cliffs, N.J.: Prentice-Hall, 1971).

Barnlund, Dean C. "Toward a Meaning-Centered Philosophy of Communication," *Journal of Communication,* 11 (1962), 198–202.

Broadbent, Donald E. *Perception and Communication* (Elmsford, N.Y.: Pergamon Press, 1958).

Broadbent, Donald E. "Attention and the Perception of Speech," in Alfred G. Smith (ed.). *Communication and Culture: Readings in the Codes of Human Interaction* (New York: Holt, Rinehart and Winston, 1966), pp. 277–282.

Brownfield, Charles A. *Isolation: Clinical and Experimental Approaches* (New York: Random House, 1965).

Cherry, Colin. *On Human Communication,* 2nd ed. (Cambridge, Mass.: M.I.T. Press, 1966).

Dance, Frank E. X. "Toward a Theory of Human Communication," in Frank E. X. Dance (ed.). *Human Communication Theory: Original Essays* (New York: Holt, Rinehart and Winston, 1967), pp. 288–309.

Dittmann, Allen T. *Interpersonal Messages of Emotion* (New York: Springer, 1972).

Festinger, Leon, and Nathan Maccoby. "On Resistance to Persuasive Communications," *Journal of Abnormal and Social Psychology,* 68 (1964), 359–366.

Freud, Sigmund. *The Psychopathology of Everyday Life,* in *The Basic Writings of Sigmund Freud.* Edited and translated by A. A. Brill (New York: Modern Library, 1938).

Gombrich, E. H. *Art and Illusion,* 2nd ed. (New York: Pantheon, 1961).

REFERENCES

James, William. *Principles of Psychology*, Vol. I (New York: Dover, 1950).

Kaplan, Abraham. *The Conduct of Inquiry: Methodology for Behavioral Science* (San Francisco: Chandler, 1964).

Kern, E. "The Brain; Part II: The Neuron," *Life*, 71 (October 22, 1971).

Lindsay, Peter H. and Donald A. Norman. *Human Information Processing: An Introduction to Psychology* (New York: Academic Press, 1972).

Mead, Margaret and James Baldwin. *A Rap on Race* (Philadelphia: J. B. Lippincott Company, 1971).

Miller, George A. *Language and Communication* (New York: McGraw-Hill, 1963).

Moray, Neville. *Listening and Attention* (Baltimore: Penguin Books, 1969).

Ruesch, Jurgen, in Jurgen Ruesch and Gregory Bateson. *Communication: The Social Matrix of Psychiatry* (New York: Norton, 1968).

Segall, M. H., D. T. Campbell, and M. J. Herskovits. "Cultural Differences in the Perception of Geometric Illusions," in D. R. Price-Williams (ed.). *Cross-Cultural Studies* (Baltimore: Penguin Books, 1969), pp. 95–101.

Simon, Herbert A. and Newell, Alan. "Models: Their Uses and Limitations," in Edwin Paul Hollander and Raymond G. Hunt (eds.). *Current Perspectives in Social Psychology* (New York: Oxford University Press), pp. 79–91.

Shakespeare, William. *Hamlet*, in H. Craig (ed.). *The Complete Works of Shakespeare* (Chicago: Scott, Foresman, 1951).

Thayer, Lee. "On Theory-Building in Communication: Some Conceptual Problems," *Journal of Communication*, 13 (1963), 217–235.

Vygotsky, Lev Semenovich. *Thought and Language*. Edited and translated by Eugenia Hanfmann and Gertrude Vakar (Cambridge, Mass.: M.I.T. Press, 1962).

Weitz, Shirley. "Attitude, Voice, and Behavior," *Journal of Personality and Social Psychology*, 24 (1972), 14–21.

Chapter Three—Social Behavior and Motivation

Allport, Floyd. *Social Psychology* (Boston: Houghton Mifflin, 1924).

REFERENCES

Aronoff, Joel and Lawrence Messé. "Motivational Determinants of Small-Group Structure," *Journal of Personality and Social Psychology,* 17 (1971), 319–324.

Bandura, Albert and Richard Walters. *Social Learning and Personality Development* (New York: Holt, Rinehart and Winston 1963).

Bandura, Albert. "Vicarious Processes: A Case of No Trial Learning," in L. Berkowitz (ed.). *Advances in Experimental Social Psychology,* Vol. II (New York: Academic Press, 1965), pp. 1–55.

Bandura, Albert, Dorothea Ross, and Sheila A. Ross. "A Comparative Test of the Status Envy, Social Power, and Secondary Reinforcement Theories of Identificatory Learning," *Journal of Abnormal and Social Psychology,* 67 (1963), 527–534.

Barker, Larry L. *Listening Behavior* (Englewood Cliffs, N.J.: Prentice-Hall, 1971).

Berlo, David K. *The Process of Communication* (New York: Holt, Rinehart and Winston, 1960).

Bostrom, Robert. "Patterns of Communicative Interaction in Small Groups," *Speech Monographs,* 37 (1970), 257–263.

Burgoon, Michael. "The Relationship between Willingness to Manipulate Others and Success in Two Different Types of Basic Speech Communication Courses," *The Speech Teacher,* 20 (1971), 178–183.

Burgoon, Michael, Gerald R. Miller, and Stewart L. Tubbs. "Machiavellianism, Justification, and Attitude Change Following Counterattitudinal Advocacy," *Journal of Personality and Social Psychology,* 22 (1972), 366–371.

Cantril, Hadley. *Gauging Public Opinion* (Princeton, N.J.: Princeton University Press, 1944).

Christie, Richard and Florence L. Geis. *Studies in Machiavellianism* (New York: Academic Press, 1970).

Church, Joseph. *Language and the Discovery of Reality* (New York: Random House, 1961).

Crane, Loren, Richard Dieker, and Charles Brown. "The Physiological Response to the Communication Modes: Reading, Listening, Writing, Speaking, and Evaluating," *Journal of Communication,* 20 (1970), 231–240.

Dittmann, Alan and Lynn G. Llewellyn. "Relationship between Vocalizations and Head Nods as Listener Responses," *Journal of Personality and Social Psychology,* 9 (1968), 79–84.

Ehrlich, H. J. and Dorothy Lee. "Dogmatism, Learning, and Resistance to Change: A Review and a New Paradigm," *Psychological Bulletin,* 71 (1969), 249–260.

Ellsworth, Phoebe and J. Carlsmith. "Effects of Eye Contact and Verbal Content on Affective Responses to a Dyadic Interaction," *Journal of Personality and Social Psychology,* 10 (1968), 15–20.

French, Elizabeth G. "Motivation as a Variable in Work-Partner Selection," *Journal of Abnormal and Social Psychology,* 53 (1956), 96–99.

Gardiner, James C. "A Synthesis of Experimental Studies of Speech Communication Feedback," *Journal of Communication,* 21 (1971), 17–35.

Giffin, Kim and Kendall Bradley. "Group Counseling for Speech Anxiety: An Approach and a Rationale," *Journal of Communication,* 19 (1969), 22–29.

Giffin, Kim and Shirley M. Gilham. "Relationships between Speech Anxiety and Motivation," *Speech Monographs,* 38 (1971), 70–73.

Ginott, Haim G. *Between Parent and Teenager* (New York: Macmillan, 1969).

Horner, Matina. "Fail: Bright Women," *Psychology Today,* 3 (1969), 36–38, 62.

Jakubowski-Spector, Patricia. *An Introduction to Assertive Training Procedures for Women* (Washington, D.C.: American Personnel and Guidance Association, 1973).

Jenkins, David. "Prediction in Interpersonal Communication," *Journal of Communication,* 11 (1961), 129–135.

Katz, Daniel. "Do Interviewers Bias Results?" *Public Opinion Quarterly,* 6 (1942), 248–268.

Keller, Paul. "Major Findings in Listening in the Past Ten Years," *Journal of Communication,* 10 (1960), 29–30.

Lehmann, I. J. "Changes in Critical Thinking, Attitudes, and Values from Freshman to Senior Years," *Journal of Educational Psychology,* 54 (1963), 305–315.

McClelland, David. "To Know Why Men Do What They Do," *Psychology Today,* 4 (1971), 35–38.

Miller, Gerald R. "Variations in the Verbal Behavior of a Second Speaker as a Function of Varying Audience Responses," *Speech Monographs,* 31 (1964), 109–115.

Nichols, Ralph and Leonard Stevens. "Listening to People," *Harvard Business Review,* 35 (1957).

REFERENCES

Rebhun, M. T. "Parental Attitudes and the Closed Belief-Disbelief System," *Psychological Reports,* 20 (1967), 260–262.

Rheingold, Harriet, Jacob Gewirtz, and Helen Ross. "Social Conditioning of Vocalizations in Infants," *Journal of Comparative and Physiological Psychology,* 52 (1959), 68–73.

Rokeach, Milton. *The Open and Closed Mind: Investigations into the Nature of Belief Systems and Personality Systems* (New York: Basic Books, 1960).

Rosenfeld, Howard. "Instrumental Affiliative Functions of Facial and Gestural Expressions," *Journal of Personality and Social Psychology,* 4 (1966), 65–72.

Schachter, Stanley. *The Psychology of Affiliation* (Stanford, Calif.: Stanford University Press, 1959).

Scheidel, Thomas and Laura Crowell. "Feedback in Small Group Communication," *Quarterly Journal of Speech,* 52 (1966), 273–278.

Thibaut, John W. and Harold H. Kelley. *The Social Psychology of Groups* (New York: Wiley, 1959).

Triplett, N. "The Dynamogenic Factors in Pacemaking and Competition," *American Journal of Psychology,* 9 (1897), 507–533.

Tubbs, Stewart L. and Gail A. Tubbs. "Speaking and Listening," *Today's Education,* 61 (1972), 23.

Tubbs, Stewart. "Learning in Organizations," in Patterson, Harry, Tony Hain, and Joseph Zima. "Organizational Behavior: A Systems Approach" (unpublished manuscript).

Widgery, Robin and Stewart L. Tubbs. "Machiavellianism and Religiosity as Determinants of Cognitive Dissonance Following Counterattitudinal Advocacy" (paper delivered at the annual convention of the International Communication Association, Atlanta, 1972).

Wiener, Norbert. *The Human Use of Human Beings: Cybernetics and Society* (New York: Avon, 1967).

Chapter Four—Person Perception

Arnold, Magda B. "A Demonstrational Analysis of the TAT in a Clinical Setting," *Journal of Abnormal and Social Psychology,* 44 (1949), 99–111.

Asch, S. E. "Forming Impressions of Personality," *Journal of Abnormal and Social Psychology,* 41 (1946), 258–290.

Barna, LaRay M. "Stumbling Blocks in Interpersonal Intercultural Communications," in Larry A. Samovar and Richard E. Porter (eds.).

REFERENCES

Intercultural Communication: A Reader (Belmont, Calif.: Wadsworth, 1972), pp. 241–245.

Bloodworth, Dennis. *The Chinese Looking Glass* (New York: Farrar, Straus and Giroux, 1967).

Brown, Roger. *Social Psychology* (New York: Free Press, 1965).

Cline, Victor B. and James M. Richards. "Accuracy of Interpersonal Perception—A General Trait?" *Journal of Abnormal and Social Psychology*, 60 (1960), 1–7.

Crockett, W. H. and Thomas Meidinger. "Authoritarianism and Interpersonal Perception," *Journal of Abnormal and Social Psychology*, 53 (1956), 378–380.

Deloria, Vine. *We Talk, You Listen* (New York: Macmillan, 1970).

Jacoby, Jacob. "Interpersonal Perceptual Accuracy as a Function of Dogmatism," *Journal of Experimental Social Psychology*, 7 (1971), 221–236.

Kelley, Harold H. "The Warm-Cold Variable in First Impressions of Persons," *Journal of Personality*, 18 (1950), 431–439.

Krech, David, Richard S. Crutchfield, and Norman Livson. *Elements of Psychology*, 2nd ed. (New York: Knopf, 1969).

Low, Ron. "A Brief Biographical Sketch of a Newly-Found Asian Male." in Amy Tachiki et al. *Roots: An Asian American Reader* (Los Angeles: UCLA Asian American Studies Center, 1971), pp. 105–108.

Luchins, A. S. "Primacy-Recency in Impression Formation," in Carl I. Hovland et al. (eds.). *The Order of Presentation in Persuasion*, Vol. I. (New Haven, Conn.: Yale University Press, 1957), pp. 33–61.

Malpass, Roy and Jerome Kravitz. "Recognition for Faces of Own and Other Race," *Journal of Personality and Social Psychology*, 13 (1969), 330–334.

Rich, Andrea L. *Interracial Communication* (New York: Harper & Row, 1974).

Secord, P. F. "Facial Features and Inference Processes in Interpersonal Perception," in Renato Tagiuri and Luigi Petrullo (eds.). *Person Perception and Interpersonal Behavior* (Stanford, Calif.: Stanford University Press, 1958).

"Igor Stravinsky: An 'Inventor of Music' Whose Works Created a Revolution," *The New York Times* (April 7, 1971), p. 48.

Tachiki, Amy et al. *Roots: An Asian American Reader* (Los Angeles: UCLA Asian American Studies Center, 1971).

Tagiuri, Renato and Luigi Petrullo (eds.). *Person Perception and*

REFERENCES

Interpersonal Behavior (Stanford, Calif.: Stanford University Press, 1958).

Tubbs, Stewart L. "Interpersonal Trust, Conformity, and Credibility" (paper delivered at the annual convention of the Speech Association of America in New York, December 1969).

Widgery, Robin and Bruce Webster. "The Effects of Physical Attractiveness upon Perceived Initial Credibility" (paper delivered at the annual convention of the National Society for the Study of Communication in Cleveland, 1969).

Wilson, Paul. "Perceptual Distortion of Height as a Function of Ascribed Academic Status," *Journal of Social Psychology,* 74 (1968), 97–102.

Chapter Five—Bases of Human Attraction

Anderson, Norman H. "Likeableness Ratings of 555 Personality-Trait Words," *Journal of Personality and Social Psychology,* 9 (1968), 354–362.

Barnlund, Dean C. *Interpersonal Communication: Survey and Studies* (Boston, Mass.: Houghton Mifflin, 1968).

Berscheid, Ellen and Elaine Walster. *Interpersonal Attraction* (Reading, Mass.: Addison-Wesley, 1969).

Blake, Brian F. and Abraham Tesser. "Interpersonal Attraction as a Function of the Other's Reward Value to the Person," *Journal of Social Psychology,* 82 (1970), 67–74.

Brewer, Robert E. "Attitude Change, Interpersonal Attraction, and Communication in a Dyadic Situation," *Journal of Social Psychology,* 75 (1968), 127–134.

Delia, Jesse. Personal communication, December 29, 1971.

Festinger, Leon, Stanley Schachter, and Kurt Back. *Social Pressures in Informal Groups* (New York: Harper & Brothers, 1950).

Gouldner, Alvin and Harry Gouldner. *Modern Sociology: An Introduction to the Study of Human Interaction* (New York: Harcourt, Brace and World, 1963).

Heider, Fritz. *The Psychology of Interpersonal Relations* (New York: Wiley, 1958).

Kerckhoff, A. C. and K. E. Davis. "Value Consensus and Need Complementarity," *American Sociological Review,* 7 (1962), 295–303.

Kramer, B. M. "Residential Contact as a Determinant of Attitudes toward Negroes" (unpublished dissertation, Harvard University, 1950).

Mann, J. H. "The Effect of Interracial Contact on Sociometric Choices and Perceptions," *Journal of Social Psychology,* 50 (1959), 143–152.

Miller, A. "Role of Physical Attractiveness in Impression Formation," *Psychonomic Science,* 19 (1970), 241–243.

Moreno, Jacob L. *Who Shall Survive?* (New York: Beacon, 1953).

Newcomb, Theodore M. *The Acquaintance Process* (New York: Holt, Rinehart and Winston, 1961).

Schachter, Stanley. *The Psychology of Affiliation* (Stanford, Calif.: Stanford University Press, 1959).

Smith, Arthur L. "Communication within Transracial Contexts," in Larry A. Samovar and Richard E. Porter (eds.) *Intercultural Communication: A Reader* (Belmont, Calif.: Wadsworth, 1972), pp. 289–298.

Thibaut, John W. and Harold H. Kelley. *The Social Psychology of Groups* (New York: Wiley, 1959).

Triandis, Harry C. *Attitude and Attitude Change* (New York: Wiley, 1971).

Walster, Elaine. "The Effect of Self-Esteem on Romantic Liking," *Journal of Experimental Social Psychology,* 1 (1965), 184–197.

Walster, Elaine and Leon Festinger. "The Effectiveness of 'Overheard' Persuasive Communications," *Journal of Abnormal and Social Psychology,* 65 (1962), 395–402.

Winch, Robert F. *Mate Selection: A Study of Complementary Needs* (New York: Harper & Brothers, 1958).

Works, E. "The Prejudice-Interaction Hypothesis from the Point of View of the Negro Minority Group," *American Journal of Sociology,* 67 (1961), 47–52.

Zajonc, Robert B. "Attitudinal Effects of Mere Exposure," *Journal of Personality and Social Psychology,* 9 (1968), 1–29.

Chapter Six—Self and Others: Relationship Aspects of Communication

Barna, LaRay M. "Stumbling Blocks in Interpersonal Intercultural Communications," in Larry A. Samovar and Richard E. Porter (eds.). *Intercultural Communication: A Reader* (Belmont, Calif.: Wadsworth, 1972), pp. 241–245.

Buber, Martin. "Distance and Relation," *Psychiatry* 20 (1957).

Cissna, Kenneth N. "Interpersonal Confirmation: A Review of Current Theory and Research" (paper delivered at the Central States Speech Association Convention, in Chicago, April, 1976).

REFERENCES

Deutsch, Morton. "The Effect of Motivational Orientation upon Trust and Suspicion," *Human Relations,* 13 (1960), 123–137.

Deutsch, Morton and Robert M. Krauss. "The Effect of Threat on Interpersonal Bargaining," *Journal of Abnormal and Social Psychology,* 61 (1960), 181–189.

Gibb, Jack R. "Defensive Communication," *Journal of Communication,* 11 (1961), 141–148.

Giovanni, Nikki and Margaret Walker. *A Poetic Equation: Conversations Between Nikki Giovanni and Margaret Walker* (Washington, D.C.: Howard University Press, 1974).

Groh, Lynn. "Smith Details Life in Russia," *The Daily Times* (February 18, 1976), p. A3.

Harrison, Roger. "Defenses and the Need to Know," in Robert Golembiewski and Arthur Blumberg (eds.). *Sensitivity Training and the Laboratory Approach* (Itasca, Ill.: Peacock, 1970), pp. 80–90.

Jourard, Sidney M. *Self-Disclosure: An Experimental Analysis of the Transparent Self* (New York: Wiley, 1971).

Jourard, Sidney M. *The Transparent Self: Self-Disclosure and Well-Being* (Princeton, N.J.: Van Nostrand, 1964).

Kafka, Franz. *Letter to His Father.* Trans. by Ernst Kaiser and Eithne Wilkins (New York: Schocken, 1966).

Leathers, Dale. "The Process Effects of Trust-Destroying Behavior," *Speech Monographs,* 37 (1970), 180–187.

Lewin, Kurt. *Resolving Social Conflicts* (New York: Harper & Brothers, 1948).

Luft, Joseph. *Of Human Interaction* (Palo Alto, Calif.: National Press, 1969).

Mellinger, Glen D. "Interpersonal Trust as a Factor in Communication," *Journal of Abnormal and Social Psychology,* 52 (1956), pp. 304–309.

Nichols, Ralph G. and Leonard A. Stevens. *Are You Listening?* (New York: McGraw-Hill, 1957).

Nisbett, Richard E. et al. "Behavior as Seen by the Actor and as Seen by the Observer," *Journal of Personality and Social Psychology,* 27 (1973), 154–164.

O'Neill, Nena and George O'Neill. *Open Marriage: A New Life Style for Couples* (New York: Evans, 1972).

Pearce, L. and S. Newton. *The Conditions of Human Growth* (New York: Citadel, 1963).

Rapoport, Anatol and Albert Chammah. *Prisoner's Dilemma: A Study in Conflict and Cooperation* (Ann Arbor, Mich.: University of Michigan Press, 1965).

Reik, Theodore. *Listening with the Third Ear.* (New York: Grove, 1948).

Roethlisberger, R. *Management and Morale* (Cambridge, Mass: Harvard University Press, 1955).

Rogers, Carl. *On Becoming a Person* (Boston: Houghton Mifflin, 1961).

Rotter, Julian. "Generalized Expectancies for Interpersonal Trust," *American Psychologist,* 26 (1971), pp. 443–452.

Ruesch, Jurgen and Gregory Bateson. *Communication: The Social Matrix of Psychiatry* (New York: Norton, 1968).

Sieberg, Evelyn and Carl Larson. "Dimensions of Interpersonal Response" (paper delivered at the annual conference of the International Communication Association, in Phoenix, April 1971).

Smith, Hedrick. *The Russians* (New York: Quadrangle, 1976).

Storms, Michael D. "Videotape and the Attribution Process: Reversing Actor's and Observer's Point of View," *Journal of Personality and Social Psychology,* 27 (1973), 165–175.

Tubbs, Stewart L. "Two Person Game Behavior, Conformity-Inducing Messages and Interpersonal Trust," *Journal of Communication,* 21 (1971), 326–341.

Watzlawick, Paul, Janet Helmick Beavin, and Don D. Jackson. *Pragmatics of Human Communication* (New York: W. W. Norton, 1967).

Chapter Seven—The Verbal Message

Arnold, William and Roger Libby. "The Semantics of Sex Related Terms" (paper delivered at the annual convention of the Speech Communication Association, in Chicago, December 1970).

Barnlund, Dean C. *Interpersonal Communication: Survey and Studies* (Boston: Houghton Mifflin, 1968).

Bernstein, Basil. "A Sociolinguistic Approach to Socialization: With Some Reference to Educability," in Frederick Williams (ed.). *Language and Poverty: Perspectives on a Theme* (Chicago: Markham, 1970).

Bostrom, Robert, John R. Basehart, and Charles Rossiter. "The Effects of Three Types of Profane Language in Persuasive Messages," *Journal of Communication,* 23 (1973), 461–475.

REFERENCES

Brown, Claude. *Manchild in the Promised Land* (New York: New American Library, 1965).

Brown, Roger and Eric H. Lenneberg. "A Study in Language and Cognition," *Journal of Abnormal and Social Psychology,* 49 (1954), 454–462.

Brown, Roger. *Words and Things: An Introduction to Language* (New York: Free Press, 1958).

Carroll, Lewis. *Through the Looking Glass and What Alice Found There* (New York: Random House, 1965).

Cherry, Colin. *On Human Communication,* 2nd ed. (Cambridge, Mass.: M.I.T. Press, 1966).

Crane, Loren, Richard Dieker, and Charles Brown. "The Physiological Response to the Communication Modes: Reading, Listening, Writing, Speaking, and Evaluating," *Journal of Communication,* 20 (1970), 231–240.

Davis, Ossie. "The English Language Is My Enemy," in Arthur L. Smith. *Language, Communication, and Rhetoric in Black America* (New York: Harper & Row, 1972), pp. 49–57.

Deese, James. *Psycholinguistics* (Boston: Allyn & Bacon, 1970).

Duncan, Wm. Walter. "How White Is Your Dictionary?" *Etc.: A Review of General Semantics,* 27 (1970), 89–91.

Haller, John. "The Semantics of Color," *Etc.: A Review of General Semantics,* 26 (1969), pp. 201–204.

Haney, William V. *Communication and Organizational Behavior,* 3rd ed. (Homewood, Ill.: Irwin, 1973).

Kochman, Thomas. "Toward an Ethnography of Black American Speech Behavior," in Arthur L. Smith. *Language, Communication, and Rhetoric in Black America* (New York: Harper & Row, 1972), pp. 58–86.

Krauss, Robert M. "The Interpersonal Regulation of Behavior," in Dwain N. Walcher (ed.). *Early Childhood: The Development of Self-Regulatory Mechanisms* (New York: Academic, 1971), pp. 187–208.

Labov, William. *Language in the Inner City: Studies in the Black English Vernacular* (Philadelphia: University of Pennsylvania, 1972).

Laing, R. D. *Self and Others,* 2nd ed. (New York: Pantheon, 1969).

Legum, Colin. "The End of Cloud-Cuckoo-Land," *The New York Times Magazine* (March 28, 1976), pp. 18–19 *et passim.*

REFERENCES

Long, Thomas. "Tek-nol'o-ji and Its Effect on Language," *Air Force and Space Digest,* 12 (March 1969), p. 87.

Mabry, Edward. "A Multivariate Investigation of Profane Language," *Central States Speech Journal,* 26 (1975), 39–44.

Maddocks, Melvin. "The Limitations of Language," *Time* (March 8, 1971), p. 36.

McNair, Malcolm, "Thinking Ahead: What Price Human Relations?" *Harvard Business Review,* 25 (1957), pp. 15–39.

Oliver, Robert T. *Culture and Communication: The Problem of Penetrating National and Cultural Boundaries* (Springfield, Ill.: Charles C. Thomas, 1962).

Osgood, Charles, George Suci, and Percy Tannenbaum. *The Measurement of Meaning* (Urbana, Ill.: University of Illinois Press, 1957), chaps. 1–4.

Osgood, Charles E. "Probing Subjective Culture Part I. Crosslinguistic Tool-making," *Journal of Communication,* 24 (1974[a]), 21–35.

Osgood, Charles E. "Probing Subjective Culture Part 2. Crosscultural Tool-using," *Journal of Communication,* 24 (1974[b]), 82–100.

Piaget, Jean. *The Language and Thought of the Child.* Trans. by Marjorie Gabain (New York: Meridian, 1955).

Rich, Andrea L. *Interracial Communication* (New York: Harper & Row, 1974).

Rossiter, Charles and Robert Bostrom. "Profanity, 'Justification,' and Source Credibility" (paper delivered at the annual conference of the National Society for the Study of Communication, in Cleveland, 1968).

Sapir, Edward. *Language: An Introduction to the Study of Speech* (New York: Harcourt, Brace, 1921).

Shenker, Israel. "If hous'wif' Becomes Obs., What Is There to Take Its Place?" *The New York Times* (February 9, 1972), p. 26.

Sithi-Amuai, Paul. "The Asian Mind," *Asia* (Spring 1968), pp. 78–91.

Smith, Arthur L. "Communication within Transracial Contexts," in Larry A. Samovar and Richard E. Porter (eds.). *Intercultural Communication: A Reader* (Belmont, Calif.: Wadsworth, 1972), pp. 289–298.

Smith, David and Clark Sturges. "The Semantics of the San Francisco Drug Scene," *Etc.: A Review of General Semantics,* 26 (1969), 168–175.

Smith, F. and G. A. Miller (eds.). *The Genesis of Language: A Psycholinguistic Approach* (Cambridge, Mass.: M.I.T. Press, 1966).

REFERENCES

Suleiman, Michael W. "The Arabs and the West: Communication Gap," in Michael H. Prosser (ed.). *Intercommunication Among Nations and Peoples* (New York: Harper & Row, 1973), pp. 287–303.

The Random House Dictionary of the English Language: College Edition. Edited by Laurence Urdang et al. (New York: Random House, 1969).

Tubbs, Stewart L. "An Introduction to General Semantics," *Kansas Speech Journal,* 29 (1967), 5–10.

Whorf, Benjamin Lee. *Language, Thought, and Reality.* John B. Carroll (ed.) (Cambridge, Mass.: M.I.T. Press, 1956).

Chapter Eight—The Nonverbal Message

Agee, James. *Agee on Film: Reviews and Comments by James Agee,* Vol. I (New York: Grosset & Dunlap, 1967).

Anderson, Virgil A. *Training the Speaking Voice,* 2nd ed. (New York: Oxford University Press, 1961).

Anonymous. *The Laws of Etiquette* (Philadelphia: Carey, Lee, and Blanchard, 1836), p. 188; quoted in Erving Goffman. *Interaction Ritual* (Garden City, N.Y.: Doubleday, 1967).

Argyle, Michael. *The Psychology of Interpersonal Behavior* (Baltimore: Penguin, 1967).

Barbara, Dominick. "Nonverbal Communication," *Journal of Communication,* 13 (1963), 166–173.

Barnlund, Dean C. *Interpersonal Communication: Survey and Studies* (Boston: Houghton Mifflin, 1968).

Bateson, Gregory et al. "Toward a Theory of Schizophrenia," *Behavioral Science,* I (1956), 251–264.

Baxter, James C. "Interpersonal Spacing in Natural Settings," *Sociometry,* 33 (1970), 444–456.

Birdwhistell, Ray L. *Introduction to Kinesics* (Louisville, Ky.: University of Louisville Press, 1952).

Blubaugh, Jon. "Effects of Positive and Negative Audience Feedback on Selected Variables of Speech Behavior," *Speech Monographs,* 36 (1969), 131–137.

Bowler, Ned. "A Fundamental Frequency Analysis of Harsh Vocal Quality," *Speech Monographs,* 31 (1964), 128–134.

Brown, Roger. *Social Psychology* (New York: Free Press, 1965).

Cobin, Martin. "Response to Eye Contact," *Quarterly Journal of Speech,* 48 (1962), 415–418.

REFERENCES

Corry, John. "An Editor Without Panache Finds He Has Many Friends," *The New York Times* (October 16, 1975), pp. 41–42.

Davitz, Joel R. and Lois Jean Davitz. "The Communication of Feeling by Content-Free Speech," *Journal of Communication,* 9 (1959[a]), 6–13.

Davitz, Joel R. and Lois Jean Davitz. "Correlates of Accuracy in the Communication of Feelings," *Journal of Communication,* 9 (1959[b]), 110–117.

Davitz, Joel R. and Lois Jean Davitz. "Nonverbal Vocal Communication of Feeling," *Journal of Communication,* 11 (1961), 81–86.

Darwin, Charles. *Evolution and Natural Selection,* Bert James Loewenberg (ed.). (Boston: Beacon, 1959).

Diehl, Charles F., Richard C. White, and Paul H. Satz. "Pitch Change and Comprehension," *Speech Monographs,* 28 (1961), 65–68.

Dittmann, Allen T. *Interpersonal Messages of Emotion* (New York: Springer, 1972).

Durrell, Lawrence. *Bitter Lemons* (London: Faber, 1957).

Eakins, Barbara J. "The Relationship of Intonation to Attitude Change, Retention, and Attitude Toward Source" (paper delivered at the annual convention of the Speech Association of America, in New York, December 1969).

Eisenson, John and Mardel Ogilvie. *Speech Correction in the Schools* (New York: Macmillan, 1963).

Ekman, Paul. "Communication Through Nonverbal Behavior" (Progress Report, Langley Porter Institute, San Francisco, 1965).

Ekman, Paul. "Differential Communication of Affect by Head and Body Cues," *Journal of Personality and Social Psychology,* 2 (1965), 726–735.

Ekman, Paul and Wallace V. Friesen. "Constants Across Cultures in the Face and Emotion," *Journal of Personality and Social Psychology,* 17 (1971), 124–129.

Ekman, Paul and Wallace V. Friesen. "Nonverbal Leakage and Clues to Deception," *Psychiatry,* 32 (1969), 88–106.

Freedman, Daniel G. "The Survival Value of Beards," *Psychology Today,* 3 (October 1969), 36–39.

Freyre, Gilberto. *New World in the Tropics: The Culture of Modern Brazil* (New York: Random House, 1963).

Goffman, Erving. *Behavior in Public Places* (New York: Free Press, 1963).

REFERENCES

Goldhaber, Gerald M. "Gay Talk: Communication Behavior of Male Homosexuals" (paper presented at the annual convention of the Speech Communication Association, in Chicago, December 27, 1974).

Gurvitch, Georges. *The Spectrum of Social Time.* Trans. by Myrtle Korenbaum (Dordrecht, Netherlands: Reidel, 1964).

Haiman, Franklyn S. "The Rhetoric of 1968: A Farewell to Rational Discourse," in Wil Linkugel, R. R. Allen, and Richard Johannesen (eds.). *Contemporary American Speeches.* 2nd ed. (Belmont, Calif.: Wadsworth, 1969), pp. 153–167.

Hall, Edward T. *The Silent Language* (New York: Fawcett, 1959).

Hall, Edward T. and William Foote Whyte. "Intercultural Communication: A Guide to Men of Action," in Alfred G. Smith (ed.). *Communication and Culture: Readings in the Codes of Human Interaction* (New York: Holt, Rinehart and Winston, 1966), pp. 567–576.

Hall, Edward T. *The Hidden Dimension* (Garden City, N.Y.: Doubleday, 1966).

Harms, L. S. "Listener Judgments of Status Cues in Speech," *Quarterly Journal of Speech,* 47 (1961), 164–168.

Harrison, Randall. "Nonverbal Communication: Explorations into Time, Space, Action, and Object," in Jim Campbell and Hal Hepler (eds.). *Dimensions in Communication* (Belmont, Calif.: Wadsworth, 1965), pp. 158–174.

Hess, E. H. "Attitude and Pupil Size," *Scientific American,* 212 (April 1965), 46–54.

Johnson, Kenneth R. "Black Kinesics: Some Nonverbal Communication Patterns in the Black Culture," in Larry A. Samovar and Richard E. Porter (eds.). *Intercultural Communication: A Reader* (Belmont, Calif.: Wadsworth, 1972), pp. 181–189.

Kinzel, August. "Towards an Understanding of Violence," *Attitude* (1969), 1.

La Barre, Weston. "The Language of Emotions and Gestures," in Warren Bennis et al. (eds.). *Interpersonal Dynamics,* 2nd ed. (Homewood, Ill.: Dorsey, 1968), pp. 197–205.

Laing, R. D. *Self and Others.* 2nd rev. ed. (New York: Pantheon, 1969).

Leathers, Dale G. *Nonverbal Communication Systems* (Boston: Allyn and Bacon, 1976).

Lefkowitz, Monroe, Robert R. Blake, and Jane Srygley Mouton, "Status Factors in Pedestrian Violation of Traffic Signals," *Journal of Abnormal and Social Psychology,* 51 (1955), 704–706.

REFERENCES

Lerner, Alan Jay and Frederick Loewe. *My Fair Lady*.

Libby, William L. and Donna Yaklevich. "Personality Determinants of Eye Contact and Direction of Gaze Aversion," *Journal of Personality and Social Psychology,* 27 (1973), 197–206.

Lindzey, Gardner and Elliot Aronson (eds.). *The Handbook of Social Psychology,* 2nd ed., Vol. II, *Research Methods* (Reading, Mass.: Addison-Wesley, 1968), pp. 390–400.

McCroskey, James C. *An Introduction to Rhetorical Communication,* 2nd ed. (Englewood Cliffs, N.J.: Prentice-Hall, 1972).

Mehrabian, Albert. "Orientation Behaviors and Nonverbal Attitude Communication," *Journal of Communication,* 17 (1967), 324–332.

Mehrabian, Albert. "Communication Without Words," *Psychology Today,* 2 (September 1968), 53–56.

Mehrabian, Albert and Martin Williams. "Nonverbal Concomitants of Perceived and Intended Persuasiveness," *Journal of Personality and Social Psychology,* 13 (1969), 37–58.

Mizener, Arthur. *The Far Side of Paradise: A Biography of F. Scott Fitzgerald* (New York: Random House, 1949).

"Notes on People: Herring Ad Irks Miss Hepburn," *The New York Times* (August 12, 1971), p. 39.

Reece, Michael and Robert N. Whitman. "Expressive Movements, Warmth, and Verbal Reinforcement," *Journal of Abnormal and Social Psychology,* 64 (1962), 234–236.

Rosenfeld, Howard M. "Effect of Approval-Seeking Induction in Interpersonal Proximity," *Psychological Reports,* 17 (1965), 120–122.

Ruesch, Jurgen and Weldon Kees. *Nonverbal Communication* (Los Angeles: University of California Press, 1956).

Scheflen, Albert E. "Quasi-Courtship Behavior in Psychotherapy," *Psychiatry,* 28 (1965), 245–257.

Sommer, Robert. *Personal Space: The Behavioral Basis of Design* (Englewood Cliffs, N.J.: Prentice-Hall, 1969).

Soskin, William F. and Paul E. Kauffman. "Judgment of Emotion in Word-Free Voice Samples," *Journal of Communication,* 11 (1961), 73–81.

Starkweather, John A. "Content-Free Speech as a Source of Information About the Speaker," *Journal of Abnormal and Social Psychology,* 52 (1956), 394–402.

Starkweather, John A. "Vocal Communication of Personality and Human Feelings," *Journal of Communication,* 11 (1961), 63–72.

REFERENCES

Steinzor, B. "The Spatial Factor in Face-to-Face Discussion Groups," *Journal of Abnormal and Social Psychology,* 45 (1950), 552–555.

"The Love that Won't Shut Up," *Time* (September 29, 1975), p. 6.

Tolstoy, Leo. *War and Peace.* Trans. by Constance Garnett (New York: Modern Library, n.d.).

Trager, George L. "Paralanguage: A First Approximation," *Studies in Linguistics,* 13 (1958), 1–12.

Van Riper, Charles. *Speech Correction,* 4th ed. (Englewood Cliffs, N.J.: Prentice-Hall, 1963).

Weakland, John. Quoted in Michael H. Prosser. "Communication, Communications, and Intercommunication," in Michael H. Prosser (ed.). *Intercommunication Among Nations and Peoples* (New York: Harper & Row, 1973), pp. 1–22.

Weick, Karl E. "Systematic Observational Methods," in Gardner Lindzey and Elliot Aronson (eds.), *The Handbook of Social Psychology,* 2nd ed., Vol. II, *Research Methods* (Reading, Mass.: Addison-Wesley, 1968).

Weitz, Shirley (ed.). *Nonverbal Communication: Readings with Commentary* (New York: Oxford University Press, 1974).

Williams, Frederick and John Tolch. "Communication by Facial Expression," *Journal of Communication,* 15 (1965), 17–21.

Wilmot, William W. *Dyadic Communication: A Transactional Perspective* (Reading, Mass.: Addison-Wesley, 1975).

Woodworth, Robert and Harold Schlosberg. *Experimental Psychology,* rev. ed. (New York: Holt, Rinehart and Winston, 1954).

Yerxa, Florence. "Encounter: A Greek Mission Impossible," *The New York Times* (January 18, 1976), Section 10, pp. 1, 16.

Chapter Nine—Two-Person Communication

Argyle, Michael. *Social Interaction* (London: Methuen, 1969).

Beckhard, Richard. *Organizational Development: Strategies and Models* (Reading, Mass.: Addison-Wesley, 1969).

Berne, Eric. *Games People Play* (New York: Grove, 1969).

Bingham, Walter Van Dyke and Bruce Victor Moore. *How to Interview* (New York: Harper & Brothers, 1924).

Cannell, Charles F. and Robert L. Kahn. "Interviewing," in Gardner Lindzey and Elliot Aronson (eds.). *The Handbook of Social Psychology,* 2nd ed., Vol. II, *Research Methods* (Reading, Mass.: Addison-Wesley, 1968).

Christie, Richard and Florence L. Geis. *Studies in Machiavellianism* (New York: Academic, 1970).

REFERENCES

Couch, Arthur and Kenneth Keniston. "Yeasayers and Naysayers: Agreeing Response Set as a Personality Variable," *Journal of Abnormal and Social Psychology,* 60 (1960), 150–174.

Ellis, Albert. *Reason and Emotion in Psychotherapy* (New York: Lyle Stuart, 1962).

Goffman, Erving. *Relations in Public: Microstudies of the Public Order* (New York: Basic Books, 1971).

Gould, Robert E. "Some Husbands Talk About Their Liberated Wives," *The New York Times Magazine* (June 18, 1972), p. 47.

Harris, Thomas. *I'm OK—You're OK* (New York: Harper & Row, 1967).

James, Muriel and Dorothy Jongeward. *Born to Win* (Reading, Mass.: Addison-Wesley, 1971).

Kahn, Robert L. and Charles F. Cannell. *The Dynamics of Interviewing* (New York: Wiley, 1957).

Lansing, J. B. and D. M. Blood. *The Changing Travel Market,* Monograph No. 38 (Ann Arbor, Mich.: Survey Research Center, 1964).

Murdoch, Peter and Dean Rosen. "Norm Formation in an Interdependent Dyad," *Sociometry,* 33 (1970), 264–275.

Potter, Stephen. *One-Upmanship* (New York: Holt, Rinehart and Winston, 1952).

Rogers, Everett M. and F. Floyd Shoemaker. *Communication of Innovations: A Cross-cultural Approach* (New York: Free Press, 1971).

Rosen, Sidney and Abraham Tesser. "On Reluctance to Communicate Undesirable Information: The MUM Effect," *Sociometry,* 33 (1970), 253–263.

Sereno, Kenneth and C. David Mortensen. "The Effects of Ego-Involved Attitudes on Conflict Negotiation in Dyads," *Speech Monographs,* 36 (1969), 8–12.

Thibaut, John W. and Harold H. Kelley. *The Social Psychology of Groups* (New York: Wiley, 1959).

Triandis, Harry C. *Attitude and Attitude Change* (New York: Wiley, 1971).

Woollams, Stanley, Michael Brown, and Huige Kristyn. *Transactional Analysis in Brief* (Ann Arbor, Mich.: Huron Valley Institute, 1974).

Chapter Ten—Small Group Communication

Bales, Robert. *Interaction Process Analysis* (Reading, Mass.: Addison-Wesley, 1950).

REFERENCES

Bales, Robert and Fred Strodbeck. "Phases in Group Problem Solving," *Journal of Abnormal and Social Psychology,* 46 (1951), 485–495.

Bavelas, Alex. "Communication Patterns in Task-Oriented Groups," *Journal of the Acoustical Society of America,* 22 (1950), 725–730.

Bennis, Warren G. and Herbert A. Shepard. "A Theory of Group Development," *Human Relations,* 9 (1956), 415–457.

Bennis, Warren G. and Herbert A. Shepard. "Group Observation," in Warren Bennis, Kenneth Benne, and Robert Chin (eds.). *The Planning of Change* (New York: Holt, Rinehart and Winston, 1961), pp. 743–756.

Bormann, Ernest. *Discussion and Group Methods,* 2nd ed. (New York: McGraw-Hill, 1976).

Bostrom, Robert. "Patterns of Communicative Interaction in Small Groups," *Speech Monographs,* 37 (1970), 257–263.

Brilhart, John. *Effective Group Discussion,* 2nd ed. (Dubuque, Iowa: Wm. C. Brown, 1974).

Cameron, N. *The Psychology of Behavior Disorders* (Boston: Houghton Mifflin, 1947).

Cartwright, Dorwin and Alvin Zander. *Group Dynamics,* 3rd ed. (New York: Harper & Row, 1968), 139–151.

Cohen, David, John W. Whitmyre, and Wilmer H. Funk. "Effect of Group Cohesiveness and Training Upon Creative Thinking," *Journal of Applied Psychology,* 44 (1960), 319–322.

Festinger, Leon. "A Theory of Social Comparison Processes," *Human Relations,* 7 (1954), 117–140.

Fisher, B. Aubrey. "Decision Emergence: Phases in Group Decision Making," *Speech Monographs,* 37 (1970), 53–66.

Fisher, B. Aubrey. *Small Group Decision Making: Communication and the Group Process* (New York: McGraw-Hill, 1974).

Gouran, Dennis. "Variables Related to Consensus in Group Discussions of Questions of Policy," *Speech Monographs,* 36 (1969), 387–391.

Gouran, Dennis. "Group Communication: Perspectives and Priorities for Future Research," *Quarterly Journal of Speech,* 59 (1973), 22–29.

Grove, Theodore. "Attitude Convergence in Small Groups," *Journal of Communication,* 15 (1965), 226–238.

Guetzkow, Harold and Herbert A. Simon. "The Impact of Certain Communication Nets Upon Organization and Performance in Task-Oriented Groups," *Management Science,* 1 (1955), 233–250.

REFERENCES

Hare, A. Paul. *Handbook of Small Group Research* (New York: Free Press, 1962).

Homans, George C. *The Human Group* (New York: Harcourt Brace, 1950).

Kelley, Harold H. and John W. Thibaut. "Group Problem Solving," in Gardner Lindzey and Elliot Aronson (eds.). *The Handbook of Social Psychology*, 2nd ed., Vol. IV, *Group Psychology and Phenomena of Interaction* (Reading, Mass.: Addison-Wesley, 1969), pp. 1–101.

Kline, John. "Indices of Orienting and Opinionated Statements in Problem-Solving Discussion," *Speech Monographs*, 37 (1970), 282–286.

Larson, Carl. "Forms of Analysis and Small Group Problem Solving," *Speech Monographs*, 36 (1969), 452–455.

Leavitt, Harold J. "Some Effects of Certain Communication Patterns on Group Performance," *Journal of Abnormal and Social Psychology*, 46 (1951), 38–50.

Lewin, Kurt. "Group Decision and Social Change," in Eleanor Maccoby, Theodore M. Newcomb, and Eugene Hartley (eds.). *Readings in Social Psychology* (New York: Holt, Rinehart and Winston, 1958), pp. 183–196.

McGrath, Joseph and Irwin Altman. *Small Group Research* (New York: Holt, Rinehart and Winston, 1966).

Mortensen, C. David. "The Status of Small Group Research," *Quarterly Journal of Speech*, 56 (1970), 304–309.

Newcomb, Theodore M. *Personality and Social Change* (New York: Dryden, 1943).

Newcomb, Theodore M. "An Approach to the Study of Communicative Acts," *Psychological Review*, 60 (1953), 393–404.

Newcomb, Theodore M. "Persistence and Regression of Changed Attitudes: Long Range Studies," *Journal of Social Issues*, 19 (1963), 3–14.

Osborn, Alex F. *Applied Imagination* (New York: Scribner, 1957), chapter 26.

Parkinson, Cyril Northcote. *Parkinson's Law* (New York: Ballantine, 1964).

Phillips, Gerald. *Communication and the Small Group* (Indianapolis: Bobbs-Merrill, 1966).

Schachter, Stanley. "Deviation, Rejection and Communication," *Journal of Abnormal and Social Psychology*, 46 (1951), 190–208.

REFERENCES

Scheidel, Thomas and Laura Crowell. "Idea Development in Small Discussion Groups," *Quarterly Journal of Speech,* 50 (1964), 140–145.

Schein, Edgar H. "The Chinese Indoctrination Program for Prisoners of War," *Psychiatry,* 19 (1956), 159–160.

Schutz, William. *FIRO: A Three-Dimensional Theory of Interpersonal Behavior* (New York: Holt, Rinehart and Winston, 1958).

Shaw, Marvin E. "Communication Networks," in Leonard Berkowitz (ed.). *Advances in Experimental Social Psychology,* Vol. I (New York: Academic, 1964), pp. 111–147.

Shaw, Marvin E. Group Dynamics: *The Psychology of Small Group Behavior,* 2nd ed. (New York: McGraw-Hill, 1976).

Sherif, Muzafer. *The Psychology of Social Norms* (New York: Harper & Row Brothers, 1936).

Sherif, Muzafer. *Social Interaction: Process and Products* (Chicago: Aldine, 1967).

Taylor, Donald W., Paul C. Berry, and Clifford H. Block. "Does Group Participation When Using Brainstorming Facilitate or Inhibit Creative Thinking?" *Administrative Science Quarterly,* 3 (1958), 23–47.

Thelen, Herbert and Watson Dickerman. "Stereotypes and the Growth of Groups," *Educational Leadership,* 6 (1949), 309–316.

Townsend, Robert. *Up the Organization* (New York: Knopf, 1970).

Tubbs, Stewart L. *A Systems Approach to Small Group Interaction* (Reading, Mass.: Addison-Wesley, 1978).

Tuckman, Bruce. "Developmental Sequence in Small Groups," *Psychological Bulletin,* 63 (1965), 384–399.

Wallach, Michael A., Nathan Kogan, and Daryl J. Bem. "Group Influence on Individual Risk-Taking," *Journal of Abnormal and Social Psychology,* 65 (1962), 75–86.

Wheeler, Ladd. *Interpersonal Influence* (Boston: Allyn & Bacon, 1970).

Supplementary Exercises appendix

Anyone who has ever taught a course in speech communication realizes that there is often a major gap between the theory and the application of that theory. This appendix includes some supplementary exercises which may be used to help bridge the above-mentioned gap. For maximum benefit, however, the behaviors stimulated by these exercises should be discussed to show their relationship to the conceptual material presented in this text and to class lectures. It is important to keep in mind that the exercises are a *means* of increasing student learning and are not an end in themselves.

ROLE-PLAY EXERCISES

TWO-PERSON ROLE-PLAY EXERCISES

1. Student-Professor Conference
    JANE: You are a college sophomore in Dr. Patterson's speech communication class. You are dissatisfied with a grade for one of your class projects and are trying to persuade Dr. Patterson that you should have received a higher grade.
    DR. PATTERSON: You have had ten students come to your office to complain about their low grades. Jane has been an uninterested student all semester long. Now she enters your office.

2. Parent-Son Episode
    PARENT: You have been looking for a lost article of your son's clothing and you find some pornographic pictures in one of the drawers of his dresser.
    NINETEEN-YEAR-OLD SON: You have just been out with some friends and you find your parent in your room.

3. Employer-Applicant Interview
    EMPLOYER: You are looking for a man or woman to hire as a summertime sales person in your department store. You are primarily looking for someone who can relate to your young college customers.
    APPLICANT: You are a twenty-year-old college student who desperately needs a summer job to help finance your way through school. You have had no sales experience but are popular and personable.

4. Employer-Employee Interview
    EMPLOYER: You have noticed that one of your employees' work has been substandard lately. He has worked for you as a used car salesman for the past five years and has been a better than aver-

APPENDIX

age salesman. You have just received a call from his wife that he has been drinking somewhat lately and that she suspects him of having spent several nights with another woman. She is completely against any drinking, and she gets upset when he drinks even one beer or mixed drink. You call him in for a discussion.

EMPLOYEE: You have been disappointed about your level of pay lately and you would like to be considered for a promotion as a used car sales manager. You have been moonlighting at a second job lately to buy your wife a special birthday gift.

5. Counselor-Student Interview

STUDENT: You are a college student who has become involved in drug use to an extent that you feel it is becoming a problem. You go to the university counseling center to get some help.

COUNSELOR: You are employed by the university counseling center to give help to students who seem to have problems of various kinds. You are eager to help in any way you can. A student has just entered your office.

GROUP ROLE-PLAY EXERCISES

The Sinking Ship

You seven people are the only survivors of a passenger ship that was hit in the South Pacific by an old World War II mine. You are now trapped in the bottom of the ship's hold, with only a small air lock to let you return to the surface. It takes approximately three minutes to operate the air lock to allow one person to escape.

The hold is steadily filling with water, and judging by the list of the ship, you have at the most fifteen minutes before the ship sinks quickly to the bottom of the 37,000-foot-deep Mariana trench.

Your problem is one of survival. You are to determine as quickly as possible the most equitable way of deciding who will be saved in the fifteen minutes' time. Remember that it takes three minutes to save each person, so the very maximum number that can be saved is five.

As each person is "saved," he or she will separate from the group and sit in a chair. Both the amount of time taken by each person in the air lock and the remaining time left for the victims will be watched closely.

To impress the disaster victims with the seriousness of their situation, it is necessary to emphasize that those who are left in the hold will suffer a most hideous death—death by drowning.

Ability Grouping Meeting

The participation group members (group A) are to assume they represent the English teachers in a senior high school. The principal of the school has asked them to meet by themselves to formulate their recommendations pertaining to ability grouping in their classes for next year. ("Ability grouping" for this situation means the use of standardized test results as a basis of placement of students in class sections.) Two years ago the students were placed in classes on the following basis: Above Average Ability, Average Ability, and Below Average Ability. The following year students were not placed in classes on the basis of ability, but were randomly placed into class sections. The principal is aware of some dissatisfaction with the grouping of students in English classes; thus, he or she is asking for the recommendation of the teachers involved.

Procedure. The participation group (group A) will meet in the center of the room for a period of twenty minutes to discuss the situation presented above. They realize that they must reach a decision before they meet with the principal. The rest of the members (group B) will observe group A's activity during their meeting. Following this twenty-minute period, group B will meet in the center of the room to discuss what they observed from group A's activity. (They will meet for approximately twenty minutes.) Group A will observe group B's evaluation. At the end of this period group A and group B will combine for a general reaction and/or summary of the two group meetings.

CASE PROBLEMS

A clinical psychologist at a university feels that interviews with a client should be recorded on tape and that the benefits to be derived from such recordings would be impaired if the client knew in advance that the recording was to be made. The psychologist sometimes uses these recordings in the classroom to illustrate lectures, always without the knowledge of the client, though the client's name is not revealed to the class.

QUESTION: Should the psychologist use these tape recordings as class demonstrations without the permission of the client?

APPENDIX

John and Mary are college students. John is nineteen years old and in his sophomore year in business administration; Mary is nearly nineteen and a sophomore in home economics. They met about a year and a half ago at school and have been dating steadily since that time. There is no question that they are really in love. Three months ago, with the consent of their parents, they became engaged, and they wish to be married within the next three months.

Neither John nor Mary is self-supporting. Their tuition and most of their expenses are paid by their parents, who in both cases are fairly well-to-do. It will take John two more full years, including summers, to complete his degree. Mary can complete her degree in about two years and should have no difficulty in getting a teaching position after graduation.

The parents, though not entirely happy about the marriage plans, have promised to continue giving the couple, until their education has been completed, the same financial support they now receive.

QUESTION: Should this couple marry now?

Jan Dorn is an attractive twenty-year-old college student majoring in art. She is a student in Dr. Thompson's small-group communication class. Jan and her husband, Jim, rent a home on the same block where Dr. Thompson lives. Jim and Dr. Thompson have met and become friends as well as neighbors. Jim is presently serving six months' duty in the army. With comfortable financial support from her parents, Jan is able to continue her education.

The first day of class Jan appears without her wedding ring, and in her self-introduction she does not reveal the fact that she is married. As the term progresses, Dr. Thompson learns that Jan has had a number of male members of the class spend the night at her house. On Easter Sunday Jan and Jim (home on leave) unexpectedly visit Dr. Thompson and his wife at their home.

QUESTION: How should Dr. Thompson react in this situation?

Two years ago Sandy (now twenty) became engaged to Thad against the wishes of her parents and the rest of her family as well. None of them liked him, especially Sandy's mother. However, since that was what Sandy wanted they all went along with it. Her parents never said she couldn't get married and were willing to pay for the wedding. After two years, Thad called Sandy and broke the engagement. Her whole family was angry and thought that Sandy had seen the light as well. She acted as if she had; in fact, she went out with some other boys and seemed to have a good time. Unknown to her family, though, she still

APPENDIX

311

loved Thad and, despite what he had done, still wanted to marry him. A few months later Thad met Sandy where she worked. She hadn't seen him for four weeks. Unexpectedly, they eloped. Her family had no idea he had come into town and didn't know what had happened until after the fact.

QUESTION: How can this couple improve the relationship between Thad and Sandy's families?

The problem lies with my communication. I don't say much in class or give much feedback. Whenever I am part of a group, whether in a class or in the fraternity, I don't feel a strong attraction toward the group. I am always putting myself in the background to observe. I feel firmly convinced that any communication on my part will not help the situation, and that by participating in the group I will lose some of my concentration on the conversation. I very rarely feel any rewards from being in a group. I can associate with a group and understand their beliefs and feelings, but I can't really become a part of it. If forced to participate or be a part of the group, I generally do a poor job and don't get much out of it. I don't like conforming with rules or goals that other people have set. There are many things that I don't wish to share with others.

QUESTION: How might this person overcome this difficulty?

My difficulty in communication isn't unusual in today's society. It is the communication gap between the young and old generations. That difficulty of communication happened between me and my parents, mainly my father.

Compared with other families we have more difficulties than usual because of his Japanese, and my Latin traditions.

When I was twelve years old I left my farm home in Brazil and went to attend high school; until then I had just a Japanese education due to the influences of my family and the Japanese colony I lived in. So, at twelve I started a complete new life far from home. I don't know if it is the peculiarity of this age, but I had no trouble in accepting changes—after one year I was completely absorbed by the Latin customs and education (that's way I don't act like a Japanese but like a Brazilian). Since then there has been a conflict between my father and me which is both a generation gap and a culture gap.

QUESTION: How might this person and the father improve their relationship?

APPENDIX

DISCLOSURE GAMES

The disclosure game* is a structured way for two people to become acquainted with one another through mutual disclosure on assigned topics. The topics are roughly graded for intimacy. Participants in the game take turns disclosing themselves to their partner on each topic. The rules of the game are simple: first, complete honesty is called for, including an honest statement of unwillingness to disclose any given subject. Second, the listener must avoid pressuring and probing, unless the other person expresses a willingness to be pressured or probed.

The long version of the game is also designed in such a way that, in addition to the two partners' mutual self-disclosure, an investigator might gather useful data on the "depth" to which two players have permitted themselves to be known. I have also used a short version of the game, which eliminates the more complicated instructions and simply invites pairs of people to begin getting acquainted by disclosing themselves to one another on just five or ten topics, such as hobbies, attitudes toward their own bodies, problems and satisfactions in work, and peronal satisfactions and problems with members of their own family. What nearly always happens is that, after initial embarrassment at the artificiality of the situation, the partners become intensely involved in mutual disclosure, spending sometimes as much as seven hours at it.

I include the game in this book so that others may play it or use it as a research tool. If it is employed in research, the investigator is advised to pretest the items, so that they may be assigned an intimacy value appropriate for the groups or individuals whom he is testing.

I have observed that many people do not know how to become acquainted with others. On large campuses, in dormitories, and other places where crowds of people reside, they live in mutual ignorance and misunderstanding. The disclosure game could be a step in the direction of increased mutual understanding.

A DISCLOSURE GAME FOR TWO PLAYERS

I am asking you to play this "game" both for serious scientific purposes and to give you an illuminating experience. You will participate in a kind of "dialogue" with a stranger.

* Found in Sidney M. Jourard. *Self-Disclosure: An Experimental Analysis of the Transparent Self* (New York: Wiley, 1971), pp. 173–178 (slightly adapted). Reprinted by permission of John Wiley & Sons, Inc.

Procedure

1. Record your name, age, occupation, religious denomination, and your partner's name.
2. Read the thirty-five topics listed below in Part 1. Check those topics that you have disclosed fully to *somebody* in your life. If there is nobody to whom you have *fully* revealed that aspect of yourself, leave the space blank.
3. In Part 2 check the topics you are willing to discuss *fully* with the partner to whom you have just been introduced, when once the dialogue between you begins. If you are reluctant for any reason to discuss a topic fully, leave that space blank.
4. After you have completed the above procedure, go through the fuller acquaintance process as instructed by the investigator. He or she may ask you to give each other back rubs, engage in ordinary conversation, or participate in some other activity.
5. After the acquaintance process, turn to Part 3 and check on the left side of the page the topics you feel willing to disclose to your partner.
6. Now, flip a coin with your partner. Whoever wins the toss asks the first question. The other person answers or declines, according to his intent. He or she then asks the same question of the other, who can answer or not. If the other person has answered the question you asked, place a check mark on the right-hand side of the page. Otherwise do not check. Take turns asking each question first, throughout the entire list.

At any time during the dialogue you can change your mind. If you intended to speak on a topic and in the course of the interview find you would rather not, then simply decline that topic. And if you intended not to disclose on a topic but decided you will, go ahead and do so. Circle the items on which you changed your mind.

Part 1

Check those topics on which you have disclosed yourself *fully* to *somebody*.

1. Your hobbies; how you like best to spend your spare time.
2. Your favorite foods and beverages, and chief dislikes in food and drink.
3. Your preferences and dislikes in music.

APPENDIX

4. The places in the world you have traveled and your reaction to these places.
5. Your educational background and your feelings about it.
6. Your personal views on politics, the presidency, foreign and domestic policy.
7. The aspects of your body you are most pleased with.
8. Aspects of your daily work that satisfy and that bother you.
9. The educational and family background of your parents.
10. What your personal goals are for the next ten years or so.
11. Your personal religious views; nature of religious participation if any.
12. Your views on the way a husband and wife should live their marriage.
13. The names of the people who helped you significantly in your life.
14. Your present financial position: income, debts, savings, sources of income.
15. The occasions in your life when you were happiest, in detail.
16. The worries and difficulties you experience now, or have experienced in the past, with your health.
17. Habits and reactions of yours that bother you at present.
18. Your usual ways of dealing with depression, anxiety, and anger.
19. The features of your appearance you are most displeased with and wish you could alter.
20. Your favorite forms of erotic play and sexual lovemaking.
21. Your most common sexual fantasies and reveries.
22. The names of the persons you have significantly helped and the ways in which you helped them.
23. Characteristics of yourself that give you cause for pride and satisfaction.
24. The unhappiest moments in your life, in detail.
25. The circumstances under which you become depressed, and when your feelings are hurt.
26. The ways in which you feel you are most maladjusted or immature.
27. The actions you have most regretted doing in your life, and why.
28. The main unfulfilled wishes and dreams and the failures in your life.
29. Your guiltiest secrets.
30. What you regard as the mistakes and failures your parents made in raising you.

APPENDIX

31. How you see and evaluate your parents' relationship with one another.
32. What you do to stay fit, if anything.
33. The sources of strain and dissatisfaction in your marriage (or relationship with the opposite sex).
34. The people with whom you have been sexually intimate; the circumstances of your relationship with each.
35. The persons in your life whom you most resent; the reasons why.

Part 2
Check those topics you are willing to reveal to your partner.

1. Your hobbies; how you like best to spend your spare time.
2. Your favorite foods and beverages, and chief dislikes in food and drink.
3. Your preferences and dislikes in music.
4. The places in the world you have traveled and your reactions to these places.
5. Aspects of your daily work that satisfy and that bother you.
6. Your educational background and your feelings about it.
7. The educational and family background of your parents.
8. Your personal views on politics, the presidency, foreign and domestic policy.
9. Your personal religious views; nature of religious participation if any.
10. What your personal goals are for the next ten years or so.
11. Your present financial position: income, debts, savings, sources of income.
12. Habits and reactions of yours that bother you at present.
13. Characteristics of yourself that give you cause for pride and satisfaction.
14. Your usual ways of dealing with depression, anxiety, and anger.
15. The unhappiest moments in your life, in detail.
16. The occasions in your life when you were happiest, in detail.
17. The circumstances under which you become depressed, and when your feelings are hurt.
18. The ways in which you feel you are most maladjusted or immature.
19. The actions you have most regretted doing in your life, and why.

APPENDIX

20. The main unfulfilled wishes and dreams and the failures in your life.
21. Your guiltiest secrets.
22. What you regard as the mistakes and failures your parents made in raising you.
23. How you see and evaluate your parents' relationship with one another.
24. Your views on the way a husband and wife should live their marriage.
25. The worries and difficulties you experience now, or have experienced in the past, with your health.
26. What you do to stay fit, if anything.
27. The aspects of your body you are most pleased with.
28. The features of your appearance you are most displeased with and wish you could alter.
29. The sources of strain and dissatisfaction in your marriage (or relationship with the opposite sex).
30. Your favorite forms of erotic play and sexual lovemaking.
31. Your most common sexual fantasies and reveries.
32. The people with whom you have been sexually intimate, the circumstances of your relationship with each.
33. The persons in your life whom you most resent; the reasons why.
34. The names of the persons you have significantly helped and the ways in which you helped them.
35. The names of the people who helped you significantly in your life.

Part 3

Check the topics you *intend to reveal* to your partner on the *left* side of page. On the right side, check those topics your partner fully discussed.

1. Your hobbies; how you like best to spend your spare time.
2. Your favorite foods and beverages, and chief dislikes in food and drink.
3. Your preferences and dislikes in music.
4. The places in the world you have traveled and your reactions to these places.
5. Aspects of your daily work that satisfy and that bother you.
6. Your educational background and your feelings about it.
7. The educational and family background of your parents.
8. Your personal views on politics, the presidency, foreign and domestic policy.

APPENDIX

9. Your personal religious views; nature of religious participation if any.
10. What your personal goals are for the next ten years or so.
11. Your present financial position: income, debts, savings, sources of income.
12. Habits and reactions of yours that bother you at present.
13. Characteristics of yourself that give you cause for pride and satisfaction.
14. Your usual ways of dealing with depression, anxiety, and anger.
15. The unhappiest moments in your life, in detail.
16. The occasions in your life when you were happiest, in detail.
17. The circumstances under which you become depressed, and when your feelings are hurt.
18. The ways in which you feel you are most maladjusted or immature.
19. The actions you have most regretted doing in your life, and why.
20. The main unfulfilled wishes and dreams and the failures in your life.
21. Your guiltiest secrets.
22. What you regard as the mistakes and failures your parents made in raising you.
23. How you see and evaluate your parents' relationship with one another.
24. Your views on the way a husband and wife should live their marriage.
25. The worries and difficulties you experience now, or have experienced in the past, with your health.
26. What you do to stay fit, if anything.
27. The aspects of your body you are most pleased with.
28. The features of your appearance you are most displeased with and wish you could alter.
29. The sources of strain and dissatisfaction in your marriage (or relationship with the opposite sex).
30. Your favorite forms of erotic play and sexual lovemaking.
31. Your most common sexual fantasies and reveries.
32. The people with whom you have been sexually intimate; the circumstances of your relationship with each.
33. The persons in your life whom you most resent; the reasons why.
34. The names of the persons you have significantly helped and the ways in which you helped them.
35. The names of people who helped you significantly in your life.

A SHORTER DISCLOSURE GAME

Interpersonal Yoga

The immediate object of Hatha Yoga is to master the various *asanas*. Each of these is a specific position which one's body assumes. A novice begins to assume one of these positions and finds that his or her muscles "protest." The means by which one fully enters an *asana* is to enter it up to one's limit and then to press gently at that limit. There can be no forcing, no cheating. The novice enters a position no further than has been "earned."

One can view authentic dialogue as a kind of interpersonal *asana*. The ultimate in dialogue is unpremeditated, uncontrived, spontaneous disclosure in response to the disclosure of the other. The following is an exercise aimed at helping a person discover his or her limits in ongoing dialogue. The first person discloses himself or herself on the first topic until both partners are satisfied there is no more to be said. Then, the other person does likewise. Then, on to the next *asana,* or topic. The rule is complete honesty, respect for one's own limits (as they are experienced in the form of embarrassment, anxiety, and so forth). As soon as this point is reached, the person declares he or she is at a limit. The partners can then discuss reasons for the reserve, and the person may overcome it.

Part 1: Disclosure
1. My hobbies, interests, and favorite leisure pursuits.
2. What I like and dislike about my body—appearance, health, and so forth.
3. My work—satisfactions, frustrations.
4. My financial situation: income, savings, debts, investments, and so forth.
5. Aspects of my parents I like and dislike; family problems encountered in growing up.
6. Religious views, philosophy of life, what gives meaning to my life.
7. My love life, past and present.
8. Problems in my marriage or in my dealings with the opposite sex at present.
9. What I like and dislike about my partner on the basis of this encounter.

Part 2: Physical Contact
The same rules of respect for one's own limits, and one's partner's, apply.

1. Massage the head and neck of the partner.
2. Massage the shoulders of the partner.
3. Give a back rub.
4. Rub the stomach of the partner.
5. Massage the partner's feet.

Index

achievement need, 63–65
acknowledgment, direct, 126
action: of appeal, 199; and communication, 11–12; language, 183–184
affiliation need, 63, 228
Agee, J., 194
aggressiveness, 59–60
agreeing response, 126
Allport, F., 57
alternatives, comparison level, 62
Altman, I., 274
Anderson, N. H., 117
angular transaction, 233, 235
answers, in interview, 240–242
anxiety: and achievement motive in women, 64; and attraction, 112
appeal: action of, 199
Argyle, M., 197
arousal and involvement, 226–227
Asch, S. E., 82, 83
assertiveness, 54
assertiveness training, 54–57
Atlas of Affective Meaning, 154
attention, selective, 25
attitude: and communication, 10; and perception, 91; salience, and similarity, 109
attraction: and proximity, 99–103; and similarity, 104–111; and situation, 111–114
authoritarianism, and perception, 91
authority, overreliance on, 65
autokinetic effect, 254
awareness: and Johari Window, 128–130; and metacommunication, 130–132; of self and others, 127–128; and self-disclosure, 132–134

Back, K., 101
balance theory, 105–108
Baldwin, J., 33
Barker, L. L., 38, 50, 59
Barna, L. M., 89
Barnlund, D. C., 99, 211
Bateson, G., 212
Batten, Barton, Durstine & Osborn, 260
Baxter, J. C., 189
beard, as visual cue, 202
behavior: game, 135–137; manipulative, 67–68; norms, 185; rehearsal, 55; sex-typed, 53–54
Berlo, D., 37
Berne, E., 232
Bernstein, B., 163, 164
Berscheid, E., 110
Birdwhistell, R. L., 194, 196, 213
Bitter Lemons (Durrell), 201
black English vernacular, 165
blacks: language use, 164–165; perception of whites, 86; street language, 158–159
Blake, R. R., 202
Bob and Carol and Ted and Alice (film), 133
body movement, 194, 198–199
Born to Win (James and Jungeward), 232
brainstorming, 260
breathiness, 210
Brewer, R. E., 104
Brilhart, J., 252
Brown, R., 81, 166

Cameron, N., 262
Cantril, H., 58
Carey, H., 173
carpentered world vs. uncarpentered, 28–29

321

INDEX

casual groups, 252
Chammah, A., 136
channels of communication, 32–34
Chaplin, C., 183
Cherry, C., 35
children, functions of language in, 160–161
Christie, R., 67, 68
chronemics, 191
Churchill, W., 34
clarifying response, 126
classical conditioning, 48–49
climate, supportive vs. defensive, 139
cliques, 115
closed question, 239
cocktail party problem, 25
codability, low, 162
cognitive consistency theories, 105–106
cohesive group, and social influence, 257
cohesiveness, in groups, 263–264
communication (*see also* interpersonal communication; language; listening; small group communication; two-person communication): channels, 32–34; defined, 3–8; filters, 25–29; input, 22–25; interference, 34–37; and metacommunication, 130–132; overlapping codes, 158; and perception, 91–93; and proximity, 101–102; receiver/sender, 37–39; sender/receiver, 21–22; stimuli, 29–32; and time, 39–42
communication network, group, 269–271
comparison level, 62
complementarity of needs, and similarity, 110
complementary transaction, 232–233, 234
conditioning: classical, 48–49; instrumental learning, 49–51
confirmation, and disconfirmation, 123–127
conflict: and group development, 265–266; interpersonal, and perceptual capacity, 29; interrole vs. intrarole, 255; resolution, group, 275–278
conflict grid, 276–277
conformity, 253–257
connotation and denotation, 152–155
consensus: in group decision making, 278; in group development, 266
consideration functions, 272
costs, in human interactions, 62
Couch, A., 241
courtship readiness, 198
creativity of groups, 260–261
critical listening, 140
Crockett, W. H., 88, 89
crossed transaction, 233, 234
Crowell, L., 59
cue: defined, 184–185; spatial vs. temporal, 185–193; visual, 193–204; vocal, 204–213
culture and set, 27–28

Dance, F. E. X., 39
Darwin, C., 195–196
decision making, group, 278–279
Deese, J., 156
defensiveness, reducing, 138–140
Delia, J., 117, 118
Deloria, V., 77
denotation, and connotation, 152–155
development, group, 264–266
Dewey, J., 274
dichotomies, 168–170
Dickerman, W., 266
direct acknowledgment, 126
disconfirmation, and confirmation, 123–127
discrimination, 51
discriminative listening, 140
Disraeli, 104
disruptive power, 222
distrust, effects of, 137–138
Dittmann, A., 33, 70, 71
dogmatism, 65–66; and perception, 91

INDEX

dominance need, 228
double bind, 212
dress, as visual cue, 202–203
drug culture, language of, 157–158
Duncan, W. W., 171
duplex transaction, 235–236
Durrell, L., 201
dyad, 221 (*see also* two-person communication)
dyadic effect, 133

educational groups, 252
egocentric speech, 161
Eisenstein, S., 183
Ekman, P., 196, 199, 200
elaborated code, language, 163–164
Ellis, A., 223
Emerson, R. W., 32
empathic listening, 140–142
empathy, 139
enacted roles, 224
encoding, message, 160–165
expected roles, 224
Expression of the Emotions in Man and Animals, The (Darwin), 195
extinction, 49
eye contact, 196–198

facial expression, 194–196
familiarity and proximity, 102
feedback, 31; influencing through, 58–60; information value, 60–61; as reinforcer, 57–58
Festinger, L., 34, 101, 257
filter, communication, 25–29
Fisher, B., 266
Fitzgerald, F. S., 203
fluency: of speech, 209
Ford, G., 173
Freedman, D. G., 202
French, D. G., 65
Freudian slip, 30
Friesen, W. V., 196
funnel sequence, 243–244

game behavior, 135–137
Games People Play (Berne), 232
Gardiner, J. C., 60

Geis, F. L., 67, 68
generalization, 50; personal, and stereotypes, 84–89
Gibb, J. R., 139
Giovanni, H., 141
Goffman, E., 196, 207
Gold, H., 172
Goldhaber, G. M., 203
Gouran, D., 278, 279
group: communication networks, 269–272; conflict resolution, 275–278; correlates, 273–274; creativity level, 260–261; decision-making patterns, 278–279; development phases, 264–266; idea development, and problem solving, 274–275; leadership, 272–273; problem-solving quality, 258–261; size, 267–269; testing effectiveness of, 279–280
group dynamics: and cohesiveness, 263–264; conformity, 253–257; and phases of group development, 264–266; and problem-solving quality, 258–261; and role of member, 261–263; social influence, 257–258
Guetzkow, H., 271

Hall, E. T., 184, 185–186, 189, 190, 192, 207
Hamlet (Shakespeare), 35
handclasping, in group decision making, 278
hand gestures, 199–201
Haney, W. V., 170
Harms, L. S., 207
Harris, T. A., 235
Harrison, R., 139
harshness, 210
Hartshorne, H., 90
hearing, vs. listening, 37
Hearst, P., 256
Heider, F., 106
helical model, 20, 39, 41–42
Hepburn, K., 205
Hess, E. H., 197
hoarseness, 210

INDEX

Homans, G. C., 252
homosexuals, and visual cues, 203–204
Horner, M., 64
huskiness, 210
hypernasality, 210

idea development and problem solving, group, 274–275
imitation, 51
I'm Ok—You're Ok (Harris), 232
impervious response, 126
impressions of others: first, 79–83; forming, 77–78; personal generalizations and stereotypes, 84–89; and private theory of personality, 78–79; and trait associations, 83
incoherent response, 126
incongruous response, 126
inferences, 167–168
influencing through feedback, 58–59
information: interpretation of, 38; in vocal cues, 205–207
information value, feedback, 60–61
Ingham, H., 128
input, communication, 22–25
instrumental learning, 49–51
intelligence and perception, 90, 91
intentional nonverbal stimuli, 31–32
Interaction Process Analysis (IPA), 261–262
intercultural communication (*see also* communication): defined, 8; and proximity, 102–103
interest, selective, 24
interference: signal-to-noise ratio, 35–36; technical and semantic, 36–37
interpersonal communication (*see also* communication): defined, 3–8; effective, 8–13
interpersonal conflict, and perceptual capacity, 29
interpretation of information, 38
interrole conflict, 224–225
interrupting response, 126

interview, questions and answers, 239–252; standardized vs. unstandardized, 238–239; structure, 242–246
intimate distance, 187
intrarole conflict, 225
involvement and arousal, 226–227
irrelevant response, 126, 241
isolates, 115; vs. overchosen people, 116–118
isolation and attraction, 113–114
issues, proportion of, and similarity, 109

James, W., 24
Jenkins, D., 60
Johari Window, 128–130
Jourard, S. M., 132–133

Kafka, F., 124
Kaplan, A., 19, 20
Kaunda, K., 175–176
Keaton, B., 183, 194–195
Kees, W., 183–202
Kelley, H. H., 61, 62, 83, 91, 111, 116, 223
Keniston, K., 241
Kern, E., 24
kinesics, 194
kinesic slip, 210
Kravitz, J., 85

La Barre, W., 196, 200
Labov, W., 165
Laing, R. D., 175, 211, 212
Langdon, H., 183
language: action, 183–184; black subculture, 158–159; dichotomies, 168–170; drug culture, 157–158; elaborated vs. restricted code, 163–164; ghetto children, 164–165; inferences, 167–168; sign, 183; single meanings, 173–177; and technology, 150; and thought, 165–167; word power, 170–173
Language and Thought of the Child, The (Piaget), 161

INDEX

Larson, C., 124, 125, 126
leadership, group, 272–273
learning: classical conditioning in, 48–49; to communicate, 47–48; instrumental, 49–51; social, 51–57
learning groups, 252
Leathers, D., 137
Leavitt, H. J., 271, 273
Lefkowitz, M., 202
Lemmon, J., 110
Lewin, K., 132
liking, reciprocal, and similarity, 109–110
linguistic coding, 163–164
listening: emphatic, 140–142; vs. hearing, 37; and learning, 48; as reinforcement, 50; selective, 25
Llewellyn, L. G., 58, 59
Lloyd, H., 183
loaded question, 240
Locke, J., 76
long-term memory, 38
Luchins, A. S., 79–80, 81, 82
Luft, J., 128, 130, 133

Maccoby, N., 34
Machiavellianism, 66–68
Maddocks, M., 173
majority vote, 278
Malpass, R., 85
manipulative behavior, 67–68
Matthau, W., 110
May, M. A., 90
McClelland, D., 63
McGrath, J., 274
McNair, M., 149
Mead, M., 33
meaning, private vs. shared, 155–160
Mehrabian, A., 193–206
Meidinger, T., 88, 89
Mellinger, G. D., 138
memory systems, 38
metacommunication, 130–132
Miller, G. R., 53
model, 19–21
modeling, in social learning, 51–53
Moray, N., 25

Moreno, J. L., 114
Mortensen, C. D., 227, 279
motivation: and achievement need, 61–65; and affiliation need, 63; and dogmatism, 65–66; and Machiavellianism, 66–68; and rewards, 61–62
Mouton, J. S., 202
Müller-Lyer illusion, 27–28
MUM effect, 231

naysayers, 241–242
need: for achievement, 63–65; for affiliation, 63, 228; complementarity of, and similarity, 110; for dominance, 228
Newcomb, T. M., 104, 108, 252, 257
Newell, A., 19
Newton, S., 151
no answer, 240
noise, 35–36
nondirective interview, 245–246
nonverbal message, interpreting, 211–212
nonverbal stimuli, 31–32; in two-person communication, 6–7
non-zero-sum, games, 135–137
norms, defined, 185; in small groups, 255; and social setting, 221–223

objectics, 203
objectivity and perception, 91
object language, 184
object perception, 73–77
objects, use of, 203–204
obvious answer, 240
oculesics, 196
Odd Couple, The (film), 110
Oliver, R. T., 155, 177
open-mindedness vs. dogmatism, 65–66
open question, 239
orientation, in group development, 265
Osgood, C., 153–154
overchosen people, 115; vs. isolates, 116–118

325

overlapping codes, communication 158
oververbalized answer, 241

pairing, in group decision making, 278
paralanguage, 205
paralinguistics, 205
Parkinson, C. N., 268–269
partial answer, 240–241
Pavlov, I., 48
Pearce, L., 139
people: and objects, perception of, 73–77; popular and unpopular, 114–118
perceived reciprocity of liking, 110
perceived similarity, 105
perception: accurate, 89–91; and communication, 91–93; of people and objects, 73–77
perceptual filters, 25–27
personal distance, 187
personality, private theory of, 78–79
personal space, 189–190
person perception, 73–74
phases, group development, 264–265
physical appearance, 202–203
physical attractiveness, 116
physical distance, and communication, 5
Piaget, J., 160–161
pitch: as vocal cue, 209–210
pleasurable listening, 140
pleasure, and communication, 9
popularity and unpopularity, 114–118
Porter, R. E., 8
positioning, 198–199
Potter, S., 230
primacy effect, 80–81
primary groups, 251
prisoner of war, as compliant group member, 256–257
Prisoner's Dilemma, 135–137
private acceptance vs. public compliance, 256–257

private meaning, vs. shared, 155–160
probing question, 239–240
problem solving: of groups, 258–261; and idea development, 274–275
problem-solving groups, 251
process model, 21
proportion of issues, and similarity, 109
proxemics, 186
proximal stimuli, 76
proximity: and attraction, 99–101; effects of, 101–102; and intercultural communication, 102–103; in two-person communication, 5
psychological set, 74–75
public compliance, vs. private acceptance, 256–257
public distance, 188–189

quality, as vocal cue, 210–211
questions, in interview, 239–240

race, and proximity, 103
railroading, in group decision making, 279
Rap on Race, A (Mead and Baldwin), 33
Rapoport, A., 136
receiver/sender communication, 37–39
recency effect, 80
reciprocal liking, and similarity, 109–110
Reece, M., 193
referents, and symbols, 150–151
rehearsal, of behavior, 55
Reik, T., 140
reinforcement, 49; in instrumental learning, 50; vicarious, 53
relationship, and communication, 11
remembering, 37–38
resonance, 210
response, confirming and disconfirming, 125–126

INDEX

restricted code, language, 161
reward: and attraction, 113–114; and motivation, 61–68
Rich, A. L., 85–86
risk, acceptance by groups, 258–261
risky shift phenomenon, 259
Rogers, C., 104, 140
Rokeach, M., 62
role, and social setting, 223–226
Roots: An Asian American Reader (Tachiki), 87
Rotter, J., 135
Ruesch, J., 183, 196
Russians, The (Smith), 142

salience, and similarity of attitude, 109
Samovar, L. A., 8
Schachter, S., 101, 112, 257, 258
Scheflen, A. E., 198
Scheidel, T., 59
Schierback, H., 77
Schramm, W., 36
Schreiner, I., 77
Secord, P. F., 88
selective attention, 25
selective interest, 24
self and others, awareness of, 127–128
self-concept: and dominance, 228–229; and feedback, 60
self-confidence, and perception, 89
self-disclosure, 132–134
self-esteem, and attraction, 112–113
self-fulfilling prophecy, 89
semantic differential, 153–155
semantic inference, 36–37
sender/receiver communication, 21–22
sensory deprivation, 23–24
sensory information storage, 38
Sereno, K., 227
sets, 35, 27–29
sex-typed behavior, 53–54
Shannon, C., 34
shared meanings, vs. private, 155–160
Shaw, M., 251

Sherif, M., 254, 255
short-term memory, 38
Sieburg, E., 125, 126, 127
signal-to-noise ratio, 35–36
sign language, 183
similarity, 104–105; and balance theory, 105–109; and proximity, 102; quantification of predictions, 108–111
Simon, H. A., 19, 271
situation and attraction, 111–114
size of group, 267, 269
Skinner, B. F., 49
small group communication (*see also* communication): and correlates of effective groups, 273–280, group dynamics, 253–266; and group structure, 267–273
Smith, A. L., 103
Smith, H., 142
social comparison theory, 257–258
social distance, 187–188
social facilitation, 57
social groups, 252
social influence, 257–258
socialized speech, 161
social learning, 51–57
social setting: norms, 221–223; role, 223–226
sociogram, 114–116
sociometric test, 114
solitary confinement, 113
Sommer, R., 189–191
space, personal, 185–191
spiral model, *see* helical model
standardized interview, 238
Starkweather, J. A., 205
status, 230–231
stereotypes: and personal generalizations, 84–89
stimuli, 23–25; communication, 29–32; nonverbal, 5–6, 31–32; proximal, 76
Storms, M. D., 127
Stravinsky, I., 90
stridency, 210
structured two-person communication, 237–246
style of communication, 40

INDEX

subgroups, 115
supportive climate, 139
supportive response, 126
symbols, and referents, 150–151

tabula rasa, 76
Tachiki, A., 87
Tagiuri, R., 76, 78
tangential response, 126
task functions, 272
task-oriented groups, 251
technical interference, 36
technology, and language, 150
territoriality, 186–190
Thayer, L., 32
Thelen, H., 266
Thematic Apperception Test (TAT), 75
theory types, 19
therapeutic groups, 252
Thibaut, J. W., 61, 62, 111, 116, 223
thought and language, 165–167
timbre, 210
time: and communication, 39–42; 191–193
touch, as communication channel, 33–34
Townsend, R., 269
Trager, G. L., 205
trait associations, 83
transaction, 5
transactional analysis, 232–236
Triplett, N., 57
trust, 134–135; and defensiveness, 138–140; and distrust, 137–138; and empathic listening, 140–142; and game behavior, 135–137
Tubbs, S. L., 136
two-person communication (*see also* communication): attitude similarity and attraction in, 105; social setting, 221–226; structured, 237–246; unstructured, 226–236

ulterior transaction, 233
uncarpentered world, vs. carpentered, 28–29

understanding, 36; and communication, 9
unintentional nonverbal stimuli, 32
unintentional verbal stimuli, 30–31
unstandardized interview, 239
unstructured two-person communication, 226–236

verbal deprivation theory, 164
verbal stimuli, 30–31
vernacular, black English, 165
vicarious reinforcement, 53
visual cues, 193–194; body movements, 194, 198–199; eye contact, 196–198, facial expression, 194–196; hand gestures, 199–201, physical appearance and use of objects, 202–204
vocal cues, 204–205; information in, 205–207; pitch, 209–210; quality, 210–211; rate and fluency, 208–209; volume, 207–208
volume, as vocal cue, 207–208
Vygotsky, L. S., 40

Walker, M., 141
Walster, E., 110, 113
Weaver, W., 34
Weick, K. E., 209
Weitz, S., 33
Wheeler, L., 259
Whitman, R. N., 193
Whorf, B. L., 166–167
Whorfian hypothesis, 166–167
Wiener, N., 57
Winch, R. F., 111
women: achievement motive and anxiety, 64
word(s): denotation and connotation, 152–155; private and shared meanings, 155–160; symbols and referents, 150–151
word power, 170–173
work groups, 252
world, carpentered vs. uncarpentered, 28–29

Yeasayers, 241–242

Zajonc, R. B., 102

About the Authors

STEWART L. TUBBS is Professor of Communication at General Motors Institute, a residential, coeducational college in Flint, Michigan, established by General Motors Corporation in 1919. Its Department of Communication and Organizational Behavior, with which Dr. Tubbs is associated, offers courses integrating communication theory and research with organizational development.

Dr. Tubbs received his doctorate jointly from the Departments of Speech and Psychology at The University of Kansas. His masters and bachelors degrees are in speech, from Bowling Green State University.

He has twice been named an Outstanding Teacher: by The University of Kansas for the Department of Speech and Drama in 1968 and by the Central States Speech Association in 1973. Dr. Tubbs is the author of *A Systems Approach to Small Group Interaction* and coauthor of *The Open Person . . . Self-Disclosure and Personal Growth*. He is also the coeditor of *Readings in Human Communication* and the editor of *New Directions in Communication* (International Communication Association). He is a member of the Speech Communication Association, the International Communication Association, and the American Psychological Association, and is listed in *American Men and Women of Science, Contemporary Authors, Directory of American Scholars,* and *Who's Who in the Midwest.*

SYLVIA MOSS is a professional writer with a strong interest in the behavioral sciences. Following her undergraduate work at Barnard (where she recalls "being appalled at first hearing a tape recording of my voice in an introductory speech course") and at The University of Wisconsin at Madison, she received a masters degree from Columbia University and pursued further graduate studies in psychology at New York University and The New School.

Ms. Moss has contributed to several textbooks in the social sciences. She also follows developments in modern poetry and translates literature in several languages. She is a poetry editor of *North River,* a forthcoming literary journal. She lives in Larchmont, New York, with her husband, who is in airline management, and their son and daughter.